Computer Spreadsheets for Library Applications

Computer Spreadsheets for Library Applications
2nd Edition

by Lawrence W.S. Auld

Formerly titled: Electronic Spreadsheets for Libraries

ORYX PRESS
1993

The rare Arabian Oryx is believed to have inspired the myth of the unicorn. This desert antelope became virtually extinct in the early 1960s. At that time several groups of international conservationists arranged to have 9 animals sent to the Phoenix Zoo to be the nucleus of a captive breeding herd. Today the Oryx population is nearly 800, and over 400 have been returned to reserves in the Middle East.

Copyright © 1986, 1993 by The Oryx Press
First edition published 1986. Second Edition 1993.
4041 North Central at Indian School Road
Phoenix, Arizona 85012-3397

Published simultaneously in Canada

Printed and Bound in the United States of America

∞ The paper used in this publication meets the minimum requirements of American National Standard for Information Science—Permanence of Paper for Printed Library Materials, ANSI Z39.48, 1984.

Library of Congress Cataloging-in-Publication Data
Auld, Lawrence W. S.
    Computer spreadsheets for library applications / by Lawrence W.S. Auld. — 2nd ed.
        p. cm.
    Includes bibliographical references.
    ISBN 0-89774-724-0
    1. Library administration—Data processing.   2. Electronic spreadsheets.   I. Title.
Z678.A87   1993   92-26884
025.1'0285—dc20   CIP

In Memory of
Dorothy Paddock Auld
1905-1990

Contents

List of Figures

List of Tables

Preface

A handwritten spreadsheet displays numbers in rows and columns with totals and subtotals laboriously written in the appropriate places. An electronic spreadsheet does the same, except that it calculates and recalculates the subtotals and totals almost instantaneously. In addition, a wide variety of other arithmetic and logical functions can also be performed, and these results, too, are displayed. In short, electronic spreadsheets offer an easy and very flexible way of recording, displaying, and analyzing data. This book is designed to help librarians, library school students, and others use spreadsheets more effectively by presenting several model templates.

Computer Spreadsheets for Library Applications is the second edition of *Electronic Spreadsheets for Libraries,* which was published in 1986. This new work updates the first edition in three areas: a few spreadsheets from the first edition have been reworked in forms that were not possible with older software; several new applications are presented; and, most important, some of these new applications use three-dimensional spreadsheet software. Like its predecessor, this book is designed as a management tool for librarians and as an instructional aid for teachers and students. At the same time, it is intended for persons who are accustomed to working with microcomputers and who are already familiar with basic spreadsheet operations.

A two-dimensional spreadsheet, composed of only rows and columns, can become quite complex; with the addition of a third dimension, one might expect that potential for complexity to be greatly increased. However, this need not be the case. When a third dimension is needed, a three-dimensional spreadsheet may actually be less complex than one in two dimensions because the additional dimension can be handled in a straightforward manner rather than by working around the limitations of two-dimensional software. Three-dimensional applications can be handled in a two-dimensional spreadsheet only with a loss of clarity and convenience.

Spreadsheets with four or more dimensions are also possible, but they are beyond the purview of this book.

Because they are not readily visualized, their use is necessarily limited to more abstract applications.

Only a few spreadsheet software packages qualify as three-dimensional. Best known among these are QubeCalc, ProQube, and 1-2-3 (release 3.0). Both QubeCalc and ProQube permit the three-dimensional matrix to be rotated so that it can be viewed from different sides. The importance of this feature depends on the nature of the particular application.

A number of other spreadsheet and spreadsheet-like programs also offer multi-dimensionality in one form or another:

- VP-Planner Plus is similar to 1-2-3 in its two-dimensional aspects; however, before its third- to fifth-dimensional capabilities can be used, it requires an extensive and complicated set-up to create what are described as multiple one-dimensional tables that are linked through a two-dimensional table. While reviewers praise VP-Planner Plus as a two-dimensional spreadsheet, they are quick to point out the complexities of using its additional dimensions.
- Lucid-D offers an interesting hypertext-like spreadsheet in which each individual cell can be "opened" to form an entire spreadsheet thereby providing a powerful ability to link together two or more spreadsheets.
- TM/1 (Table Manager/1) holds data in tables and formulas in worksheets. Output can be displayed in any of eight dimensions. More expensive than many of its competitors, it is regarded as very powerful.
- Javelin Plus, a business analysis tool, is not really a spreadsheet (lacking the customary rows and columns), but it will do many of the things that are expected of spreadsheet programs. Variables are entered as a group and are related by a separate set of equations. Data may be seen in up to 10 different views.

In general, almost any spreadsheet program can be used for the two-dimensional applications described in this book, and the results will be much the same, although

xii   *Computer Spreadsheets for Library Applications*

the processes by which the results are achieved (both programmatic and from the user's point of view) are, necessarily, somewhat different. However, the three-dimensional applications require specially designed software. Both two- and three-dimensional spreadsheet software packages were used in the preparation of this book; 1-2-3 (release 2.01) and Quattro were used for the two-dimensional applications, and ProQube was used for the three-dimensional applications. Of course, ProQube will also function in only two dimensions.

Each of the spreadsheet templates in this book presents a device in which data can be assembled, analyzed, and displayed. These data may be real, representing a particular situation, or imaginary, providing an opportunity to examine "what if" scenarios. Thus, the data may model an existing situation, project a future situation, or both.

Serious users of spreadsheets with MS-DOS machines will want no less than a full 640 K of internal memory, a graphics module, a hard disk, and a printer able to produce both condensed type and graphics. A VGA color monitor will create prettier displays with helpful color coding, and a math-coprocessor may be desirable for more rapid calculation of very large spreadsheets. While reduced configurations can be used, they will tend to require more time, consume more paper, produce less attractive output, and often promote feelings of impatience and frustration.

Although it is possible to develop spreadsheets "from scratch," it is often easier and a more economical use of time to begin with templates that have already been designed, such as those presented here or those available through exchange. Most predesigned templates may be modified easily to meet specific local needs. Chapter 2, "Design and Modification of Spreadsheets," includes two examples of modifications and a brief discussion of how such modifications can be introduced without disturbing the logic of the spreadsheet.

An excellent test of the usefulness of a spreadsheet is whether it presents data in a form that is easily understood. While the templates in this book were designed with

effective communication as one objective, users should not hesitate to make improvements, for the final test is not whether a spreadsheet looks exactly like the one in the book, but whether it accomplishes the desired task.

HOW THIS BOOK IS SET UP

Users of the first edition will recall that most of the spreadsheets were presented twice. First, the spreadsheet was shown in an expanded form, called "Cell-by-Cell Instructions," with the columns and rows identified, the formulas displayed, zeros or X's indicating where data were to be input, and most of the columns widened in order to make room for a full display of the formulas. Second, the spreadsheet was shown as it would appear when printed onto paper and with data (usually fictitious) demonstrating how the spreadsheet worked and how it would appear in use.

The dual display of each spreadsheet in the first edition was generally appreciated. One suggested alternative, a serial listing of cell-by-cell contents, would have required less space but would have failed to give the visual design cues provided in the dual displays. Because, in the author's experience, a majority of librarians are visually oriented and prefer working with visual design cues, the dual displays are used again.

A typical spreadsheet presented in this second edition is organized into an instruction area and a data and analysis area. Some also have an area containing a menu and associated macros. Since the appearance of the instruction and menu areas are unaffected by the inclusion of data, they are presented only once. The data and analysis area is usually displayed twice. First, part or all of this area is shown with the columns and rows identified, the formulas displayed, zeros or X's indicating where data are to be input, and most of the columns widened in order to make room for a full display of the formulas. Second, the area is shown as it will appear when printed onto paper and with data (usually fictitious) demonstrating how the spreadsheet works and how it will appear in use.

Acknowledgments

I want to express my appreciation to Borland International for providing a review copy of Quattro, to Lotus Development Corporation for providing a review copy of 1-2-3 (release 2.01), and to FormalSoft for providing a review copy of ProQube. My thanks go to many persons, including Patricia Palmer and Andrew Bullen, who shared their PASCAL program for determining preservation values; Norman Holmes, who shared CASMS; Tracy Moore of Oryx Press for assistance in securing software; Howard Batchelor of Oryx Press for timely advice; and John Wagner of Oryx Press for thoughtful editorial assistance.

Trademarks

The following are trademarks of the indicated companies: QubeCalc and ProQube, of FormalSoft; 1-2-3, of Lotus Development Corporation; Lucid-D, of Personal Computer Support Group; VP-Planner Plus, of Paperback Software International; Quattro, of Borland International; MS-DOS, of Microsoft Corporation; Javelin Plus, of Javelin Software Corporation; TM/1, of Sinper Corporation; dBase, of Ashton Tate; and VisiCalc, of Computer Associates.

Chapter 1
Electronic Spreadsheets: Tools for Recording, Analyzing, and Reporting Data and Statistics

Spreadsheets, or closely related documents, have been used for hundreds if not thousands of years. Accountants who lack computers manually prepare spreadsheets in order to display the structure and distribution of a budget or other financial entity, its liabilities and credits, and its status or balance. Preprinted sheets for accounting and bookkeeping, available from most stationers, vary in size from 8 1/2" x 11" to big enough to cover the top of a large desk. These sheets are preprinted with lines representing rows and columns so that their contents may be logically and conveniently displayed. Subtotals, totals, and the results of other calculations appear in appropriate places throughout the spreadsheet. However, the accountant must perform all the arithmetic operations and transcribe both the data and the results onto the spreadsheet by hand. If one item of data is changed, any calculations involving that item must also be redone. Even in a small spreadsheet, this can be an arduous and time-consuming task requiring erasures, recalculations, and reentry of totals. Because the primary object of such a manually prepared spreadsheet is for it to balance, changes are avoided whenever possible, and the result is a largely static display of information.

The concept of a spreadsheet changed in 1979 with the creation of VisiCalc for the Apple II microcomputer. The basic arrangement of rows and columns remained the same. What changed was the introduction of formulas in selected cells which displayed the results of calculations. If the content of any cell was altered, the entire spreadsheet was automatically and almost instantly recalculated.

An electronic spreadsheet can be any size within the limits imposed by the particular software and hardware, the width of each column can be adjusted, and the arithmetic operations are carried out automatically. The data need not be monetary, since any numerical data and some nonnumerical data can be used. As new or updated data are entered, the new totals are calculated immediately.

This dynamic quality makes the electronic spreadsheet very powerful and is, perhaps, its most attractive feature.

Thus, the spreadsheet, by becoming electronic, became a dynamic tool for the recording, analyzing, and reporting of data and statistics. The result is that we now approach budgetary and other quantitative analysis in very different ways from how we dealt with them before 1979. For a readable and still timely account of the birth and rapid growth of spreadsheets in business and government, see "A Spreadsheet Way of Knowledge" by Steven Levy in the November 1984 issue of *Harper's*.

Electronic spreadsheet software has developed rapidly since 1979. Today's more advanced spreadsheet programs can handle several million cells, process them more rapidly, display them in color, and draw elegant summary charts. Macros extend the user's power further by performing certain tasks through single commands. In comparison with these newer programs, VisiCalc in 1979 was primitive. Yet, there remains a sameness in spreadsheets that leads some to describe them all as spread-alike sheets. Only the three-dimensional programs can claim exemption, and even they display data in the familiar rows and columns.

USING SPREADSHEETS

Use of an electronic spreadsheet begins with a video display of an almost blank screen with the rows and columns numbered and/or lettered. One can begin entering data immediately, but usually one will want to do some planning, mentally and/or on paper, as to how the spreadsheet can best be laid out. Particular rows and columns, often the first rows and the first column of the data area are used for labels. With most spreadsheet programs, these labeled rows and columns can be "locked" in place so that they are displayed constantly regardless of what portion of the spreadsheet is shown on the screen. For this reason, it is a good idea to include meaningful keywords in these labels.

Each position or cell of a spreadsheet can be individually accessed either by moving the cursor to the position or by referring to it by column and row. Each cell can accept one of three types of input: data, a label, or a formula. Data can be numeric or alphabetic, but only numeric data are generally processed by most formulas. Labels, too, can be alphabetic, numeric, or a combination. Formulas must follow the syntax specified by the particular spreadsheet program. The lines and other marks used for indicating subtotals and totals and for separating columns are defined as a kind of label. Of course, a cell can be left blank or empty.

The lessons provided with some spreadsheet programs are helpful in guiding the newcomer through the initial steps, but, thereafter, experience at the keyboard is the best instructor.

If a spreadsheet design is not quite right, often it can be improved by inserting a column or a row; or a column or a row can be deleted. Also, while working with the spreadsheet, one frequently thinks of additional features that should be incorporated. These can also be added by inserting columns and rows or changing formulas. When inserting or deleting columns and rows, watch carefully for the effect on formulas. If a cell cited in a formula is deleted, or if a cell is added but not properly cited in a formula, the formula will no longer work correctly. (It may still appear to work, but the result will be wrong!) This problem is discussed further in Chapter 2, "Design and Modification of Spreadsheets," and some guidelines are suggested.

VIEWING AND PRINTING SPREADSHEETS

A spreadsheet may be viewed as a video terminal display, a printed page(s), a text file accessible to a word processing program, or a graphic display. Spreadsheet users should keep the general features of each format in mind.

Except for very small spreadsheets, the video display will be a "window" or portion of the entire spreadsheet. This rectangular window can be moved up and down as well as left and right permitting visual access to all parts of the spreadsheet. Operations on the spreadsheet (e.g., data entry and recalculation, insertion and deletion

of columns or rows) usually affect all of the spreadsheet, not just the portion visible in the video display. Some spreadsheet programs allow the video display to be divided into two portions or windows, either horizontal or vertical. This "split screen" capability, used to display two different portions of one spreadsheet or portions of two different spreadsheets, is particularly useful for comparing sets of data.

The entire spreadsheet, or a selected portion, can be printed out on a printer. Wide spreadsheets must be printed onto successive sheets of paper which are then decollated and assembled side by side to form the whole spreadsheet. A spreadsheet design may look fine as a video display but may need modification for best presentation on paper. Column widths may need adjustment, vertical and horizontal lines may need to be added or deleted, and some elements may need to be relocated. Other stylistic considerations may be considered, such as right, left, or center justification for certain columns or rows.

A useful feature of many spreadsheet programs is the ability to write a copy of part or all of a spreadsheet to a file as a page image(s) where it will be accessible to a word processing program. For example, a portion of a spreadsheet can be exported and inserted into the text of a document as a table. Also, some word processing programs will allow a spreadsheet to be imported directly without going through in intermediate page image step. Such compatibilities are one of the features to be considered when selecting spreadsheet and word processing software.

The graphic display capabilities of spreadsheet programs and the hardware on which they run vary all the way from none to multicolor bar and circle (so-called pie chart) graphs. The quality, nature, and analysis of the data will determine the appropriateness of a graphic display. For example, if 100 percent of a data sample falls into a given category, a bar or circle graph would be pointless.

SELECTED FEATURES OF SPREADSHEETS

In developing a spreadsheet that repeats itself in several places, it is convenient to copy portions from one place to another. When copying formulas, be aware of fixed *vs.* relative addresses. For example, if the contents of a cell are being used as a constant, that would indicate a fixed location, but if the data in a column are being summed, that would indicate a relative location. Thus, each cell address referenced in a formula may need to be identified as a fixed or a relative location.

Some spreadsheets have the ability to reference other spreadsheets, i.e., to use data in other spreadsheets through a process of linkage. This useful feature may be limited by internal memory size.

In spite of their similarities, some of which are no doubt deliberate, the various spreadsheet packages do offer different capabilities. The touch and feel may be similar, in some cases virtually the same, but there are differences in their inner workings. The difference in how the calculation and recalculation functions of two spreadsheet software packages work will serve to illustrate this point. 1-2-3 (release 2.01) recalculates the entire spreadsheet whenever the contents of a cell are changed. This results in current values being displayed in all cells. It also means that there can be an appreciable waiting time between entries in a large spreadsheet unless automatic recalculation is turned off, thereby avoiding long waits but displaying in some cells figures which are no longer current. However, recalculation of the entire spreadsheet can be accomplished at any time by pressing the [F9] key. In contrast, Quattro recalculates only those formulas affected by the entry of new data, resulting in generally faster recalculation. Again, automatic recalculation can be turned off, and recalculation can be accomplished by pressing the [F9] key. For most purposes, this difference is immaterial, but it does affect certain operations, such as the ability to work with random numbers as described in Chapters 18 and 19.

In the usual presentation of a spreadsheet, everything appears to be either a label or a value, with the calculated results of formulas appearing in the cells. (However, when a cell contains a formula, the formula will appear in the command line.) With some spreadsheets, the user has the option of changing the display so that the formulas will appear throughout the spreadsheet, and the spreadsheet can be printed with either calculated values or formulas. (For example, in 1-2-3 this is accom-

plished by selecting the "Text" option within the "Format" menu.) Usually, the column widths will need to be widened if the complete formulas are to be viewed or printed. Other spreadsheets that do not offer this "Text" option will print lists of the contents of each cell (label, value, or formula), cell-by-cell, with each cell designation and its contents on a separate line. Even a small spreadsheet can produce a surprisingly long list.

SELECTING SPREADSHEET SOFTWARE

The ideal process for selecting a spreadsheet program involves several steps:

1. Identify needs in terms of the kinds and amount of data to be processed, the kinds of analysis to be done, and the format in which the data and analyses are to be displayed.
2. Pick a software package that will satisfy these needs. Check the number of rows and columns that are available and whether the column widths can be altered. Is the spreadsheet program compatible with a word processing program? How easy or difficult is the spreadsheet to use in terms of format, commands, and lessons? How good and usable is the documentation? Does the software developer offer good customer service? Is the price affordable?
3. Pick a computer on which the spreadsheet program can run. Consider such features as the type of CPU, internal memory size, the disk or other peripheral storage space, and the price.
4. Purchase the software and the microcomputer.
5. Sit down and start using these new acquisitions!

However, the more usual spreadsheet selection process is either to use the spreadsheet at hand or to buy a spreadsheet that will run on a computer that is already owned or easily accessible. Actually, this approach works fairly well unless there are special needs or the computer is too small to function effectively.

Chapter 2
Design and Modification of Spreadsheets

A new spreadsheet is created by loading a blank spreadsheet and filling in the appropriate cells with labels, formulas, and values. The process is straightforward, since the structure is immediately visible and errors can be quickly identified and corrected. If the spreadsheet is small (not extending beyond one or two screens), this *ad hoc* approach is reasonable. However, for larger spreadsheets or even complex smaller spreadsheets, this approach can lead to confusion and errors in the overall logic. A more systematic approach to spreadsheet creation can avoid many of the problems common to the *ad hoc* approach.

Most spreadsheets have data in some cells and formulas that process these data in other cells. For convenience, the rows and columns holding the data and formulas are assigned labels. Also for convenience, the spreadsheet should be given a title, a statement describing the organization and use of the spreadsheet should be included, constants should be displayed in one area, and the filename and date of the spreadsheet should be included. A typical arrangement of these spreadsheet elements is shown in Figure 2-A.

```
Title [spelled out in whole words, not cryptic acronyms]


Statement describing the organization and use of this spreadsheet.
Include the purpose of the spreadsheet, describe the basics of how the
spreadsheet works, note any special features, indicate how data are to be
input, and cite the location of the beginning cell for each section of the
spreadsheet.

                  constant            constant

                  label     label     label     label
              -------------------------------------------------
       label  |  data      data      data      |   formula
              |
       label  |  data      data      data      |   formula
              |
       label  |  data      data      data      |   formula
              |
       label  |  data      data      data      |   formula
              |
       label  |  data      data      data      |   formula
              -------------------------------------------------
       label  |  formula   formula   formula   |   formula


            filename
            date
```

Figure 2-A: Arrangement of a Typical Spreadsheet

Persons accustomed to older software or lower-density floppy disks have been conditioned by lack of file space to be sparing in their inclusion of anything not absolutely essential to the operation of a spreadsheet. This can result in spreadsheets lacking in clarity and helpful details. Users with access to hard disks or higher density disks are not hampered by this limitation. The slight additional space used for the layout shown in Figure 2-A is quickly repaid in ease of use.

DESIGNING A SPREADSHEET TEMPLATE

When designing a new spreadsheet, a template is created in which the format is established and the label and formulas are entered; however, no data are entered, since a template is just the skeletal structure of the spreadsheet. One or more copies of the template are saved where they can be accessed conveniently. Then, a working copy is retrieved whenever it is needed for the entry of data. This copy, containing data, is saved as a spreadsheet under its own filename. Obviously, one template can be the source for several different spreadsheets, each containing a different set of data.

The first step in designing a template is usually done on paper. Start by writing down the name of the template and a brief description of what it is supposed to do. Then, begin sketching the overall arrangement of the columns and rows; assign labels; indicate where lines will be needed to mark sections, subtotals, and totals; and insert formulas and constants. Often, keeping the data in one or more contiguous areas separate from the area(s) containing the formulas happens automatically; however, when formulas draw on both data and other formulas, a haphazard arrangement may result if the column and row assignments are not carefully monitored.

This process will likely go through several drafts, each of which should be kept for future reference. This is especially the case for the statement of purpose, the latest draft, and any other drafts that contain significant shifts in thinking. Maintaining complete documentation for future reference is very important. Don't neglect it! The details of a template may seem fresh now, but in six weeks some of those same details will be obscure, and in six months they will be altogether forgotten. Thus, both you and any other persons who have to work with the template will be dependent on the documentation that has been kept. When further changes are made, be sure they are added to the documentation file, too.

The next step is to begin keyboarding the template and taking care of some basic housekeeping tasks that allow its overall shape and characteristics to be seen. Once this step is complete the details can be entered.

TEMPLATE DESIGN STEPS

The process listed below is recommended as a general procedure for designing a template; slight variations may be necessary to meet specific needs. The 28 steps provide a logical sequence for developing a two-dimensional template. (*Note:* When developing a three-dimensional template, it is easiest to complete the basic or initial data page—usually page 10 or higher—and copy it onto as many additional pages as are needed. Modify any column titles or formulas as may be necessary, particularly on the final summary page.)

1. Write the purpose and expectations for the template on a sheet of paper. This is the beginning of the documentation file.
2. Sketch the overall structure of the template on paper with lines indicating sections, subtotals, totals, etc. Write in column and row labels and the constants, and sketch in the formulas. In general, try to keep the data and formulas in separate areas, although do not worry if the separation is not absolute. Add this sketch to the documentation file.
3. Revise! Add the revisions to the documentation file.
4. Keyboard the title at the top of the template.
5. Keyboard the statement describing the organization and use of the template in one or more paragraphs following the title. (*Note:* In a three-dimensional template, enter the title and organizational statement on page 1, and repeat the title at the top of each subsequent page.)
6. Keyboard the constants. (*Note:* In a three-dimensional template, it is convenient to enter the constants on page 1, either inside or outside the instruction area.)
7. Keyboard the column titles (headings). If possible, place keywords in the row(s) that uniquely identify each column. (*Note:* In a three-dimensional template, begin entering the column titles in column B or C on page 10.)

8. Keyboard the row titles (labels). Judicious use of leading blank spaces will aid in displaying hierarchical relationships. If possible, place keywords in the column that uniquely identify each row. (*Note:* In a three-dimensional template, begin entering the row titles in column A on page 10. If the three-dimensional matrix is to be rotated, copy the row titles in as many columns on page 8 or 9 as there are pages of data.)

9. Keyboard horizontal lines for separating subtotals, totals, sections, etc. Use no more lines than are necessary for easy reading of the template. Sometimes horizontal lines are used to separate column titles from data and to separate different groups of data. Often, these lines can be referenced as the initial and final addresses for formulas.

10. Keyboard vertical lines for separating columns. Again, use no more lines than are necessary for easy reading of the template. Sometimes vertical lines are used to separate row titles from the first column of data and to separate different groups of data. Often, these lines can be referenced as the initial and final addresses for formulas. (*Note:* In a three-dimensional template, these vertical lines in column B will be copied into as many columns on page 9 as are necessary to provide conveniently placed lines when the three-dimensional matrix is rotated.)

11. Adjust the column widths as necessary to accommodate the labels and data to be keyboarded and the results to be displayed. (*Note:* Although the column widths do not have to be the same from page to page in a three-dimensional template, it is usually best to keep them uniform. The principal exception is page 1 on which the statement describing the organization and use of the template is displayed. Here, the column containing the paragraph(s) can be set to a maximum width of 76.)

12. Set the style parameters for the columns and rows (i.e., centered, left-, and right-hand justification) if they are to vary from the defaults. The default for numbers is right-justified, while the default for labels is left-justified.

13. Set the number of digits to the right of the decimal that are to be displayed for columns or rows. Digits to the right of the decimal indicate precision. Be sure the precision is congruent with that of the data and that the results of formulas do not suggest greater precision than warranted by the data.

14. Keyboard the formulas into the appropriate cells. (*Note:* When copying formulas, be alert to relative vs. absolute cell addresses, especially in three-dimensional templates. Also, it is often useful, when defining the range from which a formula draws data, to begin the range in the cell before the first datum and end the range in the cell after the last datum, thereby making it possible to insert or delete a row or column at any point among the data comprising the range. This assumes that these cells are either non-numeric or are blank. See steps 9 and 10 above.)

15. Keyboard the filename and the date below the organizational statement.

16. *Optional:* Keyboard a zero, a letter x, or other preferred symbol in each cell in which data will be input. (*Note:* While use of a zero [0] seems logical, this can be confusing, for cells with formulas will also display zeros until data are input.)

17. Save this template to disk.

18. Test the formulas in the template by keyboarding simple data. Examine the value displayed by each formula. If a formula includes any kind of logical test (e.g., an @IF statement), change the data until all possible conditions have been tested. Correct any formulas that are not performing as they should and retest them. Continue this process until the template is performing satisfactorily. (*Note:* The process of testing a template may take only a few minutes, or it may consume many hours. Persevere! Until the template is performing satisfactorily, it is unusable.)

19. Make any other refinements that will improve the usefulness and appearance of the template. This may include relocating individual cells, reorganizing sections, changing labels, rewriting the statement describing the organization and use of the spreadsheet, and making the formulas more efficient.

20. Retest the template.

21. Save the revised template to disk.

22. Make one or more back-up copies of this template. (Always make back-up copies of everything unless you particularly enjoy re-keyboarding.)

23. Print a copy of the template on paper, and add this printout to the documentation file.

24. Display the formulas (widening the columns as necessary) and print a copy on paper. (*Note:* Not all spreadsheet software will permit this step. One option may be to print a list of the section or block of the template that contains the formulas.) Add this printout to the documentation file, too.

25. Use the template to create a spreadsheet by loading a copy of the template and then keyboarding data in the appropriate cells.
26. Save the spreadsheet to disk.
27. Make a back-up copy of this spreadsheet.
28. Make a printout of the spreadsheet. Make an extra copy for the documentation file as an example of how the completed template looks when it has data in it.

MODIFYING TEMPLATES

While the sample templates provided in this text will provide both sufficient and precisely needed details for many applications, it may be necessary to alter a template to meet local needs. Provided certain rules are observed, additions, deletions, or alterations can be done easily without affecting the integrity of the template.

Most frequently, a template will be altered by the simple insertion or deletion of one or more rows or columns of data within an existing group. By carefully observing the following five rules, the range defined in a formula will expand or contract to accommodate the change, and no "orphan" rows or columns will be created.

Rule 1. Never add a row or column before the first of a series of rows or columns that are summed together or otherwise treated as a group by a formula. In other words, leave an initial row or column cited in a formula in its primary position. (*Note:* If formulas are constructed following the guideline of step 14 above, adherence to Rule 1 should not be a problem.)

Rule 2. Never add a row or column after the last of a series of rows or columns that are summed together or otherwise treated as a group by a formula. In other words, leave a final row or column cited in a formula in its terminal position. (*Note:* If formulas are constructed following the guideline of step 14 above, adherence to Rule 2 should not be a problem.)

Rule 3. Never delete the first of a series of rows or columns that are summed together or otherwise treated as a group by a formula. In other words, retain an initial row or column cited in a formula in its primary position. (*Note:* If formulas are constructed following the guideline of step 14 above, adherence to Rule 3 should not be a problem.)

Rule 4. Never delete the last of a series of rows or columns that are summed together or otherwise treated as a group by a formula. In other words, retain a final row or column cited in a formula in its terminal position. (*Note:* If formulas are constructed following the guideline of step 14 above, adherence to Rule 4 should not be a problem.)

Rule 5. Always review each formula after adding or deleting columns or rows to be sure that the formulas are still correct, i.e., be sure that the formulas are using all the desired data and only the desired data. Make any corrections that may be needed.

A less frequent modification is the introduction of a new formula or the deletion of a formula. If no other formulas are affected, either directly or indirectly, the change can be made without disrupting the integrity of the template. However, if one or more other formulas are affected, they, too, will have to be modified if integrity is to be maintained. A single change of this sort can have a "domino" effect, leading to a major restructuring of the entire template which, in turn, will require retesting of most if not all of the formulas. (See steps 18-28 above.) While such changes may be necessary if a template is to meet a particular need, the changes should be undertaken only while working with a copy of the template, the person making the changes should be sufficiently experienced to handle the process, and full documentation of the changes should be kept.

Below are two examples of how templates might be modified. The first demonstrates how rows and columns can be inserted into a two-dimensional template and the formulas modified accordingly; the second demonstrates the insertion of rows and columns into a three-dimensional template.

Modification of a Grades Template (Chapter 6)

Chapter 6, "Grades," presents a template designed to assist the library instructor by keeping track of the relative weight and the grades for each assignment, project, and examination and by calculating the final grade. It is set up with only three students, four assignments, and one examination, clearly not enough for most classes. Here are step-by-step instructions for expanding this spreadsheet to accommodate a class of 20 students, five assignments, a mid-term examination, and a final examination. Additional expansion is possible using these steps as guidelines.

1. Load a copy of the Grades template. This will become the spreadsheet for this particular class.
2. Place the cursor on AA109 and insert 17 additional rows so that there will be a total of 20 rows for students.

3. Enter the students' names and social security numbers.

4. Place the cursor on AG101 and insert two columns, one for assignment 5 and one for the mid-term examination.

5. Copy cells AF101-AF105 to the same rows in column AG; edit the assignment number in AG103 to "5."

6. Copy cells AI101-AI105 to the same rows in column AH; enter "Mid-Term" in AH102.

7. Enter "Final" in AI102.

8. Alter the assignment and examination weights in AC104 through AI104 so that the total is equal to 1.00 (i.e., 100 percent).

9. Extend the double line in cells AH126 and AI126.

10. Place the cursor on AC128 and edit the formula from "@AVG(AC106..AC108)," which can be read as "calculate the average of cells AC106 through AC108," to "@AVG(AC106..AC125)," which can be read as "calculate the average of cells AC106 through AC125." (Actually, this should have occurred when the additional rows were inserted.)

11. Copy the formula in AC128 to cells AD128 through AJ128.

12. Edit the formula in AJ106 to include the two columns that were inserted by extending the formula. To do this, add "+(AH106*$AH$104)+(AI106*$AI$104)" to the end of the formula.

13. Copy the formula in AJ106 into cells AJ107 through AJ125.

14. Examine the formula in AL106. It is set up with A = 92-100 (i.e., >91 and <101), B = 84-91 (i.e., >83 and <92), C = 76-83 (i.e., >75 and <84), D = 68-75 (i.e., >67 and <76), and F = 67 or lower (i.e., <68). Edit the formula as needed to establish different ranges of points for the letter grades.

15. Copy the the formula in AL106 into cells AL107 through AL125.

16. Save this customized spreadsheet under an appropriate filename.

17. Save a back-up copy.

Modification of a CD-ROM Use Template (Chapter 14)

Chapter 14, "CD-ROM Use," presents a three-dimensional template designed to assist the librarian by keeping track of the use of CD-ROM databases. It is set up with only six databases and five categories of users.

Below are step-by-step instructions for expanding this spreadsheet to accommodate 20 databases and seven categories of users. Additional expansion is possible using these steps as guidelines.

1. Load a copy of the CD-ROM Use template. This will become the spreadsheet in which the data will be recorded and analyzed.

2. Place the cursor in cell A16 of page 10 (i.e., the cell at the intersection of column A and row 16 on page 10; written as A16;10) and insert 14 rows in pages 10-22 (A16;10..A30;22). This will create space for a total of 20 CD-ROM databases. If more databases are anticipated, space can be made for them now.

3. On page 10, beginning with A10, enter the names of the CD-ROM databases.

4. Copy the names of the CD-ROM databases in A10-A30 to the same location on pages 11-22.

5. Place the cursor in cell F1 of page 10 and insert two columns in pages 10-22 (F1;10..G1;22). This will create space for a total of seven user categories.

6. Extend the lines in rows 9 and 31, pages 10-22, to columns F and G.

7. On page 10, edit the user categories in B9 through H9 to reflect the seven user categories.

8. Copy the user categories in B9-H9 on page 10 to the same location on pages 11-22.

9. Examine the formula in B32 on page 10 (B32;10) to be sure that all 20 databases are included in the total. The formula should read "=@SUM(B9;10..B31;10)." If necessary, edit the formula and copy it into C32 through H32 on page 10 (C32;10..H32;10). Also, copy the formula into B32 through H32 on pages 11 through 22 (B32;11..H32;22).

10. Examine the formula in I10 on page 10 (I10;10) to be sure that all seven user categories are included in the total. The formula should read "=@SUM(B10;10..H10;10." If necessary, edit the formula and copy it into B11 through B30 on page 10 (B11;10..B30;10). Also, copy the formula in B10 through B30 on pages 11 through 22 (B10;11..B30;22).

11. Examine the formula in I32 on page 10 (I32;10) to be sure that all 20 databases and all seven user categories are included in the total. The formula should read "=@IF(@SUM(B32;10..H32;10)=@SUM(I9;10..I31;10),@SUM(I9;10..I31;10),"ERROR")." If necessary, edit the formula and copy it into I32 on pages 11 through 22 (I32;11..I32;22).

12. Copy the formula in F10 on page 22 into cells G10 through G30 and H10 through H30 (G10;22..H10;22).
13. Save this customized spreadsheet under an appropriate filename.
14. Save a back-up copy.

The above two examples illustrate how spreadsheets can be modified by inserting rows and columns and adjusting formulas. By approaching this process systematically and logically, writing down the changes on paper in advance, and introducing the changes one step at a time, a potentially complex operation can be accomplished simply and without problems. Also, because the changes are being made on a copy of the template, the process is fail-safe, and at worst, a ruined copy can be discarded and the process started over on a fresh copy.

Chapter 3
Macros, Graphics, Word Processing, and Databases

The basic benchmarks against which a spreadsheet software program is measured are its ability to calculate the values represented by formulas and the ease with which it is used, including editing and layout. Further benchmarks include the program's ability to accept macros, sets of instructions that function like programs; to generate graphic displays of part or all of the data; and to interact with word processors and databases. The following comments are intended to help spreadsheet users understand these features without going into detail about how they work.

MACROS

A macro represents a sequence of recorded keystrokes that can be played back on demand, a very convenient feature that allows for the automatic execution of many repetitive tasks. Macros are intimidating on first sight. They look strange because they are written in a special program language that follows a set of strict syntactical rules. However, understanding macros can make using spreadsheets much easier. Further, macros can be structured so as to provide customized menus that can greatly simplify the use of complicated spreadsheets. The two-dimensional spreadsheets in this book include macros organized into menus.

Like any computer program, a macro must be absolutely logical and exactly sequenced if it is to perform the intended task. A macro with a flaw in its logic or a wrong sequence of statements may appear to work, but the results will likely not be those expected. Thus, accurate keyboarding is essential for macros to function properly. Further, the addition or deletion of rows or columns from a spreadsheet can inadvertently render a macro inoperable. Thus, it is a good idea to protect the range containing macros, and the data and analysis areas should be located where their operation cannot interfere with the macros.

GRAPHICS

It is, perhaps, unfortunate that the rows and columns of data in a spreadsheet can be so easily displayed in graphic form. Just because a string of data can be depicted as a graph does not mean that the display is appropriate or even meaningful. Graphs are properly used as visual displays of summary data and statistics, and the same basic guidelines apply to both.

Before attempting to construct any graphs, review the differences between nominal, ordinal, interval, and ratio data, and between continuous and noncontinuous data, in a basic statistics text. This review should make clear why nominal, ordinal, and non-continuous data are displayed only in bar and circle graphs, while interval and ratio data, which are continuous, can be displayed in a line graph.

A well-designed graph can be an effective communication tool, but a poorly designed graph will interfere with communication. Good design can be realized if some basic rules of thumb are followed: Avoid a cluttered appearance. Simplify the layout by combining appropriate sets of data. Provide key numbers and words to identify the various elements of the graph. For complicated data, make two or three graphs instead of attempting to combine everything into one, and build a summary graph in which only the results are displayed. If one approach to a display does not work, try reversing the axes, or consider a different graphic format.

Edward R. Tufte has written two outstanding works on the effective display of information, *Envisioning Information* (1990) and *The Visual Display of Quantitative Information* (1983). Reference to these fascinating books can help in the design of clear and meaningful tabular and graphic displays.

WORD PROCESSORS

Most spreadsheet software will output part or all of the spreadsheet in the form of page images that can be imported by most word processors. To export a spreadsheet, go to the spreadsheet menu under Print and select the File option; the page image(s) is written to a designated file which can, in turn, be inserted into a word processor text file where it can be edited and shaped as needed.

The chief problem occurs when the constraints of the text file are forgotten, and the page image won't fit properly. For example, text files are usually set up and printed in "portrait" format, e.g., on a sheet 8.5 inches wide and 11 inches long. Obviously, a landscape page image, designed for a sheet 11 inches wide and 8.5 inches long, will be out of place unless your word processor and printer can handle this format.

When preparing page images for export to a word processor, visualize the text format and how the page image will fit into the text. The page image will need to be compatible with the text margins, although it may be possible to use a smaller font with more characters per line. Chapter 14, "Formats of Component Parts and Sample Layouts," in the 5th edition of Turabian's *A Manual for Writers of Term Papers, Theses, and Dissertations* offers excellent advice and examples for the design of effective tables.

Some word processors are capable of importing a spreadsheet, or a portion of a spreadsheet, directly without having to go through an intermediary page image stage. Some also allow linkage so that updates to the spreadsheet are automatically reflected in the word processor file.

DATABASES

Some spreadsheet software programs will accept dBase, DIF (Data Interchange Format), and ASCII files as input. This is a particularly useful feature when one wants to analyze data already keyboarded in another format. In general, each imported record is displayed as a row, and each field as a cell within the row. Consult the spreadsheet and source file manuals and documentation for specific instructions.

The advantages of this approach quickly become evident when working with a large and complex set of data such as might be gained from a questionnaire. After keyboarding the data into a database, selected fields can be imported into a spreadsheet for analysis and display. Other combinations of fields can be imported into other spreadsheets for additional analyses and displays. In this way, a given field may be used in several spreadsheets without the necessity of rekeyboarding any of the data, and it is possible to examine a set of data from several points of view. Additionally, this approach enables analysis of data sets that are too large for a single spreadsheet.

Chapter 4
Three-Dimensional Spreadsheets

We live in a three-dimensional world in which objects have length, width, and height. Because we take this for granted, we find the idea of a two-dimensional world somewhat peculiar. The limits and characteristics of a two-dimensional world were explored by Edwin A. Abbott in *Flatland; A Romance of Many Dimensions* (1884). Just as the Flatlanders existed in a world of length and width but not height, most of the spreadsheets in use during the last decade have been laid out in two dimensions. Cells are arranged in rows and columns in a two-dimensional array in which the rows form the horizontal or x axis and columns form the vertical or y axis. However, if one visualizes a spreadsheet as having multiple pages, one behind the other (i.e., along the z axis), it can be said to be three-dimensional. Thus, a three-dimensional spreadsheet has cells arranged in an array with three axes, x, y, and z.

In addition to allowing the customary calculations with rows and columns, three-dimensional spreadsheets also allow calculations to be performed on a group of cells on two or more pages. For example, the cells D5;2 (i.e., the cell at the intersection of column D and row 5 on page 2), D5;3, and D5;4 can be totalled and the result displayed in D5;5 (column D, row 5, page 5) as is shown in Figure 4-A. In order to do this, the pages are formatted so that each cell on a page is consistent with the cells in that same location on the other pages.

This feature is useful in any application in which the same rows and columns can be repeated on two or more pages. Time series and other sets of data in which the same categories are repeated are especially appropriate candidates for this treatment. Or, data for each of several locations or persons can be gathered on separate pages.

Tables 4-1 to 4-4 show an example of a simple three-dimensional spreadsheet, so simple, in fact, that it is not particularly useful. (To be useful, it would need to be expanded to include much greater detail.) It is shown here to demonstrate several features of three-dimensional spreadsheets, including calculations summarizing several pages, rotation of the spreadsheet to permit viewing from different sides or perspectives, and the placement of additional and variant row and column labels which are necessary for viewing the spreadsheet from different sides and for correctly identifying multiple-page totals.

A page from this sample three-dimensional spreadsheet displays row labels for Salaries, Supplies, and Books and the Total of these three rows. Column labels for Allocations, Expenditures, and Balance are displayed with the year shown immediately above. Page 2 for 1988 is shown in Table 4-1. Pages 3 and 4 for 1989 and 1990 are shown in Tables 4-2 and 4-3.

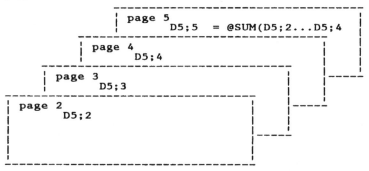

Figure 4-A: Schematic of Pages of a Three-Dimensional Spreadsheet

Table 4-1: Sample Three-Dimensional Spreadsheet, Page 2

	1988 Allocations	1988 Expenditures	1988 Balance
Salaries	100000	97400	2600
Supplies	23000	26750	-3750
Books	75000	74890	110
Total	198000	199040	-1040

Table 4-2: Sample Three-Dimensional Spreadsheet, Page 3

	1989 Allocations	1989 Expenditures	1989 Balance
Salaries	112500	111250	1250
Supplies	25000	24998	2
Books	79000	78987	13
Total	216500	215235	1265

Table 4-3: Sample Three-Dimensional Spreadsheet, Page 4

	1990 Allocations	1990 Expenditures	1990 Balance
Salaries	117850	117824	26
Supplies	25000	25340	-340
Books	87400	87085	315
Total	230250	230249	1

Page 5 (Table 4-4) contains totals for the previous pages: the column headings have been modified accordingly, and the values displayed are the result of formulas that add cells in pages 2-4. Alternatively, the formulas in page 5 can be displayed instead of the values as is shown in Table 4-5. For example, the formula in B5;5 (cell B5 of page 5) contains the formula @SUM(B5;2..B5;4), which can be read as "add the values in cells B5 of pages 2, 3, and 4 and display the sum in cell B5 of page 5." Analogous formulas occupy the other cells in which values are displayed.

Table 4-4: Sample Three-Dimensional Spreadsheet, Page 5

	1988-1990 Total Allocations	1988-1990 Total Expenditures	1988-1990 Total Balance
Salaries	330350	326474	3876
Supplies	73000	77088	-4088
Books	241400	240962	438
Total	644750	644524	226

Table 4-5: Sample Three-Dimensional Spreadsheet, Page 5 with Formulas Displayed

```
            A              B                 C                 D
     |----------|-------------------|-------------------|-------------------|
01   |                1988-1990          1988-1990          1988-1990
02   |                    Total              Total              Total
03   |                Allocations        Expenditures           Balance
04   |
05   Salaries     @SUM(B5;2..B5;4)   @SUM(C5;2..C5;4)   @SUM(D5;2..D5;4)
06   Supplies     @SUM(B6;2..B6;4)   @SUM(C6;2..C6;4)   @SUM(D6;2..D6;4)
07   Books        @SUM(B7;2..B7;4)   @SUM(C7;2..C7;4)   @SUM(D7;2..D7;4)
08                ================   ================   ================
09   Total        @SUM(B9;2..B9;4)   @SUM(C9;2..C9;4)   @SUM(D9;2..D9;4)
```

ROTATION

With some three-dimensional software the spreadsheet can be rotated and viewed from different sides. Imagine the spreadsheet as having the shape of a cube, as shown in Figure 4-B, with the front, right, and top sides visible. The remaining three sides, the back, left, and bottom, are mirror images of the front, right, and top.

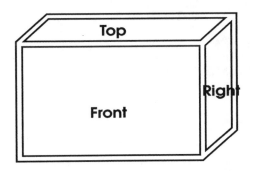

Figure 4-B: Three-Dimensional Spreadsheet Cube

The spreadsheet in Tables 4-1 to 4-5 was shown as viewed from the front. When the cube is rotated so that a different side is facing the user, the display will shift accordingly. For example, when rotated to the right side, the spreadsheet shows separate pages for Allocations, Expenditures, and Balance. Table 4-6 shows a view from the right, in this case, the Expenditures page. A top view reveals separate pages for Salaries, Supplies, Books, and Total. Table 4-7 shows a view from the top, in this case, the Salaries page.

If this spreadsheet is rotated to the right side, there will be no row labels; in fact column A is blank. This problem can be taken care of by copying the row labels from column A of page 2 into columns B, C, and D of page 1 where they will appear as row labels for right side displays. (This is why page 1 of this spreadsheet was left blank until now.) While page 1 is superfluous when viewed from the front, it is necessary for easy reading when viewed from the right.

Labels can be inserted to make the top view more easily read, too. Working from the front, enter the year in cells F5-F7 and F9 of pages 2-5; "(Total)" in cells G5-G7 of page 5; and "(Allocation)" in B5, "(Expenditure)" in C5, and "(Balance)" in D5 of page 6. The resulting top views are not as neat and trim as the front or right side; for example, the row and column labels are redundant because of the formatting for the front and right side views. While the parenthetical row and column labels shown at the right and at the bottom are not elegant, they serve their purpose. It should be noted that some pages (e.g., page 8, which is simply a series of lines) are meaningless from this point of view.

Table 4-6: Sample Three-Dimensional Spreadsheet—Right-Side View, Page 3

1988-1990	1988 Expenditures	1989 Expenditures	1990 Expenditures	Total Expenditures
Salaries	97400	111250	117824	326474
Supplies	26750	24998	25340	77088
Books	74890	78987	87085	240962
Total	199040	215235	230249	644524

Table 4-7: Sample Three-Dimensional Spreadsheet—Top View, Page 5

```
          Salaries  Salaries  Salaries  Salaries
Salaries    100000    112500    117850    330350  (Allocations)
Salaries     97400    111250    117824    326474  (Expenditures)
Salaries      2600      1250        26      3876  (Balance)

            (1988)    (1989)    (1990)   (1988-1990)
                                           (Total)
```

DESIGNING A THREE-DIMENSIONAL SPREADSHEET

Designing a three-dimensional spreadsheet is somewhat different from designing a two-dimensional spreadsheet. Indeed, the process can be the mental equivalent of first building and then finding one's way around a three-dimensional maze. Not only must one know the current cell location on the current page, one must also know which page and the locations of cells on other pages. As a result, designing even a small three-dimensional spreadsheet for the first time can be a slow process requiring a surprising amount of time and effort. Larger or more complicated three-dimensional spreadsheets will require proportionately more time and effort. As a rule of thumb, a three-dimensional spreadsheet will take at least three times the time and effort as a two-dimensional spreadsheet with the same number of rows and columns.

Because of the greater complexity and the greater opportunity to mis-cite cell addresses, it is particularly important to map out a three-dimensional spreadsheet on paper before beginning to construct it on the screen. First, sketch out the structure of a typical middle page. Then, sketch out the first, second, and final data pages, and make specific notes about how the pages are interrelated and how the summary page relates to the whole spreadsheet.

The typical page, probably any page other than the initial label page or the summary page, is the first page to be developed in detail. The basic structure is established here in terms of both the single page and the interrelationships among the pages. The rows and columns are labeled and formatted, cells in which values will be entered are identified, cells for totals are located, and formulas are specified.

If the spreadsheet is to be rotated, the first page will probably repeat the row labels from column A of page 2. Otherwise, treat the first page as the initial data page. Also, it may be useful to add row and column labels in strategic locations (e.g., at the right or the bottom of pages so that viewing the spreadsheet from the top will be meaningful).

The initial data page will probably look much like the typical page except that there will be no previous page from which cells can be copied. Therefore, most values on this page will probably need to be keyboarded.

The final page will probably be a summary page. (It is possible to designate the initial data page as the summary page, but we tend to think of quantitative summaries as coming at the end rather than at the beginning.) While the structure of the summary page will be reminiscent of the typical page, the row and column labels will probably be altered to indicate the summary function, and most cells will contain functions or formulas that gather and process data from the preceding pages.

Chapter 5
Fines

Most libraries have a policy of collecting fines for overdue materials. The spreadsheet presented in this chapter is for those who are averse to calculating these fines themselves. Of course, a simple formula can be used to calculate the number of days an item is overdue and the resulting fine, but this would be impractical unless the spreadsheet were kept running continuously and could be used on demand. (One version of such a formula, with a three-day grace period subtracted, is (@NOW-@DATE(93,6,3)-3)*.10, in which the due date [@DATE(93,6,3)] is subtracted from today's date [@NOW], the three grace days are subtracted [-3], and the days are multiplied by the daily fine rate [$.10].)

A more practical approach is a spreadsheet that displays a table in which one looks down the columns to the number of days an item is overdue and, by moving to the right, can see the fine due. The spreadsheet is shown here with fines from 1 to 200 days; however, additional days can be added easily. Also, the daily fine can be changed. The table can be printed and duplicated, although it is possible to look up fines on the screen.

To set up the Fines Table template, follow the general instructions and guidelines in Chapter 2, "Design and Modification of Spreadsheets."

The specifications, labels, and formulas for setting up the Fines Table template are shown below. Most of the columns are set at the default of nine spaces. Columns set at other widths are: B and D = 3; C = 50; AC, AF, and AI = 3; BA-BJ = 20-65 depending on need.

Begin by keyboarding the organizational statement.

FINES SPREADSHEET: CELL-BY-CELL INSTRUCTIONS

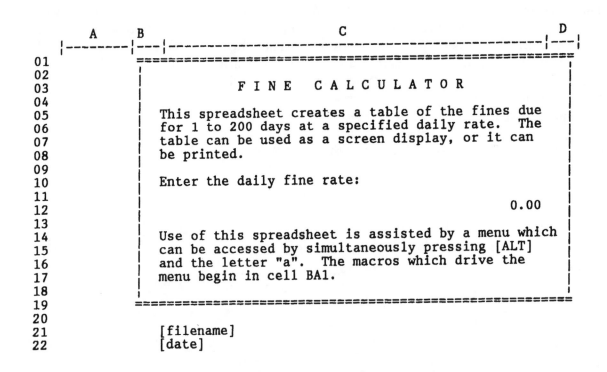

Keyboard the basic template into columns AA-AK, rows 1-53. Only the beginning and ending rows are shown below.

	AA number of days	AB amount due	AC	AD number of days	AE amount due	AF
01	number of	amount		number of	amount	
02	days	due		days	due	
03	=====	=====	===	=====	=====	===
04	1	+AA4*$C$12		51	+AD4*$C$12	
05	2	+AA5*$C$12		52	+AD5*$C$12	
06	3	+AA6*$C$12		53	+AD6*$C$12	
07	4	+AA7*$C$12		54	+AD7*$C$12	
08	5	+AA8*$C$12		55	+AD8*$C$12	
47	44	+AA47*$C$12		94	+AD47*$C$12	
48	45	+AA48*$C$12		95	+AD48*$C$12	
49	46	+AA49*$C$12		96	+AD49*$C$12	
50	47	+AA50*$C$12		97	+AD50*$C$12	
51	48	+AA51*$C$12		98	+AD51*$C$12	
52	49	+AA52*$C$12		99	+AD52*$C$12	
53	50	+AA53*$C$12		100	+AD53*$C$12	

	AG number of days	AH amount due	AI	AJ number of days	AK amount due
01	number of	amount		number of	amount
02	days	due		days	due
03	=====	=====	===	=====	=====
04	101	+AG4*$C$12		151	+AJ4*$C$12
05	102	+AG5*$C$12		152	+AJ5*$C$12
06	103	+AG6*$C$12		153	+AJ6*$C$12
07	104	+AG7*$C$12		154	+AJ7*$C$12
08	105	+AG8*$C$12		155	+AJ8*$C$12
47	144	+AG47*$C$12		194	+AJ47*$C$12
48	145	+AG48*$C$12		195	+AJ48*$C$12
49	146	+AG49*$C$12		196	+AJ49*$C$12
50	147	+AG50*$C$12		197	+AJ50*$C$12
51	148	+AG51*$C$12		198	+AJ51*$C$12
52	149	+AG52*$C$12		199	+AJ52*$C$12
53	150	+AG53*$C$12		200	+AJ53*$C$12

Note: Throughout the book, spreadsheet columns that run horizontally across the computer screen are stacked vertically to save space.

After keyboarding columns BA-BJ, rows 1-9, name the range AB1 "\0." This will cause the organizational statement to be displayed whenever the spreadsheet is loaded. Name the range BD1 "\a" so that the menu will be displayed when [ALT] and the letter "a" are pressed simultaneously.

```
         BA              BB            BC              BD                      BE
     |--------|--------------|---------|------------------|---------------|
01   |\0          /WTC           \a         {MENUBRANCH BE1}~ Rate
02               {GOTO}AA1~                                  Set fine rate
03               {QUIT}                                      /WTC
04                                                           {GOTO}A1~
05                                                           {RIGHT 2}~
06                                                           {DOWN 11}~
07                                                           {QUIT}
```

```
                   BF                                      BG
     |------------------------------------|--------------------------------------|
01   View                                  Print
02   See the table of calculated fines     Print the table of calculated fines
03   /WTC                                   /WTC
04   {GOTO}AA1~                             /PP
05   {QUIT}                                 RAA1~
06                                          R.
07                                          AA1..AK53~
08                                          GPQ
09                                          {QUIT}
```

```
                 BH                                    BI
     |----------------------------|--------------------------------------|
01   Save                          Quit
02   Save the spreadsheet          Exit Lotus 1-2-3.  SAVE FILE FIRST!
03   /WTC                          /WTC
04   /FS{?}~                       /QY~
05   {QUIT}                        {QUIT}
```

```
                          BJ
     |-------------------------------------------------------------|
01   Macro
02   Utility to move the cursor to the beginning of the menu program
03   /WTC
04   {GOTO}BA1~
05   {QUIT}
```

Save this template and make a working copy. A sample of the printed spreadsheet is shown in Table 5-1.

Table 5-1: Fines: 1 to 200 Days—11¢ per Day

number of days	amount due	number of days	amount due	number of days	amount due	number of days	amount due
1	0.11	51	5.61	101	11.11	151	16.61
2	0.22	52	5.72	102	11.22	152	16.72
3	0.33	53	5.83	103	11.33	153	16.83
4	0.44	54	5.94	104	11.44	154	16.94
5	0.55	55	6.05	105	11.55	155	17.05
6	0.66	56	6.16	106	11.66	156	17.16
7	0.77	57	6.27	107	11.77	157	17.27
8	0.88	58	6.38	108	11.88	158	17.38
9	0.99	59	6.49	109	11.99	159	17.49
10	1.10	60	6.60	110	12.10	160	17.60
11	1.21	61	6.71	111	12.21	161	17.71
12	1.32	62	6.82	112	12.32	162	17.82
13	1.43	63	6.93	113	12.43	163	17.93
14	1.54	64	7.04	114	12.54	164	18.04
15	1.65	65	7.15	115	12.65	165	18.15
16	1.76	66	7.26	116	12.76	166	18.26
17	1.87	67	7.37	117	12.87	167	18.37
18	1.98	68	7.48	118	12.98	168	18.48
19	2.09	69	7.59	119	13.09	169	18.59
20	2.20	70	7.70	120	13.20	170	18.70
21	2.31	71	7.81	121	13.31	171	18.81
22	2.42	72	7.92	122	13.42	172	18.92
23	2.53	73	8.03	123	13.53	173	19.03
24	2.64	74	8.14	124	13.64	174	19.14
25	2.75	75	8.25	125	13.75	175	19.25
26	2.86	76	8.36	126	13.86	176	19.36
27	2.97	77	8.47	127	13.97	177	19.47
28	3.08	78	8.58	128	14.08	178	19.58
29	3.19	79	8.69	129	14.19	179	19.69
30	3.30	80	8.80	130	14.30	180	19.80
31	3.41	81	8.91	131	14.41	181	19.91
32	3.52	82	9.02	132	14.52	182	20.02
33	3.63	83	9.13	133	14.63	183	20.13
34	3.74	84	9.24	134	14.74	184	20.24
35	3.85	85	9.35	135	14.85	185	20.35
36	3.96	86	9.46	136	14.96	186	20.46
37	4.07	87	9.57	137	15.07	187	20.57
38	4.18	88	9.68	138	15.18	188	20.68
39	4.29	89	9.79	139	15.29	189	20.79
40	4.40	90	9.90	140	15.40	190	20.90
41	4.51	91	10.01	141	15.51	191	21.01
42	4.62	92	10.12	142	15.62	192	21.12
43	4.73	93	10.23	143	15.73	193	21.23
44	4.84	94	10.34	144	15.84	194	21.34
45	4.95	95	10.45	145	15.95	195	21.45
46	5.06	96	10.56	146	16.06	196	21.56
47	5.17	97	10.67	147	16.17	197	21.67
48	5.28	98	10.78	148	16.28	198	21.78
49	5.39	99	10.89	149	16.39	199	21.89
50	5.50	100	11.00	150	16.50	200	22.00

Chapter 6
Grades

Librarians who teach courses, such as bibliographic instruction, must assign a grade for each student's work. A librarian conducting in-service training sessions may also need to assign grades. This spreadsheet is designed to assist in the task of keeping track of the grades for each assignment, project, and examination and their relative weights by calculating the final grade.

Create a generic template as directed below. The template is set up with only three students, four assignments, and an examination with the percentage weight assigned to each. To enter the template and add students' names, assignments, and examinations, follow the general instructions and guidelines in Chapter 2, "Design and Modification of Spreadsheets." The specifications, labels, and formulas for setting up the template are shown below. Set the column widths as follows: B and D = 3, AA = 25, AB = 12, AC-AH = 10, AI = 3, and BA-BK = 9-65 as necessary to display macros.

Begin by keyboarding the organizational statement.

GRADES SPREADSHEET: CELL-BY-CELL INSTRUCTIONS

```
            A         B   C                                                   D
     |----------|---|-------------------------------------------------|---|
01             ==================================================================
02             |                                                                |
03             |            G R A D E   C A L C U L A T O R                     |
04             |                                                                |
05             |   This spreadsheet calculates grades based on                  |
06             |   project and examination scores.  Use of this                 |
07             |   spreadsheet is assisted by a menu which can be               |
08             |   activated by simultaneously pressing [ALT] and               |
09             |   the letter "a".                                              |
10             |                                                                |
11             |   Select "Setup" to customize the spreadsheet.                 |
12             |   Modify columns, change percentages, edit formulas,           |
13             |   and enter names and social security numbers.                 |
14             |                                                                |
15             |   Select "Enter" to input project and test scores.             |
16             |   Entry will be faster if automatic recalculation              |
17             |   is turned off.  Select "Calculate" to recalculate            |
18             |   the spreadsheet.                                             |
19             |                                                                |
20             |   Edit the formulas in column AJ to include all                |
21             |   projects and tests; also, set the lower and upper            |
22             |   limits for each letter grade.                                |
23             |                                                                |
24             |   The macros which drive the menu begin at BA1.                |
25             |                                                                |
26             ==================================================================
27
28             [filename]
29             [date]
```

Keyboard the basic template into columns AA through AJ, rows 101-111. Follow the instructions in Chapter 2 for adding more students and additional assignments and examinations or for changing the criteria for grades.

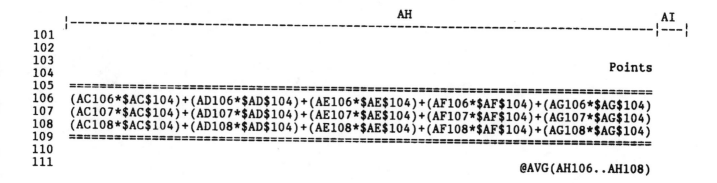

	AA	AB	AC	AD
			Assign/ percent	Assign/ percent
101	Bibliographic Instruction : Grades			
102	[date]			
103			1	2
104	Name	SS#	0.00	0.00
105	================================	==========	==============	==============
106	xxxx, xxxx	xxx-xx-xxxx	0	0
107	xxxx, xxxx	xxx-xx-xxxx	0	0
108	xxxx, xxxx	xxx-xx-xxxx	0	0
109	================================	==========	==============	==============
110				
111	Average		@AVG(AC106..AC108)	@AVG(AD106..AD108)

	AE	AF	AG
	Assign/ percent	Assign/ percent	
101			
102			
103	3	4	Exam
104	0.30	0.15	0.25
105	=========	=========	=========
106	0	0	0
107	0	0	0
108	0	0	0
109	=========	=========	=========
110			
111	@AVG(AE106..AE108)	@AVG(AF106..AF108)	@AVG(AG106..AG108)

	AH	AI
101		
102		
103		
104	Points	
105	===	====
106	(AC106*$AC$104)+(AD106*$AD$104)+(AE106*$AE$104)+(AF106*$AF$104)+(AG106*$AG$104)	
107	(AC107*$AC$104)+(AD107*$AD$104)+(AE107*$AE$104)+(AF107*$AF$104)+(AG107*$AG$104)	
108	(AC108*$AC$104)+(AD108*$AD$104)+(AE108*$AE$104)+(AF108*$AF$104)+(AG108*$AG$104)	
109	===	====
110		
111	@AVG(AH106..AH108)	

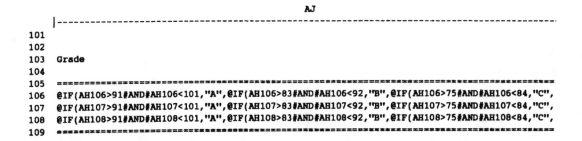

```
                                          AJ
      |----------------------------------------------------------------------------
  101
  102
  103  Grade
  104
  105  ===========================================================================
  106  @IF(AH106>91#AND#AH106<101,"A",@IF(AH106>83#AND#AH106<92,"B",@IF(AH106>75#AND#AH106<84,"C",
  107  @IF(AH107>91#AND#AH107<101,"A",@IF(AH107>83#AND#AH107<92,"B",@IF(AH107>75#AND#AH107<84,"C",
  108  @IF(AH108>91#AND#AH108<101,"A",@IF(AH108>83#AND#AH108<92,"B",@IF(AH108>75#AND#AH108<84,"C",
  109  ===========================================================================
```

```
                              AJ (continued)
      ----------------------------------------------------------------|



          ============================================================
          @IF(AH106>67#AND#AH106<76,"D",@IF(AH106<68,"F","ERROR")))))
          @IF(AH107>67#AND#AH107<76,"D",@IF(AH107<68,"F","ERROR")))))
          @IF(AH108>67#AND#AH108<76,"D",@IF(AH108<68,"F","ERROR")))))
          ============================================================
```

After keyboarding columns BA-BK, name the range BB1 "\0" so that the introductory box will be displayed automatically when the spreadsheet is loaded. Name the range BD1 "\a" so that the menu will be displayed when [ALT] and the letter "a" are pressed simultaneously.

```
        BA            BB          BC            BD
   |----------|------------|----------|----------------------|
01 |\0        |/WTC        |\a        |{MENUBRANCH BE1}~      |
02 |          |{GOTO}A1~   |          |                      |
03 |          |{QUIT}      |          |                      |
```

```
                        BE                                              BF
   |----------------------------------------------------------|-----------------------------------|
01 |Setup                                                     |Enter                              |
02 |Set up assignments, add names to list, etc.              |Add project and test scores        |
03 |/WTC                                                      |/WTC                               |
04 |{GOTO}AA101~                                              |{GOTO}AA101~                       |
05 |{QUIT}                                                    |{RIGHT 2}                          |
06 |                                                          |{DOWN 5}                           |
07 |                                                          |/WTB                               |
08 |                                                          |{QUIT}                             |
```

```
                BG                                  BH
   |-------------------------------|--------------------------|
01 |Calculate                      |Print                     |
02 |Recalculates the spreadsheet   |Prints the spreadsheet    |
03 |/WTC                           |/WTC                      |
04 |{CALC}                         |/PP                       |
05 |{QUIT}                         |RAA101~                   |
06 |                               |R.                        |
07 |                               |{DOWN 2}                  |
08 |                               |{END}{DOWN}               |
09 |                               |{RIGHT 9}                 |
10 |                               |{DOWN 2}                  |
11 |                               |GPPQ                      |
12 |                               |{QUIT}                    |
```

```
                BI                                         BJ
   |------------------------------------|---------------------------------------------|
01 |File                                |Quit                                         |
02 |Saves the spreadsheet to disk       |Exits Lotus 1-2-3.  SAVE FILE FIRST!         |
03 |/WTC                                |/WTC                                         |
04 |/FS{?}~                             |/QY                                          |
05 |{QUIT}                              |{QUIT}                                       |
```

```
                                BK
   |-----------------------------------------------------------------|
01 |Macro                                                            |
02 |Utility to move the cursor to the beginning of the menu program  |
03 |/WTC                                                             |
04 |{GOTO}BA1~                                                       |
05 |{QUIT}                                                           |
```

Save this completed template. Load a copy of the template and enter the class name and date in cells AA101 and AA102. Make the necessary adjustments for the number of students, assignments, and examinations. Enter the students' names and social security numbers in columns AA and AB. Enter the weight of each assignment and examination beginning in cell AC104. Adjust the grade ranges in AJ106 and copy this revised formula in the cells below. Finally, enter the data for assignments and examinations. An example of the completed spreadsheet, with fictitious data, is shown below in Table 6-1.

Table 6-1: Grades

Bibliographic Instruction: Grades February 21, 1992		Assign/ percent 1	Assign/ percent 2	Assign/ percent 3	Assign/ percent 4	Exam	Points	Grade
Name	SS#	0.20	0.10	0.30	0.15	0.25		
Brown, Judy	123-45-6789	99	95	98	99	100	98.6	A
Black, Ralph	987-65-4321	80	78	83	81	82	81.4	C
Blue, Janice	444-55-6666	65	73	70	69	74	70.2	D
Average		81.3	82.0	83.7	83.0	85.3	83.4	

Chapter 7
Currency Exchange Rates

A frequent problem in acquisitions and serials units is converting the amounts on invoices billed in other currencies into the domestic currency. The inverse problem of converting from the domestic currency to another currency occurs less frequently because libraries tend to pay for materials and services in their domestic currency. The Currency Exchange Rates template easily performs both types of conversion.

The prevailing currency exchange rates can be secured from banks and some other financial institutions. Some newspapers also quote exchange rates. *The Wall Street Journal* lists bank-to-bank exchange rates. Most institutions follow the official rate, although this rate may be very different from the one quoted to tourists or available through black market or other sources.

Many libraries approve invoices and then forward them to a business office for payment. Because of the inherent time lag, too often measured in weeks or even months, the amount actually paid may be significantly different from the earlier estimate made by the library. Nevertheless, it is necessary for the library to consider currency exchange rates as a part of the process of fund encumbrance and dispersal.

The Currency Exchange Rates template provides spaces for the names of monetary units, the prevailing exchange rates, and the dates the rates were entered. Then, specific amounts can be calculated to or from the domestic currency.

To set up the Currency Exchange Rates template, follow the general instructions and guidelines in Chapter 2, "Design and Modification of Spreadsheets." Only six currencies are shown in the template. Additional currencies can be added by keyboarding a currency name into the first available blank line, entering the exchange rate, and noting the date. The specifications, labels, and formulas for setting up the Currency Exchange Rates template are shown below.

These columns are set at widths other than the default of nine spaces:

B = 3	AE = 12	AK = 15	BH = 60
C = 45	AF = 4	BB = 12	BI = 75
D = 3	AG = 15	BD = 30	BJ = 75
AA = 20	AH = 15	BE = 25	BK = 40
AB = 3	AI = 4	BF = 55	BL = 65
AD = 3	AJ = 15	BG = 60	

Set the display of currency numbers to Currency with two digits after the decimal. Begin by keyboarding the organizational statement in columns B-D, rows 2-29.

CURRENCY EXCHANGE RATES SPREADSHEET: CELL-BY-CELL INSTRUCTIONS

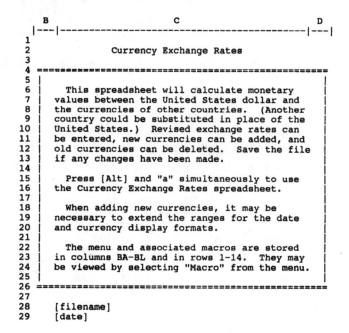

Keyboard the basic template into columns AA through AK, rows 101-115.

```
            AA              AB      AC    AD      AE        AF
    |-------------------|---|----------|---|----------|----|
101 |
102 |
103 |
104 |                    |            |            | |
105 |                    |  Exchange  |  Exchange  | |
106 | National           |  Rate in   |  Rate Date | |
107 | Currency           |  Dollars   | (mmm dd, yr)| |
108 |-------------------|-----------|------------| |-
109 |                    |            |            | |
110 | currency 1         |     0      |     0      | |
111 | currency 2         |     0      |     0      | |
112 | currency 3         |     0      |     0      | |
113 | currency 4         |     0      |     0      | |
114 | currency 5         |     0      |     0      | |
115 | currency 6         |     0      |     0      | |
```

```
            AG              AH            AI    AJ           AK
    |----------------|----------------|---|-----------|-----------------
101 | Currency Exchange Rates
102 |
103 |    To U.S. Dollars                    From U.S. Dollars
104 |================================| |================================
105 |                                  | |
106 | National          US             | |    US         National
107 | Currency          Dollars        | |    Dollars    Currency
108 |--------------------------------| |--------------------------------
109 |                                  | |
110 |        0      +AG110*AC110       | |      0      +AJ110/AC110
111 |        0      +AG111*AC111       | |      0      +AJ111/AC111
112 |        0      +AG112*AC112       | |      0      +AJ112/AC112
113 |        0      +AG113*AC113       | |      0      +AJ113/AC113
114 |        0      +AG114*AC114       | |      0      +AJ114/AC114
115 |        0      +AG115*AC115       | |      0      +AJ115/AC115
```

After keyboarding columns BA-BL, name the range BB1 "\0" so that the instructions will be displayed automatically when the spreadsheet is retrieved. Name the range BD1 "\a" so that the menu will be displayed when [ALT] and the letter "a" are pressed simultaneously.

```
        BA          BB          BC              BD
    |--------|---------------|--------|-----------------------------|
 1  | \0      '/WTC            \a       {MENUBRANCH BE1}~
 2  |         {GOTO}A1~
 3  |         {RIGHT 2}~
 4  |         {DOWN 5}~
 5  |         {QUIT}
 6  |
 7  |
 8  |
 9  |
```

```
                            BE
   |-------------------------------------|
   |                                     |
 1 Rate
 2 Enter new exchange rate
 3 {WINDOWSOFF}~
 4 '/WTC
 5 {GOTO}AA101~
 6 {RIGHT 2}~
 7 DOWN 9}~
 8 'WTB
 9 {WINDOWSON}~
10 {QUIT}
```

```
                            BF
   |------------------------------------------------|
   |                                                |
 1 US
 2 Convert a national currency to United States dollars
 3 {WINDOWSOFF}~
 4 '/WTC
 5 {GOTO}AA101~
 6 {RIGHT 2}~
 7 {DOWN 9}~
 8 '/WTB
 9 {RIGHT 8}~
10 {LEFT 4}~
11 {WINDOWSON}~
12 {QUIT}
```

```
                            BG
   |----------------------------------------------------------|
   |                                                          |
 1 National
 2 Convert United States Dollars to another national currency
 3 {WINDOWSOFF}~
 4 '/WTC
 5 {GOTO}AA101~
 6 {RIGHT 2}~
 7 {DOWN 9}~
 8 '/WTB
 9 {RIGHT 11}~
10 {LEFT 4}~
11 {WINDOWSON}~
12 {QUIT}
```

```
                            BH
   |----------------------------------------------------------|
   |                                                          |
 1 Save
 2 Saves the spreadsheet to disk.  Supply a filename as needed
 3 '/WTC
 4 '/FS{?}~
 5 {QUIT}
```

```
                              BI
 |----------------------------------------------------------------|
 1 Print
 2 Sends the list of currency names, exchange rates, and dates to
     the printer
 3 '/WTC
 4 '/PPRAA101~
 5 R.
 6 {DOWN 9}~
 7 {END}{DOWN}
 8 {RIGHT 4}~
 9 G
10 P
11 Q
12 {QUIT}
```

```
                              BJ
 |----------------------------------------------------------------|
 1 File
 2 Writes the list of currencies, exchange rates, and dates in a
     disk file
 3 '/WTC
 4 '/PF{?}
 5 {GOTO}AA101~
 6 R.AA101~
 7 R.
 8 {DOWN 9}~
 9 {END}{DOWN}
10 {RIGHT 4}~
11 G
12 P
13 Q
14 {QUIT}
```

```
                    BK
 |--------------------------------------------|
 1 Quit
 2 Exits Lotus 1-2-3.  SAVE FILES FIRST!
 3 '/WTC
 4 '/QY
 5 {QUIT}
```

```
                         BL
 |--------------------------------------------------------------|
 1 Macro
 2 Utility to move the cursor to the beginning of the menu program
 3 '/WTC
 4 {GOTO}BA1~
 5 {QUIT}
```

Save this completed template. Load a copy of the template and enter currency names, rates, and dates. If more currencies are needed, copy the formulas in AH115 and AK115 into as many additional lines as are needed. An example of the completed spreadsheet is shown below in Table 7-1.

Table 7-1: Currency Exchange Rates

| National Currency | Exchange Rate in Dollars | Exchange Rate Date (mmm dd, yr) | To U.S. Dollars | | From U.S. Dollars | |
			National Currency	US Dollars	US Dollars	National Currency
England	1.88	Jan 13, 92	23.50	44.18	32.60	17.34
Germany	0.66	Jan 13, 92	147.75	97.52	32.60	49.39
France	0.19	Jan 13, 92	219.00	41.61	32.60	171.58
Japan	0.008	Jan 13, 92	4800.00	38.40	32.60	4,075.00
Canada	0.91	Jan 13, 92	87.20	79.35	32.60	35.82
Switzerland	0.75	Jan 13, 92	54.40	40.80	32.60	43.47

A visual representation of the relative differences among the six currencies and the U.S. dollar are shown below in Figure 7-A. The horizontal mid-point line represents the value of one dollar.

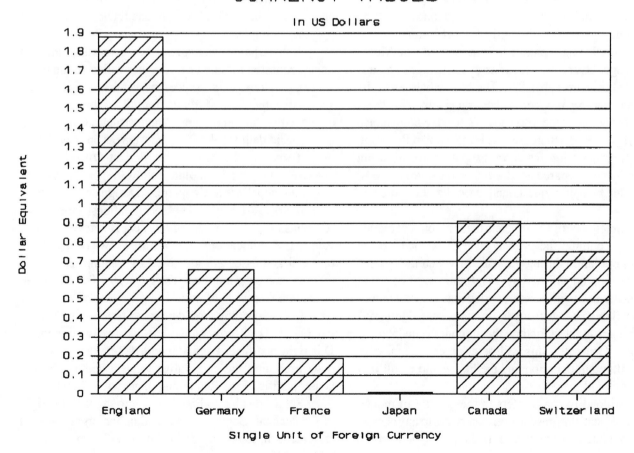

Figure 7-A: Currency Values in U.S. Dollars

Chapter 8
Multi-Year Budget Overview

A template for preparing a one-year budget request was presented in Chapter 4 of *Electronic Spreadsheets for Libraries*. The approach followed was to set the requested budget in the context of the previous two years so that data for three years could be viewed together: the expenditure level for the first year, the initial request and the final allocation for the second year, and the request for the third year. In this chapter that earlier template is expanded, using software for a three-dimensional spreadsheet, to accommodate several years' requests with the data for each year's detailed request on a separate page. With the addition of successive years' requests, a time series is developed that shows the budget history.

A sample page (page 10, front view) of the Multi-Year Budget Overview: Requests & Allocations spreadsheet is shown in Table 8-1. The row labels are self-explanatory as are most of the column labels. However, three of the column labels need to be defined: Maintenance of Effort, Workload Increase, and Expansion of Program. By keeping these three categories separate, the librarian will be better prepared to document budgetary needs, defend the budget request, and describe the expected benefits.

Maintenance of Effort refers to the amount of money needed to continue the present level of services to the present population during the year for which the request is being prepared. If there is no inflation, cost of living adjustments, salary increases, or price changes, the amount needed will not change from the previous year. However, with changes in these factors, the amount needed will be different. Generally, this will be a larger amount than before, although deflation and the like would result in a smaller amount.

Workload Increase refers to the amount of money needed to extend the present level of services to any change in the population being served. If the population served changes because of such things as annexation or greater enrollment, Workload Increase will be a positive amount. However, if the population served changes because of such things as migration away from the community, plant closure, or a decrease in enrollment, Workload Increase will be a negative amount. In a nation with a growing population and industrial and economic expansion, the Workload Increase factor is usually a positive amount.

Expansion of Program refers to the amount of money needed to introduce new services which have not previously been provided. The addition of video tapes and CD-ROM disks, the inauguration of bookmobile service, and the establishment of a telephone reference center are possible examples.

A single page of this spreadsheet presents the amount being requested for one year together with a summary of the two previous years. Successive years are displayed on successive pages, and totals for all of the years are displayed on the final page. The instructions appear on page 1, and data for the first year appear on page 10.

To set up the Multi-Year Budget Overview: Requests & Allocations template, follow the general instructions and guidelines in Chapter 2, "Design and Modification of Spreadsheets." The specifications, labels, and formulas for setting up the Multi-Year Budget Overview: Requests & Allocations template are shown below. Note that cell addresses are identified by column letter, row number, and page number. Thus, C5;10 refers to the cell in column C, row 5, of page 10.

Column widths should be set as follows: Page 1: B = 3, C = 50, D = 3; column B is left-justified, while column D is right-justified. Page 8: width = 22. Page 9 and the page preceding the cumulative totals: width = 3; use center justification. Remaining pages: A = 22, B-H-12.

Set the display to Fixed with zero digits to the right of the decimal. Begin by keyboarding the organizational statement in columns B-D, rows 2-35, on page 1 (B2;1..D35;1).

MULTI-YEAR BUDGET OVERVIEW SPREADSHEET: CELL-BY-CELL INSTRUCTIONS

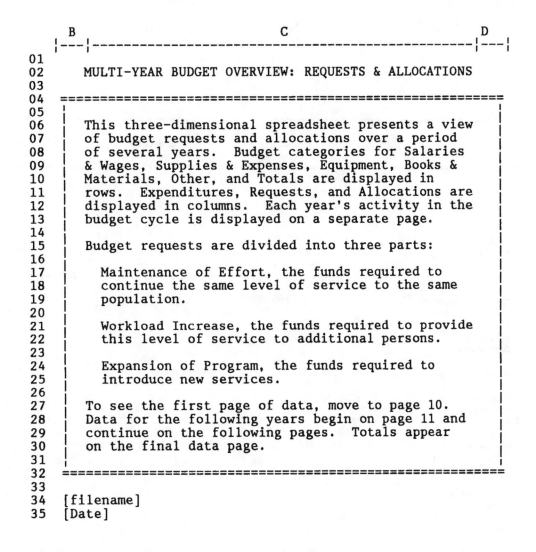

```
           B                          C                          D
      !---!----------------------------------------------!---!
   01 !
   02 !     MULTI-YEAR BUDGET OVERVIEW: REQUESTS & ALLOCATIONS
   03
   04 ================================================================
   05 !                                                              !
   06 !     This three-dimensional spreadsheet presents a view       !
   07 !     of budget requests and allocations over a period         !
   08 !     of several years.  Budget categories for Salaries        !
   09 !     & Wages, Supplies & Expenses, Equipment, Books &         !
   10 !     Materials, Other, and Totals are displayed in            !
   11 !     rows.  Expenditures, Requests, and Allocations are       !
   12 !     displayed in columns.  Each year's activity in the       !
   13 !     budget cycle is displayed on a separate page.            !
   14 !                                                              !
   15 !     Budget requests are divided into three parts:            !
   16 !                                                              !
   17 !       Maintenance of Effort, the funds required to           !
   18 !       continue the same level of service to the same         !
   19 !       population.                                            !
   20 !                                                              !
   21 !       Workload Increase, the funds required to provide       !
   22 !       this level of service to additional persons.           !
   23 !                                                              !
   24 !       Expansion of Program, the funds required to            !
   25 !       introduce new services.                                !
   26 !                                                              !
   27 !     To see the first page of data, move to page 10.          !
   28 !     Data for the following years begin on page 11 and        !
   29 !     continue on the following pages.  Totals appear          !
   30 !     on the final data page.                                  !
   31 !                                                              !
   32 ================================================================
   33
   34 [filename]
   35 [Date]
```

Keyboard the basic template into columns A-H, rows 1-54, on page 10 (A1;10..H54;10). It is not necessary to include the page number in a formula if it refers only to cells on the same page; however, the software will insert the page numbers.

	A	B	C	D
01				
02				
03				
04	===		
05				
06		Expended	Requested	Allocated
07		year 1	year 2	year 2
08	===		
09				
10	Salaries & Wages			
11	Professional	0	0	0
12	LTA	0	0	0
13	Clerical	0	0	0
14	Hourly	0	0	0
15	Benefits*	@SUM(B11..B13)*B52	@SUM(C11..C13)*B53	@SUM(D11..D13)*B53
16		-----------	-----------	-----------
17	Sub-Total	@SUM(B11..B15)	@SUM(C11..C15)	@SUM(D11..D15)
18				
19	Supplies & Expenses			
20	Communications	0	0	0
21	Stationery	0	0	0
22	Utilities	0	0	0
23	Contractual	0	0	0
24		-----------	-----------	-----------
25	Sub-Total	@SUM(B20..B23)	@SUM(C20..C23)	@SUM(D20..D23)
26				
27	Equipment			
28	Furniture	0	0	0
29	Motor vehicle	0	0	0
30		-----------	-----------	-----------
31	Sub-Total	@SUM(B28..B29)	@SUM(C28..C29)	@SUM(D28..D29)
32				
33	Books & Materials			
34	Books	0	0	0
35	Periodicals	0	0	0
36	Audiovisual	0	0	0
37	Services	0	0	0
38	Binding	0	0	0
39		-----------	-----------	-----------
40	Sub-Total	@SUM(B34..B38)	@SUM(C34..C38)	@SUM(D34..D38)
41				
42	Other			
43	Building & Repairs	0	0	0
44	Contingency	0	0	0
45		-----------	-----------	-----------
46	Sub-Total	@SUM(B43..B44)	@SUM(C43..C44)	@SUM(D43..D44)
47				
48		===========	===========	===========
49	TOTAL	+B17+B25+B31+B40+B46	+C17+C25+C31+C40+C46	+D17+D25+D31+D40+D46
50				
51	*benefits:			
52	year 1 =	0		
53	year 2 =	0		
54	year 3 =	0		

The yearly benefit rates will need to be adjusted in lines 51-54, columns A and B, from year to year.

```
               E                  F                    G                  H
  |-------------------|---------------------|---------------------|----------------|
01
02
03 ===============================================================================
04        Maintenance          Workload            Expansion
05         of effort           increase           of program            Total
06         requested           requested           requested          requested
07           year 3              year 3              year 3             year 3
08 ===============================================================================
09
10
11             0                   0                   0           @SUM(E11..G11)
12             0                   0                   0           @SUM(E12..G12)
13             0                   0                   0           @SUM(E13..G13)
14             0                   0                   0           @SUM(E14..G14)
15  @SUM(E11..E13)*B54   @SUM(F11..F13)*B54   @SUM(G11..G13)*B54   @SUM(E15..G15)
16     -----------          -----------          -----------         -----------
17  @SUM(E11..E15)      @SUM(F11..F15)      @SUM(G11..G15)      @SUM(E17..G17)
18
19
20             0                   0                   0           @SUM(E20..G20)
21             0                   0                   0           @SUM(E21..G21)
22             0                   0                   0           @SUM(E22..G22)
23             0                   0                   0           @SUM(E23..G23)
24     -----------          -----------          -----------         -----------
25  @SUM(E20..E23)      @SUM(F20..F23)      @SUM(G20..G23)      @SUM(E25..G25)
26
27
28             0                   0                   0           @SUM(E28..G28)
29             0                   0                   0           @SUM(E29..G29)
30     -----------          -----------          -----------         -----------
31  @SUM(E28..E29)      @SUM(F28..F29)      @SUM(G28..G29)      @SUM(E31..G31)
32
33
34             0                   0                   0           @SUM(E34..G34)
35             0                   0                   0           @SUM(E35..G35)
36             0                   0                   0           @SUM(E36..G36)
37             0                   0                   0           @SUM(E37..G37)
38             0                   0                   0           @SUM(E38..G38)
39     -----------          -----------          -----------         -----------
40  @SUM(E34..E38)      @SUM(F34..F38)      @SUM(G34..G38)      @SUM(E40..G40)
41
42
43             0                   0                   0           @SUM(E43..G43)
44             0                   0                   0           @SUM(E44..G44)
45     -----------          -----------          -----------         -----------
46  @SUM(E43..E44)      @SUM(F43..F44)      @SUM(G43..G44)      @SUM(E46..G46)
47
48  ===========          ===========          ===========         ===========
49 +E17+E25+E31+E40+E46 +F17+F25+F31+F40+F46 +G17+G25+G31+G40+G46 @SUM(E49..G49)
50
51
```

Copy the row labels in column A of page 10 onto page 8 in as many columns, beginning with column B, as there are annual data pages. This will provide row labels when the spreadsheet is rotated and viewed from the right side.

Enter vertical lines on page 9 beginning with column B, rows 1-54, and on the page preceding the cumulative totals, again beginning with column B, rows 1-54, in as many columns as there are annual data pages. This will permit insertion or deletion of pages without affecting the cumulative total formulas on the final page.

Copy page 10 onto page 11. On page 11, edit column C as shown below. This is necessary because, for the second year, formulas are used which carry forward the request totals from the previous year. After the formulas have been keyboarded onto page 11, this page can be copied into succeeding pages for as many years as are needed, and each will carry forward the request totals from the previous year.

```
                             C
         !------------------!
01       !                  !
02
03       ====================
04
05                    Total
06                Requested
07                   year 3
08       ====================
09
10
11                   H11;10
12                   H12;10
13                   H13;10
14                   H14;10
15                   H15;10
16       ------------------
17                   H17;10
18
19
20                   H20;10
21                   H21;10
22                   H22;10
23                   H23;10
24       ------------------
25                   H25;10
26
27
28                   H28;10
29                   H29;10
30       ------------------
31                   H31;10
32
33
34                   H34;10
35                   H35;10
36                   H36;10
37                   H37;10
38                   H38;10
39       ------------------
40                   H40;10
41
42
43                   H43;10
44                   H44;10
45       ------------------
46                   H46;10
47
48       ====================
49                   H49;10
50
51
```

Keyboard the labels and formulas for the final or total page as shown below. Because these formulas refer to more than one page, it is necessary to include the page numbers.

Save this completed template. Load a copy of the template and enter the data in the appropriate cells.

```
               A                    B                   C                  D
     |-------------------- |--------------------|-------------------|--------------------|
  01 ========================================================================================
  02
  03
  04                              Total               Total              Total
  05                             Expended           Requested          Allocated
  06                              Years               Years              Years
  07                               1-5                 2-6                2-6
  08 ========================================================================================
  09
  10 Salaries & Wages
  11    Professional         @SUM(B11;9..B11;15)  @SUM(C11;9..C11;15)  @SUM(D11;9..D11;15)
  12    LTA                  @SUM(B12;9..B12;15)  @SUM(C12;9..C12;15)  @SUM(D12;9..D12;15)
  13    Clerical             @SUM(B13;9..B13;15)  @SUM(C13;9..C13;15)  @SUM(D13;9..D13;15)
  14    Hourly               @SUM(B14;9..B14;15)  @SUM(C14;9..C14;15)  @SUM(D14;9..D14;15)
  15    Benefits             @SUM(B15;9..B15;15)  @SUM(C15;9..C15;15)  @SUM(D15;9..D15;15)
  16                            ----------          ----------          ----------
  17    Sub-Total            @SUM(B17;9..B17;15)  @SUM(C17;9..C17;15)  @SUM(D17;9..D17;15)
  18
  19 Supplies & Expenses
  20    Communications       @SUM(B20;9..B20;15)  @SUM(C20;9..C20;15)  @SUM(D20;9..D20;15)
  21    Stationery           @SUM(B21;9..B21;15)  @SUM(C21;9..C21;15)  @SUM(D21;9..D21;15)
  22    Utilities            @SUM(B22;9..B22;15)  @SUM(C22;9..C22;15)  @SUM(D22;9..D22;15)
  23    Contractual          @SUM(B23;9..B23;15)  @SUM(C23;9..C23;15)  @SUM(D23;9..D23;15)
  24                            ----------          ----------          ----------
  25    Sub-Total            @SUM(B25;9..B25;15)  @SUM(C25;9..C25;15)  @SUM(D25;9..D25;15)
  26
  27 Equipment
  28    Furniture            @SUM(B28;9..B28;15)  @SUM(C28;9..C28;15)  @SUM(D28;9..D28;15)
  29    Motor vehicle        @SUM(B29;9..B29;15)  @SUM(C29;9..C29;15)  @SUM(D29;9..D29;15)
  30                            ----------          ----------          ----------
  31    Sub-Total            @SUM(B31;9..B31;15)  @SUM(C31;9..C31;15)  @SUM(D31;9..D31;15)
  32
  33 Books & Materials
  34    Books                @SUM(B34;9..B34;15)  @SUM(C34;9..C34;15)  @SUM(D34;9..D34;15)
  35    Periodicals          @SUM(B35;9..B35;15)  @SUM(C35;9..C35;15)  @SUM(D35;9..D35;15)
  36    Audiovisual          @SUM(B36;9..B36;15)  @SUM(C36;9..C36;15)  @SUM(D36;9..D36;15)
  37    Services             @SUM(B37;9..B37;15)  @SUM(C37;9..C37;15)  @SUM(D37;9..D37;15)
  38    Binding              @SUM(B38;9..B38;15)  @SUM(C38;9..C38;15)  @SUM(D38;9..D38;15)
  39                            ----------          ----------          ----------
  40    Sub-Total            @SUM(B40;9..B40;15)  @SUM(C40;9..C40;15)  @SUM(D40;9..D40;15)
  41
  42 Other
  43    Building & Repairs   @SUM(B43;9..B43;15)  @SUM(C43;9..C43;15)  @SUM(D43;9..D43;15)
  44    Contingency          @SUM(B44;9..B44;15)  @SUM(C44;9..C44;15)  @SUM(D44;9..D44;15)
  45                            ----------          ----------          ----------
  46    Sub-Total            @SUM(B46;9..B46;15)  @SUM(C46;9..C46;15)  @SUM(D46;9..D46;15)
  47
  48                            ==========          ==========          ==========
  49    TOTAL                @SUM(B49;9..B49;15)  @SUM(C49;9..C49;15)  @SUM(D49;9..D49;15)
```

	E	F	G	H
	Total Maintenance of Effort Requested Years 3-7	Total Workload Increase Requested Years 3-7	Total Expansion of Program Requested Years 3-7	Total Requested Years 3-7
11	@SUM(E11;9..E11;15)	@SUM(F11;9..F11;15)	@SUM(G11;9..G11;15)	@SUM(H11;9..H11;15)
12	@SUM(E12;9..E12;15)	@SUM(F12;9..F12;15)	@SUM(G12;9..G12;15)	@SUM(H12;9..H12;15)
13	@SUM(E13;9..E13;15)	@SUM(F13;9..F13;15)	@SUM(G13;9..G13;15)	@SUM(H13;9..H13;15)
14	@SUM(E14;9..E14;15)	@SUM(F14;9..F14;15)	@SUM(G14;9..G14;15)	@SUM(H14;9..H14;15)
15	@SUM(E15;9..E15;15)	@SUM(F15;9..F15;15)	@SUM(G15;9..G15;15)	@SUM(H15;9..H15;15)
16	----------	----------	----------	----------
17	@SUM(E17;9..E17;15)	@SUM(F17;9..F17;15)	@SUM(G17;9..G17;15)	@SUM(H17;9..H17;15)
20	@SUM(E20;9..E20;15)	@SUM(F20;9..F20;15)	@SUM(G20;9..G20;15)	@SUM(H20;9..H20;15)
21	@SUM(E21;9..E21;15)	@SUM(F21;9..F21;15)	@SUM(G21;9..G21;15)	@SUM(H21;9..H21;15)
22	@SUM(E22;9..E22;15)	@SUM(F22;9..F22;15)	@SUM(G22;9..G22;15)	@SUM(H22;9..H22;15)
23	@SUM(E23;9..E23;15)	@SUM(F23;9..F23;15)	@SUM(G23;9..G23;15)	@SUM(H23;9..H23;15)
24	----------	----------	----------	----------
25	@SUM(E25;9..E25;15)	@SUM(F25;9..F25;15)	@SUM(G25;9..G25;15)	@SUM(H25;9..H25;15)
28	@SUM(E28;9..E28;15)	@SUM(F28;9..F28;15)	@SUM(G28;9..G28;15)	@SUM(H28;9..H28;15)
29	@SUM(E29;9..E29;15)	@SUM(F29;9..F29;15)	@SUM(G29;9..G29;15)	@SUM(H29;9..H29;15)
30	----------	----------	----------	----------
31	@SUM(E31;9..E31;15)	@SUM(F31;9..F31;15)	@SUM(G31;9..G31;15)	@SUM(H31;9..H31;15)
34	@SUM(E34;9..E34;15)	@SUM(F34;9..F34;15)	@SUM(G34;9..G34;15)	@SUM(H34;9..H34;15)
35	@SUM(E35;9..E35;15)	@SUM(F35;9..F35;15)	@SUM(G35;9..G35;15)	@SUM(H35;9..H35;15)
36	@SUM(E36;9..E36;15)	@SUM(F36;9..F36;15)	@SUM(G36;9..G36;15)	@SUM(H36;9..H36;15)
37	@SUM(E37;9..E37;15)	@SUM(F37;9..F37;15)	@SUM(G37;9..G37;15)	@SUM(H37;9..H37;15)
38	@SUM(E38;9..E38;15)	@SUM(F38;9..F38;15)	@SUM(G38;9..G38;15)	@SUM(H38;9..H38;15)
39	----------	----------	----------	----------
40	@SUM(E40;9..E40;15)	@SUM(F40;9..F40;15)	@SUM(G40;9..G40;15)	@SUM(H40;9..H40;15)
43	@SUM(E43;9..E43;15)	@SUM(F43;9..F43;15)	@SUM(G43;9..G43;15)	@SUM(H43;9..H43;15)
44	@SUM(E44;9..E44;15)	@SUM(F44;9..F44;15)	@SUM(G44;9..G44;15)	@SUM(H44;9..H44;15)
45	----------	----------	----------	----------
46	@SUM(E46;9..E46;15)	@SUM(F46;9..F46;15)	@SUM(G46;9..G46;15)	@SUM(H46;9..H46;15)
48	==========	==========	==========	==========
49	@SUM(E49;9..E49;15)	@SUM(F49;9..F49;15)	@SUM(G49;9..G49;15)	@SUM(H49;9..H49;15)

Selected pages of the completed spreadsheet, with fictitious data, are shown below. Table 8-1 displays the first data page. Table 8-2 displays the cumulative totals for each category. Table 8-3 is a rotated view of the spreadsheet displaying page 7—allocations—as seen from the right-hand side.

Table 8-1: Multi-Year Budget Overview: Requests and Allocations—Front View, Page 10

	Expended year 1	Requested year 2	Allocated year 2	Maintenance of effort requested year 3	Workload increase requested year 3	Expansion of program requested year 3	Total requested year 3
Salaries & Wages							
Professional	220000	275000	225000	226800	24000	48000	298800
LTA	110000	222000	119000	121000	14500	102500	238000
Clerical	156000	204000	180000	185000	21000	31000	237000
Hourly	14500	28000	14500	13800	2000	17000	32800
Benefits*	87480	126180	94320	98568	11007	33577	143153
Sub-Total	587980	855180	632820	645168	72507	232077	949753
Supplies & Expenses							
Communications	40000	60000	40000	41000	3000	22000	66000
Stationery	20000	40000	18000	18600	6000	25000	49600
Utilities	80000	110000	88000	94000	8000	29800	131800
Contractual	15000	18000	16000	16000	1500	5000	22500
Sub-Total	155000	228000	162000	169600	18500	81800	269900
Equipment							
Furniture	4000	17000	4000	6000	950	2500	9450
Motor vehicle	0	17500	0	0	0	18890	18890
Sub-Total	4000	34500	4000	6000	950	21390	28340
Books & Materials							
Books	88000	110000	91000	95000	7400	14000	116400
Periodicals	22000	31000	23000	26000	1950	11000	38950
Audiovisual	2500	7000	2800	3200	780	5500	9480
Services	2300	4000	2400	2800	455	3500	6755
Binding	3500	15000	3500	3900	900	12000	16800
Sub-Total	118300	167000	122700	130900	11485	46000	188385
Other							
Building & Repairs	9400	17500	9600	12500	0	0	12500
Contingency	0	75000	0	75000	0	25000	100000
Sub-Total	9400	92500	9600	87500	0	25000	112500
TOTAL	874680	1377180	931120	1039168	103442	406267	1548878

```
*Benefit rates:
    year 1 =    0.18
    year 2 =    0.18
    year 3 =    0.185
```

Table 8-2: Budget Overview: Requests and Allocations—Front View, Page 16

	Total Expended Years 1-5	Total Requested Years 2-6	Total Allocated Years 2-6	Total Maintenance of Effort Requested Years 3-7	Total Workload Increase Requested Years 3-7	Total Expansion of Program Requested Years 3-7	Total Requested Years 3-7
Salaries & Wages							
Professional	1100000	1375000	1125000	1134000	120000	240000	1494000
LTA	550000	1110000	595000	605000	72500	512500	1190000
Clerical	780000	1020000	900000	925000	105000	155000	1185000
Hourly	72500	159200	72500	69000	10000	85000	164000
Benefits	447120	706530	487320	500832	55930	170610	727372
Sub-Total	2949620	4661930	3179820	3233832	363430	1163110	4760372
Supplies & Expenses							
Communications	200000	324000	200000	205000	15000	110000	330000
Stationery	100000	238400	90000	93000	30000	125000	248000
Utilities	400000	637200	440000	470000	40000	149000	659000
Contractual	75000	108000	80000	80000	7500	25000	112500
Sub-Total	775000	1307600	810000	848000	92500	409000	1349500
Equipment							
Furniture	20000	54800	20000	30000	4750	12500	47250
Motor vehicle	0	93060	0	0	0	94450	94450
Sub-Total	20000	147860	20000	30000	4750	106950	141700
Books & Materials							
Books	440000	575600	455000	475000	37000	70000	582000
Periodicals	110000	186800	115000	130000	9750	55000	194750
Audiovisual	12500	44920	14000	16000	3900	27500	47400
Services	11500	31020	12000	14000	2275	17500	33775
Binding	17500	82200	17500	19500	4500	60000	84000
Sub-Total	591500	920540	613500	654500	57425	230000	941925
Other							
Building & Repairs	47000	67500	48000	62500	0	0	62500
Contingency	0	475000	0	375000	0	125000	500000
Sub-Total	47000	542500	48000	437500	0	125000	562500
TOTAL	4383120	7580430	4671320	5203832	518105	2034060	7755997

Table 8-3: Budget Overview: Requests and Allocations—Right-Side View, Page 7

	Allocated year 2	Allocated year 3	Allocated year 4	Allocated year 5	Allocated year 6	Total Allocated Years 2-6
Salaries & Wages						
Professional	225000	225000	225000	225000	225000	1125000
LTA	119000	119000	119000	119000	119000	595000
Clerical	180000	180000	180000	180000	180000	900000
Hourly	14500	14500	14500	14500	14500	72500
Benefits*	94320	96940	96940	99560	99560	487320
Sub-Total	632820	635440	635440	638060	638060	3179820
Supplies & Expenses						
Communications	40000	40000	40000	40000	40000	200000
Stationery	18000	18000	18000	18000	18000	90000
Utilities	88000	88000	88000	88000	88000	440000
Contractual	16000	16000	16000	16000	16000	80000
Sub-Total	162000	162000	162000	162000	162000	810000
Equipment						
Furniture	4000	4000	4000	4000	4000	20000
Motor vehicle	0	0	0	0	0	0
Sub-Total	4000	4000	4000	4000	4000	20000
Books & Materials						
Books	91000	91000	91000	91000	91000	455000
Periodicals	23000	23000	23000	23000	23000	115000
Audiovisual	2800	2800	2800	2800	2800	14000
Services	2400	2400	2400	2400	2400	12000
Binding	3500	3500	3500	3500	3500	17500
Sub-Total	122700	122700	122700	122700	122700	613500
Other						
Building & Repairs	9600	9600	9600	9600	9600	48000
Contingency	0	0	0	0	0	0
Sub-Total	9600	9600	9600	9600	9600	48000
TOTAL	931120	933740	933740	936360	936360	4671320

Chapter 9
Salaries by Sources of Funding

The bookkeeping for the employee whose salary is paid from one source during the entire fiscal year is relatively simple, but, when the salary is paid from two or more sources, the records become more complicated. This is especially true when the sources vary during the fiscal year as when an employee is paid from grants or other special allocations for less than a full year. When a change coincides with the beginning and end of a payroll period, the process is simply a matter of designating what percentage of the salary will be drawn from each source. However, when the changes occur at times other than the beginning and end of the payroll period, the determination of the number of salary days to be charged to each source is more complicated. The Salaries by Sources of Funding spreadsheet provides a mechanism for allocating the salaries of employees who are paid from more than one source for varying periods of time.

In spite of the varying number of days shown on the calendar for each month of the year, many organizations follow the practice of pretending that each month of the year is 30 days in length. Thus, for payroll purposes, February and March are each 30 days in length, not 28 or 29, or 31, respectively. For example, the employee hired on February 16 will receive a full half of a month's paycheck at the end of February. Similarly, the employee hired on March 16 will receive only one half of a month's paycheck at the end of March. (The alternatives create other problems. For example, prorating the daily pay by the number of days in the month will produce greater or lesser daily/hourly pay rates depending on the length of the month.)

This spreadsheet observes the fiction of 30-day months, trimming 31-day months to 30 days and boosting February to a full 30 days. The effect is that any slippage in budget is taken from the base salary rather than from a grant or contract, while the employees' salaries are unaffected.

If a person is awarded a different rate of pay during the year, the new rate may be treated as a new funding source with the old pay rate terminating the preceding day.

To set up the Salaries by Sources of Funding template, follow the general instructions and guidelines in Chapter 2, "Design and Modification of Spreadsheets." The following specifications, labels, and formulas for setting up the Salaries by Sources of Funding template are shown below. Set the column widths as follows: A = 20, B-C = 15, D-R = 12, S = 3, T = 11, U-AF = 12, AG = 3, and AH = 12. Set the display formats to match those shown in Table 9-1. Begin by keyboarding the organizational statement.

SALARIES BY SOURCES OF FUNDING SPREADSHEET: CELL-BY-CELL INSTRUCTIONS

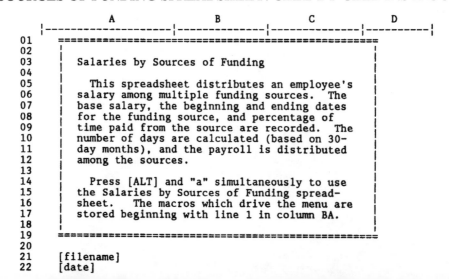

Columns A-F, rows 101-118, contain the basic employment data for one employee. (The Mary Blue and Paul White entries in rows 119-146 demonstrate how this area will appear when data for employees are input.) As shown here, there is space for eight contracts/funding sources for the library for the year. If spaces for more contracts/funding sources are needed, they can be inserted immediately before line 14. By using the same uniform list of contracts/funding sources for all employees, subsidiary analyses can be done more easily.

Copy columns A-F, rows 105-118, as many times as are needed for additional employees beginning with line 119.

```
                 A                  B                C              D                 E            F
        |----------------|--------------------|---------------|--------------------|------------------|---------|
101     SALARIES -Sources         Annual/                          Contract Period
102                               Daily                            Begin.              End
103     Name                      Rate             Contract        Date                Date         FTE
104     ================================================================================================
105     Brown, Jack          [salary]  Base Pay        @DATE(yr,mo,day)    @DATE(yr,mo,day)      x.x
106       date hired:      (B5/12)/30    [contract name]   @DATE(yr,mo,day)    @DATE(yr,mo,day)      x.xxx
107     @DATE(yr,mo,day)                [contract name]   @DATE(yr,mo,day)    @DATE(yr,mo,day)      x.xxx
108       last raise:                   [contract name]   @DATE(yr,mo,day)    @DATE(yr,mo,day)      x.xxx
109     @DATE(yr,mo,day)                [contract name]   @DATE(yr,mo,day)    @DATE(yr,mo,day)      x.xxx
110                                     [contract name]   @DATE(yr,mo,day)    @DATE(yr,mo,day)      x.xxx
111                                     [contract name]   @DATE(yr,mo,day)    @DATE(yr,mo,day)      x.xxx
112                                     [contract name]   @DATE(yr,mo,day)    @DATE(yr,mo,day)      x.xxx
113                                     [contract name]   @DATE(yr,mo,day)    @DATE(yr,mo,day)      x.xxx
114
115
116
117
118     ================================================================================================
119     Blue, Mary              37000  Basic           @DATE(91,7,1)       @DATE(92,6,30)          1
120       date hired:      (B19/12)/30   Acme
121     @DATE(87,5,1)                   Brown
122       last raise:                   Corporation     @DATE(91,7,1)       @DATE(92,3,31)          1
123     @DATE(91,7,1)                   Green
124                                     Hunter
125                                     Mission         @DATE(92,4,1)       @DATE(92,6,30)          0.5
126                                     Parrott
127                                     Western         @DATE(92,4,1)       @DATE(92,6,30)          0.5
128
129
130
131
132     ================================================================================================
133     White, Paul             24000  Basic           @DATE(91,7,1)       @DATE(92,6,30)          1
134       date hired:        +B33/364   Acme
135     @DATE(90,9,15)                  Brown           @DATE(88,9,16)      @DATE(93,1,20)          0.25
136       last raise:                   Corporation
137     @DATE(91,7,1)                   Green           @DATE(92,1,21)      @DATE(92,5,31)          0.33
138                                     Hunter
139                                     Mission
140                                     Parrott
141                                     Western         @DATE(92,4,1)       @DATE(92,6,30)          0.125
142
143
144
145
146     ================================================================================================
```

Keyboard column G, lines 101-104.

```
                       G
      !--------------------------------!
  101 @DATE(yr,mo,day)
  102 @DATE(yr,mo,day)
  103
  104 ============================
```

Then, keyboard the following formula, which calculates the number of days to be paid from each contract/funding source, into G105:

```
@IF($D105>G$102,0,(@IF($E105<G$101,0,(@IF
($D105>=G$101#AND#$E105<=G$102,$E105-
$D105+1,(@IF($D105>G$101#AND#$E105>G$102,G
$102-$D105+1,(@IF($D105<G$101#AND#$E105
<G$102,$E105-G$101+1,G$102-G$101+1))))))))
```

Copy this formula into rows G106-G113. This completes the first month for one employee.

Copy G101-104 into columns H-R. Then, copy the formula in G105 into the range H105-R113. Copy column G, row 118, into the range H118-R118. This completes 12 months for one employee.

Keyboard columns S-U, lines 101-105. Copy U101-U105 into columns V-AF.

```
      S      T                 U
      !---!----------!---------------------------!
  101                            @DATE(yr,mo,day)
  102          Fund              @DATE(yr,mo,day)
  103          Source
  104 =================================================
  105          Base Pay         (($B$105/12)*$F105)
```

Keyboard columns T-U, lines 106-118. The formula in U115 calculates the month's pay from contracts; the formula in U116 calculates the month's pay from the base salary fund; and the formula in U117 calculates the total pay for the month. Copy U106-U118 into columns V-AF. Note that the formulas for months with less than 31 days must be altered as follows: in columns AD (April), AF (June), AI (September), and AK (November), change the element "<=30" to "<=29," and in column AB (February), change the element "<=30" to "<=28" for leap years and "<=27" for other years.

```
             T                              U
      !----------------!---------------------------------------------!
  106 [contract name]      +$B$106*(@IF(G106<=30,G106,30))*$F106
  107 [contract name]      +$B$106*(@IF(G107<=30,G107,30))*$F107
  108 [contract name]      +$B$106*(@IF(G108<=30,G108,30))*$F108
  109 [contract name]      +$B$106*(@IF(G109<=30,G109,30))*$F109
  110 [contract name]      +$B$106*(@IF(G110<=30,G110,30))*$F110
  111 [contract name]      +$B$106*(@IF(G111<=30,G111,30))*$F111
  112 [contract name]      +$B$106*(@IF(G112<=30,G112,30))*$F112
  113 [contract name]      +$B$106*(@IF(G113<=30,G113,30))*$F113
  114 ---------------------------------------------
  115 sub-total                            @SUM(U106..U114)
  116 from base                                +U105-U115
  117 Total                                    +U115+U116
  118 =========================================================
```

Keyboard columns T-U, rows 147-160, immediately following the entry for the last employee. These formulas, which calculate the grand totals for each contract and other funding source, follow three employees as shown here. An additional element must be added to each formula for each additional employee. Also, each additional employee will cause this group of rows to be located 14 lines further down in the spreadsheet. For example, a fourth employee would require that the first formula be revised to +U105+U119+U133+U147, and what is shown below as row 147 would become row 161.

```
            T                    U
     |----------------|------------------|
147  Base Pay           +U105+U119+U133
148  [contract name]    +U106+U120+U134
149  [contract name]    +U107+U121+U135
150  [contract name]    +U108+U122+U136
151  [contract name]    +U109+U123+U137
152  [contract name]    +U110+U124+U138
153  [contract name]    +U111+U125+U139
154  [contract name]    +U112+U126+U140
155  [contract name]    +U113+U127+U141
156                    ------------------
157  sub-total          @SUM(U148..U156)
158  from base          +U147-U157
159  Total              +U157+U158
160  =====================================
```

Keyboard columns AG-AH, rows 101-118, which calculate the year's total for each row. Copy AH105-AH118 to the right of each employee and to the right of the grand total area.

```
         AG        AH
      !---!|-------------------!
101
102
103          Total
104   =========================
105          @SUM(U105..AF105)
106          @SUM(U106..AF106)
107          @SUM(U107..AF107)
108          @SUM(U108..AF108)
109          @SUM(U109..AF109)
110          @SUM(U110..AF110)
111          @SUM(U111..AF111)
112          @SUM(U112..AF112)
113          @SUM(U113..AF113)
114   -------------------------
115          @SUM(AH116..AH114)
116          +AH115-AH115
117          +AH115+AH116
118   =========================
```

After keyboarding columns BA-BK, rows 1-13, name the range BB1 "\0" so that the introductory statement will be displayed automatically when the spreadsheet is loaded. Name the range BD1 "\a" so that the menu will be displayed when [ALT] and the letter "a" are pressed simultaneously.

Save this completed template. Load a copy of the template, insert additional rows as necessary to accommo-

```
         BA            BB           BC           BD
      !--------!|-------------!|--------!|------------------!
01    \0         {GOTO}A1~      \a        {MENUBRANCH BE1}~
02               {QUIT}
```

```
                      BE                          BF
      !------------------------------------!|----------------!
01    Names                                  Contracts
02    View names and employment data         View contracts
03    {WINDOWSOFF}~                           {WINDOWSOFF}~
04    /WTC                                    /WTC
05    {GOTO}H101~                             {GOTO}H101~
06    {GOTO}A101~                             {GOTO}A101~
07    {DOWN 4}~                               {DOWN 4}~
08    /WTH                                    {RIGHT 1}~
09    {WINDOWSON}~                            /WTB
10    {QUIT}                                  {RIGHT 3}~
11                                            {LEFT 2}
12                                            {WINDOWSON}~
13                                            {QUIT}
```

```
                          BG                                   BH
     |-----------------------------------------|--------------------------------|
01   | Salaries                                 File
02   | View salaries by sources and totals      Saves the spreadsheet to disk
03   | {WINDOWSOFF}~                             /WTC
04   | /WTC                                      /FS{?}~
05   | {GOTO}H101~                               {QUIT}
06   | {GOTO}A101~
07   | {DOWN 4}~
08   | {RIGHT 1}~
09   | /WTB
10   | {RIGHT 22}~
11   | {LEFT 4}~
12   | {WINDOWSON}~
13   | {QUIT}
```

```
                          BI                             BJ
     |-----------------------------------------|--------------------|
01   | Periods                                  Quit
02   | View monthly pay periods                 Exits Lotus 1-2-3.   SAVE FILE FIRST!
03   | {WINDOWSOFF}                             /WTC
04   | /WTC                                      /QY
05   | {GOTO}H101~                               {QUIT}
06   | {GOTO}A101~
07   | {DOWN 4}~
08   | {RIGHT 1}~
08   | /WTB
09   | {RIGHT 8}~
10   | {LEFT 3}~
11   | {WINDOWSON}~
12   | {QUIT}
```

```
                                  BK
     |----------------------------------------------------------------|
01   | Macro
02   | Utility to move the cursor to the beginning of the menu program
03   | /WTC
04   | {GOTO}BA1~
05   | {QUIT}
```

date all employees, and enter the data in the appropriate cells. An example of the completed spreadsheet, with fictitious data, is shown below in Table 9-1. The printed spreadsheet is large, requiring several sheets of paper which can be trimmed and taped together to form one continuous display.

Table 9-1: Salaries by Sources of Funding

Name	Annual/ Daily Rate	Contract	Contract Period Begin. Date	End Date	FTE
Brown, Jack	$35,000.00	Base Pay	20-Jun-91	20-Aug-92	1.000
date hired:	$97.22	Acme	21-Aug-91	25-Aug-91	0.500
01-Jan-85		Brown	01-Sep-91	20-Oct-91	0.125
last raise:		Corporation	21-Jan-91	20-Aug-92	0.125
01-Jul-91		Green	10-Nov-91	20-Dec-91	0.200
		Hunter	01-Jan-92	10-Feb-92	0.100
		Mission	15-Feb-92	31-Mar-92	0.200
		Parrott	15-Apr-92	30-Apr-92	0.125
		Western	01-May-91	31-May-92	0.333
Blue, Mary	$37,000.00	Basic	01-Jul-91	30-Jun-92	1.000
date hired:	$102.78	Acme			
01-May-87		Brown			
last raise:		Corporation	01-Jul-91	31-Mar-92	1.000
01-Jul-91		Green			
		Hunter			
		Mission	01-Apr-92	30-Jun-92	0.500
		Parrott			
		Western	01-Apr-92	30-Jun-92	0.500
White, Paul	$24,000.00	Basic	01-Jul-91	30-Jun-92	1.000
date hired:	$65.93	Acme			
15-Sep-90		Brown	16-Sep-88	20-Jan-93	0.250
last raise:		Corporation			
01-Jul-91		Green	21-Jan-92	31-May-92	0.330
		Hunter			
		Mission			
		Parrott			
		Western	01-Apr-92	30-Jun-92	0.125

Table 9-1: Salaries by Sources of Funding (Continued)

01-Jul-91 31-Jul-91	01-Aug-91 31-Aug-91	01-Sep-91 30-Sep-91	01-Oct-91 31-Oct-91	01-Nov-91 30-Nov-91	01-Dec-91 31-Dec-91	01-Jan-92 31-Jan-92	01-Feb-92 29-Feb-92	01-Mar-92 31-Mar-92	01-Apr-92 30-Apr-92	01-May-92 31-May-92	01-Jun-92 30-Jun-92
31	31	30	31	30	31	31	29	31	30	31	30
0	5	0	0	0	0	0	0	0	0	0	0
0	0	30	20	0	0	0	0	0	0	0	0
31	31	30	31	30	31	31	29	31	30	31	30
0	0	0	0	21	20	0	0	0	0	0	0
0	0	0	0	0	0	31	10	0	0	0	0
0	0	0	0	0	0	0	15	31	0	0	0
0	0	0	0	0	0	0	0	0	16	0	0
31	31	30	31	30	31	31	29	31	30	31	0
31	31	30	31	30	31	31	29	31	30	31	30
0	0	0	0	0	0	0	0	0	0	0	0
0	0	0	0	0	0	0	0	0	0	0	0
31	31	30	31	30	31	31	29	31	0	0	0
0	0	0	0	0	0	0	0	0	0	0	0
0	0	0	0	0	0	0	0	0	0	0	0
0	0	0	0	0	0	0	0	0	30	31	30
0	0	0	0	0	0	0	0	0	0	0	0
0	0	0	0	0	0	0	0	0	30	31	30
31	31	30	31	30	31	31	29	31	30	31	30
0	0	0	0	0	0	0	0	0	0	0	0
31	31	30	31	30	31	31	29	31	30	31	30
0	0	0	0	0	0	0	0	0	0	0	0
0	0	0	0	0	0	11	29	31	30	31	0
0	0	0	0	0	0	0	0	0	0	0	0
0	0	0	0	0	0	0	0	0	0	0	0
0	0	0	0	0	0	0	0	0	30	31	30

Table 9-1: Salaries by Sources of Funding (Continued)

Fund Source	01-Jul-91 31-Jul-91	01-Aug-91 31-Aug-91	01-Sep-91 30-Sep-91	01-Oct-91 31-Oct-91	01-Nov-91 30-Nov-91	01-Dec-91 31-Dec-91	01-Jan-92 31-Jan-92	01-Feb-92 29-Feb-92	01-Mar-92 31-Mar-92	01-Apr-92 30-Apr-92	01-May-92 31-May-92	01-Jun-92 30-Jun-92	Total
Base Pay	$2,916.67	$2,916.67	$2,916.67	$2,916.67	$2,916.67	$2,916.67	$2,916.67	$2,916.67	$2,916.67	$2,916.67	$2,916.67	$2,916.67	$35,000.00
Acme	$0.00	$243.06	$0.00	$0.00	$0.00	$0.00	$0.00	$0.00	$0.00	$0.00	$0.00	$0.00	$243.06
Brown	$0.00	$0.00	$364.58	$243.06	$0.00	$0.00	$0.00	$0.00	$0.00	$0.00	$0.00	$0.00	$607.64
Corporation	$364.58	$364.58	$364.58	$364.58	$364.58	$364.58	$364.58	$352.43	$364.58	$364.58	$364.58	$364.58	$4,362.85
Green	$0.00	$0.00	$0.00	$0.00	$408.33	$388.89	$0.00	$0.00	$0.00	$0.00	$0.00	$0.00	$797.22
Hunter	$0.00	$0.00	$0.00	$0.00	$0.00	$0.00	$291.67	$97.22	$0.00	$0.00	$0.00	$0.00	$388.89
Mission	$0.00	$0.00	$0.00	$0.00	$0.00	$0.00	$0.00	$291.67	$583.33	$0.00	$0.00	$0.00	$875.00
Parrott	$0.00	$0.00	$0.00	$0.00	$0.00	$0.00	$0.00	$0.00	$0.00	$194.44	$0.00	$0.00	$194.44
Western	$971.25	$971.25	$971.25	$971.25	$971.25	$971.25	$971.25	$938.88	$971.25	$971.25	$971.25	$0.00	$10,651.38
sub-total	$1,335.83	$1,578.89	$1,700.42	$1,578.89	$1,744.17	$1,724.72	$1,627.50	$1,680.19	$1,919.17	$1,530.28	$1,335.83	$364.58	$18,120.47
from base	$1,580.83	$1,337.78	$1,216.25	$1,337.78	$1,172.50	$1,191.94	$1,289.17	$1,236.47	$997.50	$1,386.39	$1,580.83	$2,552.08	$16,879.53
Total	$2,916.67	$2,916.67	$2,916.67	$2,916.67	$2,916.67	$2,916.67	$2,916.67	$2,916.67	$2,916.67	$2,916.67	$2,916.67	$2,916.67	$35,000.00
Base Pay	$3,083.33	$3,083.33	$3,083.33	$3,083.33	$3,083.33	$3,083.33	$3,083.33	$3,083.33	$3,083.33	$3,083.33	$3,083.33	$3,083.33	$37,000.00
Acme	$0.00	$0.00	$0.00	$0.00	$0.00	$0.00	$0.00	$0.00	$0.00	$0.00	$0.00	$0.00	$0.00
Brown	$0.00	$0.00	$0.00	$0.00	$0.00	$0.00	$0.00	$0.00	$0.00	$0.00	$0.00	$0.00	$0.00
Corporation	$3,083.33	$3,083.33	$3,083.33	$3,083.33	$3,083.33	$3,083.33	$3,083.33	$2,980.56	$3,083.33	$0.00	$0.00	$0.00	$27,647.22
Green	$0.00	$0.00	$0.00	$0.00	$0.00	$0.00	$0.00	$0.00	$0.00	$0.00	$0.00	$0.00	$0.00
Hunter	$0.00	$0.00	$0.00	$0.00	$0.00	$0.00	$0.00	$0.00	$0.00	$0.00	$0.00	$0.00	$0.00
Mission	$0.00	$0.00	$0.00	$0.00	$0.00	$0.00	$0.00	$0.00	$0.00	$1,541.67	$1,541.67	$1,541.67	$4,625.00
Parrott	$0.00	$0.00	$0.00	$0.00	$0.00	$0.00	$0.00	$0.00	$0.00	$0.00	$0.00	$0.00	$0.00
Western	$0.00	$0.00	$0.00	$0.00	$0.00	$0.00	$0.00	$0.00	$0.00	$1,541.67	$1,541.67	$1,541.67	$4,625.00
sub-total	$3,083.33	$3,083.33	$3,083.33	$3,083.33	$3,083.33	$3,083.33	$3,083.33	$2,980.56	$3,083.33	$3,083.33	$3,083.33	$3,083.33	$36,897.22
from base	$0.00	$0.00	$0.00	$0.00	$0.00	$0.00	$0.00	$102.78	$0.00	$0.00	$0.00	$0.00	$102.78
Total	$3,083.33	$3,083.33	$3,083.33	$3,083.33	$3,083.33	$3,083.33	$3,083.33	$3,083.33	$3,083.33	$3,083.33	$3,083.33	$3,083.33	$37,000.00
Base Pay	$2,000.00	$2,000.00	$2,000.00	$2,000.00	$2,000.00	$2,000.00	$2,000.00	$2,000.00	$2,000.00	$2,000.00	$2,000.00	$2,000.00	$24,000.00
Acme	$0.00	$0.00	$0.00	$0.00	$0.00	$0.00	$0.00	$0.00	$0.00	$0.00	$0.00	$0.00	$0.00
Brown	$494.51	$494.51	$494.51	$494.51	$494.51	$494.51	$494.51	$478.02	$494.51	$494.51	$494.51	$494.51	$5,917.58
Corporation	$0.00	$0.00	$0.00	$0.00	$0.00	$0.00	$0.00	$0.00	$0.00	$0.00	$0.00	$0.00	$0.00
Green	$0.00	$0.00	$0.00	$0.00	$0.00	$0.00	$239.34	$630.99	$652.75	$652.75	$652.75	$0.00	$2,828.57
Hunter	$0.00	$0.00	$0.00	$0.00	$0.00	$0.00	$0.00	$0.00	$0.00	$0.00	$0.00	$0.00	$0.00
Mission	$0.00	$0.00	$0.00	$0.00	$0.00	$0.00	$0.00	$0.00	$0.00	$0.00	$0.00	$0.00	$0.00
Parrott	$0.00	$0.00	$0.00	$0.00	$0.00	$0.00	$0.00	$0.00	$0.00	$0.00	$0.00	$0.00	$0.00
Western	$0.00	$0.00	$0.00	$0.00	$0.00	$0.00	$0.00	$0.00	$0.00	$247.25	$247.25	$247.25	$741.76
sub-total	$0.00	$494.51	$494.51	$494.51	$494.51	$494.51	$733.85	$1,109.01	$1,147.25	$1,394.51	$1,394.51	$741.76	$9,487.91
from base	$2,000.00	$1,505.49	$1,505.49	$1,505.49	$1,505.49	$1,505.49	$1,266.15	$890.99	$852.75	$605.49	$605.49	$1,258.24	$14,512.09
Total	$2,000.00	$2,000.00	$2,000.00	$2,000.00	$2,000.00	$2,000.00	$2,000.00	$2,000.00	$2,000.00	$2,000.00	$2,000.00	$2,000.00	$24,000.00
Base Pay	$8,000.00	$8,000.00	$8,000.00	$8,000.00	$8,000.00	$8,000.00	$8,000.00	$8,000.00	$8,000.00	$8,000.00	$8,000.00	$8,000.00	$96,000.00
Acme	$0.00	$243.06	$0.00	$0.00	$0.00	$0.00	$0.00	$0.00	$0.00	$0.00	$0.00	$0.00	$243.06
Brown	$494.51	$494.51	$859.09	$737.56	$494.51	$494.51	$494.51	$478.02	$494.51	$494.51	$494.51	$494.51	$6,525.22
Corporation	$3,447.92	$3,447.92	$3,447.92	$3,447.92	$3,447.92	$3,447.92	$3,447.92	$3,332.99	$3,447.92	$364.58	$364.58	$364.58	$32,010.07
Green	$0.00	$0.00	$0.00	$0.00	$408.33	$388.89	$239.34	$630.99	$652.75	$652.75	$652.75	$0.00	$3,625.79
Hunter	$0.00	$0.00	$0.00	$0.00	$0.00	$0.00	$291.67	$97.22	$0.00	$0.00	$0.00	$0.00	$388.89
Mission	$0.00	$0.00	$0.00	$0.00	$0.00	$0.00	$0.00	$291.67	$583.33	$1,541.67	$1,541.67	$1,541.67	$5,500.00
Parrott	$0.00	$0.00	$0.00	$0.00	$0.00	$0.00	$0.00	$0.00	$0.00	$194.44	$0.00	$0.00	$194.44
Western	$971.25	$971.25	$971.25	$971.25	$971.25	$971.25	$971.25	$938.88	$971.25	$2,760.17	$2,760.17	$1,788.92	$16,018.13
sub-total	$4,913.67	$5,156.73	$5,278.26	$5,156.73	$5,322.01	$5,302.56	$5,444.68	$5,769.76	$6,149.75	$6,008.12	$5,813.67	$4,189.67	$64,505.61
from base	$3,086.33	$2,843.27	$2,721.74	$2,843.27	$2,677.99	$2,697.44	$2,555.32	$2,230.24	$1,850.25	$1,991.88	$2,186.33	$3,810.33	$31,494.39
Total	$8,000.00	$8,000.00	$8,000.00	$8,000.00	$8,000.00	$8,000.00	$8,000.00	$8,000.00	$8,000.00	$8,000.00	$8,000.00	$8,000.00	$96,000.00

Chapter 10
Circulation in 2-D: Whole Year

Circulation data accumulate day by day and are often recorded class by class as well as service point by service point. Recording these data is a relatively simple task; however, cumulating these data in a spreadsheet is more difficult. How this cumulation problem is handled depends on whether these data are arranged in two- or three-dimensional spreadsheets. The spreadsheets in Chapters 10, 11, and 12 are based on two-dimensional solutions to this problem; a three-dimensional solution is shown in Chapter 13.

Circulation data can be recorded easily in flat (2-D) spreadsheets. However, space limitations dictate that a given spreadsheet be dedicated either to data for one service point or format for an entire year or that it be dedicated to only one month for several service points or formats. A summary spreadsheet, which draws data from these other spreadsheets, can display monthly and year-to-date totals for either approach. The choice is mostly a matter of taste.

Both the year-at-a-time and the single-month approaches are used in the models developed in this and the following two chapters. In the first model, shown in this chapter, the data are arranged sequentially day by day for the entire year for one service point. In the second model, shown in Chapter 11, the data for an entire year are displayed in month-by-month blocks for one service point. In the third model, shown in Chapter 12, data for several service points are brought together in a separate spreadsheet for each month. In each of the three models, year-to-date data are summarized in a separate spreadsheet. While the first model is somewhat simpler to construct, the second offers a visually separate display of each month, and the third brings all of one month's activities together in one spreadsheet. Again, the choice is primarily a matter of taste.

In the model described in this chapter, the data are arranged sequentially day by day for the entire year for one service point with columns for each Decimal Class. (LC class letters can be substituted, although this will require that additional columns be inserted and that the menu macros be moved and appropriately altered.) A month-by-month summary is appended at the bottom of the spreadsheet. Matching spreadsheets are assigned to other service points. Finally, the year-to-date totals are brought together in a summary spreadsheet. This relationship is illustrated below in Figure 10-A.

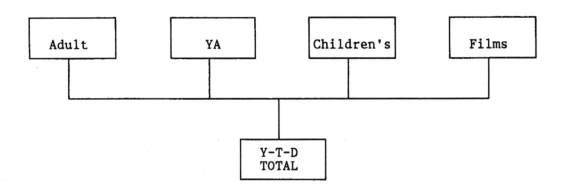

Figure 10-A: Relationship of Individual Circulation Spreadsheets to Year-to-Date Total Spreadsheet

To set up the Circulation: Whole-Year template follow the cell-by-cell instructions that appear below, creating a generic template. Refer as needed to the general instructions and guidelines in Chapter 2, "Design and Modification of Spreadsheets." Most of the columns are set at the default of nine spaces. Column B is set at 10 spaces, while columns AA-AN are set at varying widths sufficient to display the texts of the menu macros.

Begin by keyboarding the organizational statement.

CIRCULATION SPREADSHEET—WHOLE YEAR: CELL-BY-CELL INSTRUCTIONS

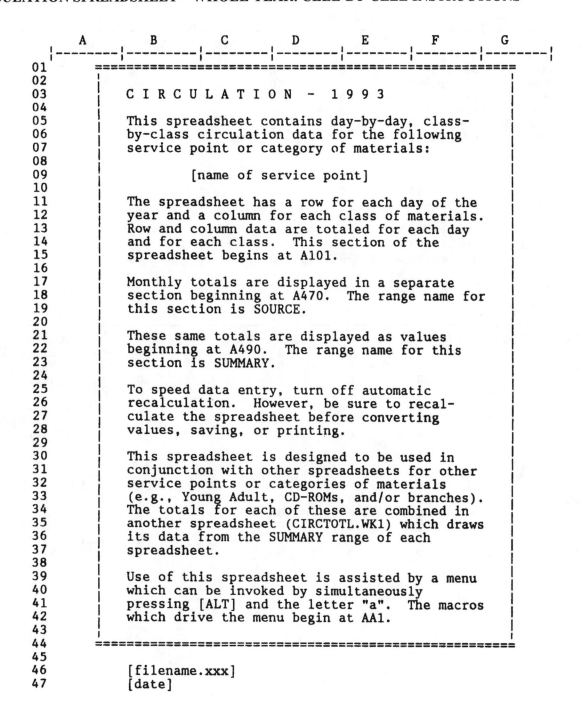

Keyboard the basic template into columns A-O, rows 101-466. Only the beginning and ending rows are shown below. Use the data fill command (/df) to enter the dates. (The beginning value for January 1, 1993, is 33970, while the concluding value for December 31, 1993, is 34334. For 1994, the beginning and concluding values are 34335 and 34699, while for 1995 they are 34700 and 35064.) Copy the zeros and formula in row 102 into rows 103 through 466.

	A	B	C	D	E	F	G	H
101	DAY	DATE	-000-	-100-	-200-	-300-	-400-	-500-
102	Fri	01-Jan-93	0	0	0	0	0	0
103	Sat	02-Jan-93	0	0	0	0	0	0
104	Sun	03-Jan-93	0	0	0	0	0	0
105	Mon	04-Jan-93	0	0	0	0	0	0
106	Tues	05-Jan-93	0	0	0	0	0	0
107	Wed	06-Jan-93	0	0	0	0	0	0
108	Thur	07-Jan-93	0	0	0	0	0	0
461	Sun	26-Dec-93	0	0	0	0	0	0
462	Mon	27-Dec-93	0	0	0	0	0	0
463	Tues	28-Dec-93	0	0	0	0	0	0
464	Wed	29-Dec-93	0	0	0	0	0	0
465	Thur	30-Dec-93	0	0	0	0	0	0
466	Fri	31-Dec-93	0	0	0	0	0	0

	I	J	K	L	M	N	O
101	-600-	-700-	-800-	-900-	-Biog-	-Fict-	-Total-
102	0	0	0	0	0	0	@SUM(C102..N102)
103	0	0	0	0	0	0	@SUM(C103..N103)
104	0	0	0	0	0	0	@SUM(C104..N104)
105	0	0	0	0	0	0	@SUM(C105..N105)
106	0	0	0	0	0	0	@SUM(C106..N106)
107	0	0	0	0	0	0	@SUM(C107..N107)
108	0	0	0	0	0	0	@SUM(C108..N108)
461	0	0	0	0	0	0	@SUM(C461..N461)
462	0	0	0	0	0	0	@SUM(C462..N462)
463	0	0	0	0	0	0	@SUM(C463..N463)
464	0	0	0	0	0	0	@SUM(C464..N464)
465	0	0	0	0	0	0	@SUM(C465..N465)
466	0	0	0	0	0	0	@SUM(C466..N466)

Keyboard row 467, copying the formula in C467 into D467-N467.

```
            A         B               C                /\ /              N
        |-----|-----------|-------------------|       / \/     |-----------------|
   467  Totals           @SUM(C102..C466)    / /\\/  /          @SUM(N102..N466)
                                               / \/
                                          O
        |-------------------------------------------------------------------------|
   467  @IF(@SUM(O102..O466)=@SUM(C467..N467),@SUM(C467..N467),"ERROR")
```

After keyboarding the Summary Table into columns A-O, rows 470-486, name the range C474-N485 "SOURCE." This is used in the updating process to tranfer values to the SUMMARY range.

```
           A           B              C                                    N
      |---------|-----------|-------------------|            |-----------------|
 470  Summary Table With Formulas; range name = SOURCE
 471    Main - Adult
 472  Summary - 1993
 473              Month          -000-                            -Fict-
 474              Jan        @SUM(C102..C132)                 @SUM(N102..N132)
 475              Feb        @SUM(C133..C160)                 @SUM(N133..N160)
 476              Mar        @SUM(C161..C191)                 @SUM(N161..N191)
 477              Apr        @SUM(C192..C221)      /\ /       @SUM(N192..N221)
 478              May        @SUM(C222..C250)     / \/        @SUM(N222..N250)
 479              Jun        @SUM(C253..C282)     /\ /        @SUM(N253..N282)
 480              Jul        @SUM(C283..C313)    / \/         @SUM(N283..N313)
 481              Aug        @SUM(C314..C344)                 @SUM(N314..N344)
 482              Sep        @SUM(C345..C375)                 @SUM(N345..N375)
 483              Oct        @SUM(C376..C405)                 @SUM(N376..N405)
 484              Nov        @SUM(C406..C435)                 @SUM(N406..N435)
 485              Dec        @SUM(C436..C466)                 @SUM(N436..N466)
 486              Total      @SUM(C474..C485)                 @SUM(N474..N485)

                                        O
      |-------------------------------------------------------------------|
 473                                                            -Total-
 474                                                        @SUM(C474..N474)
 475                                                        @SUM(C475..N475)
 476                                                        @SUM(C476..N476)
 477                                                        @SUM(C477..N477)
 478                                                        @SUM(C478..N478)
 479                                                        @SUM(C479..N479)
 480                                                        @SUM(C480..N480)
 481                                                        @SUM(C481..N481)
 482                                                        @SUM(C482..N482)
 483                                                        @SUM(C483..N483)
 484                                                        @SUM(C484..N484)
 485                                                        @SUM(C485..N485)
 486  @IF(@SUM(O474..O485)=@SUM(C486..N486),@SUM(C486..N486),"ERROR")
```

After keyboarding the Summary Range into columns A-O, rows 489-505, name the range C493-N504 "SUMMARY." This range is referenced by the spreadsheet CIRCTOTL.WK1 in which year-to-date cumulations are gathered.

	A	B	C	D	E
489	Summary Table With Values; Range name - SUMMARY				
490	Main - Adult				
491	Summary 1993				
492		Month	-000-	-100-	-200-
493		Jan	0	0	0
494		Feb	0	0	0
495		Mar	0	0	0
496		Apr	0	0	0
497		May	0	0	0
498		Jun	0	0	0
499		Jul	0	0	0
500		Aug	0	0	0
501		Sep	0	0	0
502		Oct	0	0	0
503		Nov	0	0	0
504		Dec	0	0	0
505		Total	@SUM(C493..C504)	@SUM(D493..D504)	@SUM(E493..E504)

	O
492	-Total-
493	@SUM(C493..N493)
494	@SUM(C494..N494)
495	@SUM(C495..N495)
496	@SUM(C496..N496)
497	@SUM(C497..N497)
498	@SUM(C498..N498)
499	@SUM(C499..N499)
500	@SUM(C500..N500)
501	@SUM(C501..N501)
502	@SUM(C502..N502)
503	@SUM(C503..N503)
504	@SUM(C504..N504)
505	@IF(@SUM(O493..O504)=@SUM(C505..N505),@SUM(C505..N505),"ERROR")

After keyboarding columns AA-AN, rows 1-9, name the range AB1 "\0." This will cause the instructional statement to be displayed whenever the spreadsheet is loaded. Name the range AE1 "\a." This will display the menu when [ALT] and "a" are pressed simultaneously.

```
        AA          AB        AC     AD            AE
    !---------!-------------!-----!---------!-----------------!
01  \0            {GOTO}A1~        \a        {MENUBRANCH AG1}~
```

```
                                AG
    !-----------------------------------------------------!
01  Enter
02  Enter data. Holds date and class titles on screen
03  /WTC
04  {GOTO}A101~
05  {RIGHT 2}~
06  {DOWN 1}~
07  /WTB
08  {QUIT}
```

```
                    AH
    !-----------------------------!
01  Recalculate
02  Recalculates the spreadsheet
03  {CALC}
04  {QUIT}
```

```
                            AI
    !-------------------------------------------------------!
01  Update
02  Recalculates spreadsheet and updates summary range values
03  /WTC
04  {CALC}
05  /RV
05  Source~
06  Summary~
07  {CALC}
08  {QUIT}
```

```
                            AJ
    !-------------------------------------------------------!
01  Y-T-D
02  Recalculates spreadsheet and displays year-to-date summary
03  /WTC
04  {CALC}
05  {GOTO}A470~
06  {RIGHT 2}~
07  {DOWN 3}~
08  /WTB
09  {QUIT}
```

```
                            AK
    !-------------------------------------------------------!
01  Save
02  Saves the spreadsheet to disk.  Supply a filename as needed
03  /WTC
04  /FS{?}~
05  {QUIT}
```

```
                       AL
       |-----------------------------------|
   01  Print
   02  Prints the year-to-date summary
   03  /WTC
   04  /PPR
   05  A470..O485~
   06  G
   07  P
   08  Q
   09  {QUIT}
```

```
                                  AM
       |-------------------------------------------------------|
   01  Quit
   02  Exits Lotus 1-2-3.  RECALCULATE, UPDATE, and SAVE FILES FIRST!
   03  /WTC
   04  /QY
   05  {QUIT}
```

```
                                  AN
       |-------------------------------------------------------|
   01  Macro
   02  Utility to move the cursor to the beginning of the menu program
   03  /WTC
   04  {GOTO}AA1~
   05  {QUIT}
```

Save this generic template. Make a copy for each service point, and assign an appropriate filename to each (e.g., CIRCADLT.WK1 for adult circulation). Begin entering data.

The next step is to create the summary template. Begin by keyboarding the organizational statement in columns B-D, rows 1-28.

SUMMARY SPREADSHEET: CELL-BY-CELL INSTRUCTIONS

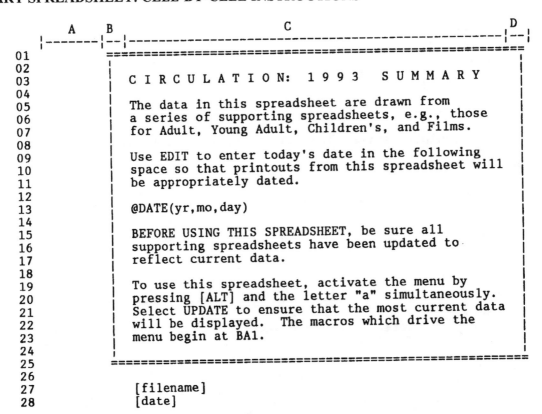

```
                  A     B                    C                      D
              |-------|--|------------------------------------------|--|
   01              =================================================
   02              |                                                |
   03              |  C I R C U L A T I O N:  1 9 9 3   S U M M A R Y |
   04              |                                                |
   05              |  The data in this spreadsheet are drawn from    |
   06              |  a series of supporting spreadsheets, e.g., those |
   07              |  for Adult, Young Adult, Children's, and Films.  |
   08              |                                                |
   09              |  Use EDIT to enter today's date in the following |
   10              |  space so that printouts from this spreadsheet will |
   11              |  be appropriately dated.                        |
   12              |                                                |
   13              |  @DATE(yr,mo,day)                               |
   14              |                                                |
   15              |  BEFORE USING THIS SPREADSHEET, be sure all     |
   16              |  supporting spreadsheets have been updated to   |
   17              |  reflect current data.                          |
   18              |                                                |
   19              |  To use this spreadsheet, activate the menu by  |
   20              |  pressing [ALT] and the letter "a" simultaneously. |
   21              |  Select UPDATE to ensure that the most current data |
   22              |  will be displayed.  The macros which drive the |
   23              |  menu begin at BA1.                             |
   24              |                                                |
   25              =================================================
   26
   27              [filename]
   28              [date]
```

Keyboard the labels, zeros, and formulas in columns A-O, rows 101-179. Use the COPY command to copy column C, rows 3 through 79, into columns D through N. Then, keyboard column O. As shown here, the template will accommodate data from spreadsheets for four service points. If additional service points are inserted, the formulas in rows 167-178 will need to be adjusted accordingly. Also, the Update macro (AE1..AE21) in the menu will need to recognize the filename used for each service point.

```
            A          B                  C                             N
     |--------|--------|-----------------------------|      |----------------|
101   Adult Circulation - 1993
102            Month                    -000-                     -Fict-
103            Jan                        0            /\ /            0
104            Feb                        0           / \/            0
105            Mar                        0          / \/ /            0
106            Apr                        0         /\ /              0
107            May                        0        / \/               0
108            Jun                        0       /\ /                0
109            Jul                        0      / \/                0
110            Aug                        0                          0
111            Sep                        0                          0
112            Oct                        0                          0
113            Nov                        0                          0
114            Dec                        0                          0
115            Total          @SUM(C103..C114)          @SUM(N103..N114)
116
117   Young Adult Circulation - 1993
118            Month                    -000-                     -Fict-
119            Jan                        0                          0
120            Feb                        0                          0
121            Mar                        0                          0
122            Apr                        0                          0
123            May                        0                          0
124            Jun                        0                          0
125            Jul                        0                          0
126            Aug                        0                          0
127            Sep                        0                          0
128            Oct                        0                          0
129            Nov                        0                          0
130            Dec                        0                          0
131            Total          @SUM(C119..C130)          @SUM(N119..N130)
132
133   Children's Circulation - 1993
134            Month                    -000-                     -Fict-
135            Jan                        0                          0
136            Feb                        0                          0
137            Mar                        0                          0
138            Apr                        0                          0
139            May                        0                          0
140            Jun                        0                          0
141            Jul                        0                          0
142            Aug                        0                          0
143            Sep                        0                          0
144            Oct                        0                          0
145            Nov                        0                          0
146            Dec                        0                          0
147            Total          @SUM(C135..C146)          @SUM(N135..N146)
148
```

	A	B	C	N
149	Films Circulation - 1993			
150		Month	-000-	-Fict-
151		Jan	0	0
152		Feb	0	0
153		Mar	0	0
154		Apr	0	0
155		May	0	0
156		Jun	0	0
157		Jul	0	0
158		Aug	0	0
159		Sep	0	0
160		Oct	0	0
161		Nov	0	0
162		Dec	0	0
163		Total	@SUM(C152..C163)	@SUM(N152..N163)
164				
165	TOTAL Circulation - 1993			
166		Month	-000-	-Fict-
167		Jan	+C103+C119+C135+C151	+N103+N119+N135+N151
168		Feb	+C104+C120+C136+C152	+N104+N120+N136+N152
169		Mar	+C105+C121+C137+C153	+N105+N121+N137+N153
170		Apr	+C106+C122+C138+C154	+N106+N122+N138+N154
171		May	+C107+C123+C139+C155	+N107+N123+N139+N155
172		Jun	+C108+C124+C140+C156	+N108+N124+N140+N156
173		Jul	+C109+C125+C141+C157	+N109+N125+N141+N157
174		Aug	+C110+C126+C142+C158	+N110+N126+N142+N158
175		Sep	+C111+C127+C143+C159	+N111+N127+N143+N159
176		Oct	+C112+C128+C144+C160	+N112+N128+N144+N160
177		Nov	+C113+C129+C145+C161	+N113+N129+N145+N161
178		Dec	+C114+C130+C146+C162	+N114+N130+N146+N162
179		Total	@SUM(C167..C178)	@SUM(N167..N178)

	AO
101	
102	-Total-
103	@SUM(C103..N103)
104	@SUM(C104..N104)
105	@SUM(C105..N105)
106	@SUM(C106..N106)
107	@SUM(C107..N107)
108	@SUM(C108..N108)
109	@SUM(C109..N109)
110	@SUM(C110..N110)
111	@SUM(C111..N111)
112	@SUM(C112..N112)
113	@SUM(C113..N113)
114	@SUM(C114..N114)
115	@IF(@SUM(O103..O114)=@SUM(C115..N115),@SUM(C115..N115),"ERROR")
116	

```
117
118                                                        -Total-
119                                             @SUM(C119..N119)
120                                             @SUM(C120..N120)
121                                             @SUM(C121..N121)
122                                             @SUM(C122..N122)
123                                             @SUM(C123..N123)
124                                             @SUM(C214..N214)
125                                             @SUM(C125..N125)
126                                             @SUM(C126..N126)
127                                             @SUM(C127..N127)
128                                             @SUM(C128..N128)
129                                             @SUM(C129..N129)
130                                             @SUM(C130..N130)
131      @IF(@SUM(O119..O130)=@SUM(C131..N131),@SUM(C131..N131),"ERROR")
132
133
134                                                        -Total-
135                                             @SUM(C135..N135)
136                                             @SUM(C136..N136)
137                                             @SUM(C137..N137)
138                                             @SUM(C138..N138)
139                                             @SUM(C139..N139)
140                                             @SUM(C140..N140)
141                                             @SUM(C141..N141)
142                                             @SUM(C142..N142)
143                                             @SUM(C143..N143)
144                                             @SUM(C144..N144)
145                                             @SUM(C145..N145)
146                                             @SUM(C146..N146)
147      @IF(@SUM(O135..O146)=@SUM(C147..N47),@SUM(C147..N147),"ERROR")
148
149
150                                                        -Total-
151                                             @SUM(C151..N151)
152                                             @SUM(C152..N152)
153                                             @SUM(C153..N153)
154                                             @SUM(C154..N154)
155                                             @SUM(C155..N155)
156                                             @SUM(C156..N156)
157                                             @SUM(C157..N157)
158                                             @SUM(C158..N158)
159                                             @SUM(C159..N159)
160                                             @SUM(C160..N160)
161                                             @SUM(C161..N161)
162                                             @SUM(C162..N162)
163      @IF(@SUM(O151..O162)=@SUM(C163..N163),@SUM(C163..N163),"ERROR")
164
165
166                                                        -Total-
167                                             @SUM(C167..N167)
168                                             @SUM(C168..N168)
169                                             @SUM(C169..N169)
170                                             @SUM(C170..N170)
171                                             @SUM(C171..N171)
172                                             @SUM(C172..N172)
173                                             @SUM(C173..N173)
174                                             @SUM(C174..N174)
175                                             @SUM(C175..N175)
176                                             @SUM(C176..N176)
177                                             @SUM(C177..N177)
178                                             @SUM(C178..N178)
179      @IF(@SUM(O167..O178)=@SUM(C179..N179),@SUM(C179..N179),"ERROR")
```

After keyboarding columns BA-BQ, rows 1-21, name the range BB1 "\0" so that the instructional statement will be displayed automatically when the spreadsheet is retrieved. Name the range BD1 "\a" so that the menu will be displayed when [ALT] and the letter "a" are pressed simultaneously. Supply the filenames referenced in BE (Update), matching those assigned to the source spreadsheets. Insert additional service points following row 19. This will also require expansion of the print options. Be sure to make room for additional service points by using the Move command. DO NOT use the Insert Row command, as this will disrupt other parts of the spreadsheet.

```
        BA            BB          BC            BD
     |---------|-------------|--------|------------------|
  01  \0            /WTC          \a      {MENUBRANCH BE1}~
  02                {GOTO}A1~
  03                {QUIT}
```

```
                              BE
     |------------------------------------------------------------|
  01  Update
  02  Updates totals by importing data from supporting spreadsheets
  03  /WTC
  04  {GOTO}C103~
  05  /FCCN~
  06  SUMMARY~
  07  CIRCADLT.WK1~
  08  {GOTO}C119~
  09  /FCCN
  10  SUMMARY~
  11  CIRCYA.WK1~
  12  {GOTO}C135~
  13  /FCCN
  14  SUMMARY~
  15  CIRCCHLD.WK1~
  16  {GOTO}C151~
  17  /FCCN
  18  SUMMARY~
  19  CIRCFILM.WK1~
  20  {GOTO}A101~
  21  {QUIT}
```

```
          BF                        BG
     |-----------------|-------------------------------------|
  01  View               Save
  02  See summary data   Writes the year-to-date totals to disk
  03  /WTC               /WTC
  04  {GOTO}A101~        /FS{?}~
  05  {QUIT}             {QUIT}
```

```
          BH                          BI
     |-----------------|----------------------------------|
  01  Print              Quit
  02  Prints year-to-date totals   Exits Lotus 1-2-3.  SAVE FILES FIRST!
  03  {MENUBRANCH BL1}~  /WTC
  04                     /QY
  05                     {QUIT}
```

```
                                      BJ
        |-----------------------------------------------------------------|
01      Macro
02      Utility to move the cursor to the beginning of the menu program
03      /WTC
04      {GOTO}BA1~
05      {QUIT}
```

```
                    BL                                    BM
        |-----------------------------------|  |-----------------------------------|
01      Adult                                  YA
02      Prints Adult year-to-date totals       Prints Young Adult year-to-date totals
03      /WTC                                    /WTC
04      /PP                                     /PP
05      RA101..0115~                            RA117..0131~
06      GPQ                                     GPQ
07      {QUIT}                                  {QUIT}
```

```
                    BN                                    BO
        |-----------------------------------|  |-----------------------------------|
01      Children's                             Films
02      Prints Children's year-to-date totals  Prints Films year-to-date totals
03      /WTC                                    /WTC
04      /PP                                     /PP
05      RA133..0147~                            RA149..0163~
06      GPQ                                     GPQ
07      {QUIT}                                  {QUIT}
```

```
                    BP                                    BQ
        |-----------------------------------|  |-----------------------------------|
01      Summary                                Totals
02      Prints year-to-date summary            Prints all year-to-date totals
03      /WTC                                    /WTC
04      /PP                                     /PP
05      RA165..0179~                            RA101..0179~
06      GPQ                                     GPQ
07      {QUIT}                                  {QUIT}
```

Save this template. Make a copy, and label it with the appropriate title and date. The set of spreadsheets is now ready to use. The total activity for the year at one service point, using fictitious data, is displayed in Table 10-1; this was extracted from the spreadsheet for adult services. The total activity for the year at all service points, using fictitious data, is displayed in Table 10-2; this was printed from the Summary spreadsheet.

Table 10-1: Circulation—Main—Adult—1993: Monthly Totals

```
Summary Table With Formulas; range name = SOURCE
Main - Adult
Summary - 1993
```

Month	-000-	-100-	-200-	-300-	-400-	-500-	-600-	-700-	-800-	-900-	-Biog-	-Fict-	-Total-
Jan	3750	4471	3977	3591	3831	4095	5041	3854	3954	4774	4685	4311	50334
Feb	4048	3898	3844	4224	4576	4807	3528	3687	3868	4176	4925	4142	49724
Mar	3979	4140	5160	4698	5081	4846	5465	4148	4639	4961	4203	4998	56317
Apr	3370	5155	4263	3379	4047	3361	3717	3976	4964	4578	4189	3816	48815
May	4362	3689	3928	4246	3902	3784	4431	4997	3769	4747	3247	4229	49330
Jun	4887	4809	4520	4797	3168	4864	5102	5279	4720	4343	4359	4211	55060
Jul	4426	5128	4127	5103	4551	5180	4914	5125	4768	4103	4828	4978	57232
Aug	3513	5143	3990	4555	4031	4205	5286	4195	3745	4632	4752	4651	52699
Sep	4927	5743	4985	4880	4423	4458	4672	3656	4409	4393	4214	3965	54725
Oct	5842	4769	4302	3848	3862	4708	4388	4822	4787	4268	4682	4493	54772
Nov	3657	3182	4277	3840	4116	3561	4255	4103	4499	4452	4307	4478	48726
Dec	4309	4503	4158	4378	4061	4111	3994	4622	5178	4005	3738	4041	51098
Total	51070	54629	51533	51538	49649	51980	54792	52465	53300	53432	52130	52314	628832

Table 10-2: Circulation—Y-T-D

Adult Circulation - 1993　　　　02/28/93

Month	-000-	-100-	-200-	-300-	-400-	-500-	-600-	-700-	-800-	-900-	-Biog-	-Fict-	-Total-
Jan	5472	6885	6433	5590	4826	6355	6188	6013	6516	5158	6547	6382	72367
Feb	6605	6145	6789	5486	6266	5296	5767	4958	6110	6297	4922	5894	70534
Mar	0	0	0	0	0	0	0	0	0	0	0	0	0
Apr	0	0	0	0	0	0	0	0	0	0	0	0	0
May	0	0	0	0	0	0	0	0	0	0	0	0	0
Jun	0	0	0	0	0	0	0	0	0	0	0	0	0
Jul	0	0	0	0	0	0	0	0	0	0	0	0	0
Aug	0	0	0	0	0	0	0	0	0	0	0	0	0
Sep	0	0	0	0	0	0	0	0	0	0	0	0	0
Oct	0	0	0	0	0	0	0	0	0	0	0	0	0
Nov	0	0	0	0	0	0	0	0	0	0	0	0	0
Dec	0	0	0	0	0	0	0	0	0	0	0	0	0
Total	12077	13030	13222	11077	11092	11651	11955	10971	12626	11455	11469	12277	142901

Young Adult Circulation - 1993　　　　02/28/93

Month	-000-	-100-	-200-	-300-	-400-	-500-	-600-	-700-	-800-	-900-	-Biog-	-Fict-	-Total-
Jan	3958	4035	4242	4655	3393	4375	3691	4292	3286	4068	3804	3572	47370
Feb	4241	3482	3242	3006	4070	3890	3033	3638	3403	3921	3519	3357	42802
Mar	0	0	0	0	0	0	0	0	0	0	0	0	0
Apr	0	0	0	0	0	0	0	0	0	0	0	0	0
May	0	0	0	0	0	0	0	0	0	0	0	0	0
Jun	0	0	0	0	0	0	0	0	0	0	0	0	0
Jul	0	0	0	0	0	0	0	0	0	0	0	0	0
Aug	0	0	0	0	0	0	0	0	0	0	0	0	0
Sep	0	0	0	0	0	0	0	0	0	0	0	0	0
Oct	0	0	0	0	0	0	0	0	0	0	0	0	0
Nov	0	0	0	0	0	0	0	0	0	0	0	0	0
Dec	0	0	0	0	0	0	0	0	0	0	0	0	0
Total	8199	7516	7484	7661	7463	8265	6723	7930	6689	7989	7323	6929	90172

Children's Circulation - 1993　　　　02/28/93

Month	-000-	-100-	-200-	-300-	-400-	-500-	-600-	-700-	-800-	-900-	-Biog-	-Fict-	-Total-
Jan	8371	7557	9097	7120	7012	7416	6481	6756	8424	8449	6853	7440	90975
Feb	7074	7440	5891	6197	7712	6212	7443	7642	6663	7325	8112	6424	84136
Mar	0	0	0	0	0	0	0	0	0	0	0	0	0
Apr	0	0	0	0	0	0	0	0	0	0	0	0	0
May	0	0	0	0	0	0	0	0	0	0	0	0	0
Jun	0	0	0	0	0	0	0	0	0	0	0	0	0
Jul	0	0	0	0	0	0	0	0	0	0	0	0	0
Aug	0	0	0	0	0	0	0	0	0	0	0	0	0
Sep	0	0	0	0	0	0	0	0	0	0	0	0	0
Oct	0	0	0	0	0	0	0	0	0	0	0	0	0
Nov	0	0	0	0	0	0	0	0	0	0	0	0	0
Dec	0	0	0	0	0	0	0	0	0	0	0	0	0
Total	15445	14996	14988	13318	14724	13628	13924	14398	15087	15774	14965	13864	175111

Films Circulation - 1993　　　　02/28/93

Month	-000-	-100-	-200-	-300-	-400-	-500-	-600-	-700-	-800-	-900-	-Biog-	-Fict-	-Total-
Jan	1137	1057	1318	1238	1075	1061	940	1041	1203	917	1060	1056	13103
Feb	1268	1059	1029	972	957	938	1030	985	888	1053	986	1071	12239
Mar	0	0	0	0	0	0	0	0	0	0	0	0	0
Apr	0	0	0	0	0	0	0	0	0	0	0	0	0
May	0	0	0	0	0	0	0	0	0	0	0	0	0
Jun	0	0	0	0	0	0	0	0	0	0	0	0	0
Jul	0	0	0	0	0	0	0	0	0	0	0	0	0
Aug	0	0	0	0	0	0	0	0	0	0	0	0	0
Sep	0	0	0	0	0	0	0	0	0	0	0	0	0
Oct	0	0	0	0	0	0	0	0	0	0	0	0	0
Nov	0	0	0	0	0	0	0	0	0	0	0	0	0
Dec	0	0	0	0	0	0	0	0	0	0	0	0	0
Total	2405	2117	2347	2210	2032	1999	1971	2026	2091	1971	2046	2127	25341

TOTAL Circulation - 1993　　　　02/28/93

Month	-000-	-100-	-200-	-300-	-400-	-500-	-600-	-700-	-800-	-900-	-Biog-	-Fict-	-Total-
Jan	18938	19534	21090	18604	16305	19208	17300	18102	19428	18592	18265	18450	223815
Feb	19189	18125	16952	15662	19006	16336	17273	17223	17064	18596	17539	16746	209711
Mar	0	0	0	0	0	0	0	0	0	0	0	0	0
Apr	0	0	0	0	0	0	0	0	0	0	0	0	0
May	0	0	0	0	0	0	0	0	0	0	0	0	0
Jun	0	0	0	0	0	0	0	0	0	0	0	0	0
Jul	0	0	0	0	0	0	0	0	0	0	0	0	0
Aug	0	0	0	0	0	0	0	0	0	0	0	0	0
Sep	0	0	0	0	0	0	0	0	0	0	0	0	0
Oct	0	0	0	0	0	0	0	0	0	0	0	0	0
Nov	0	0	0	0	0	0	0	0	0	0	0	0	0
Dec	0	0	0	0	0	0	0	0	0	0	0	0	0
Total	38127	37659	38041	34265	35311	35543	34573	35325	36492	37188	35803	35196	433525

Chapter 11
Circulation in 2-D: Month by Month

In this second two-dimensional model, the data for an entire year are displayed in month-by-month blocks for one service point in each spreadsheet. (LC class letters can be substituted for the Decimal Classification numbers, although this will require that additional columns be inserted and that the menu macros be moved and appropriately altered.) Matching spreadsheets are assigned to other service points. Finally, the year-to-date totals are brought together in a summary spreadsheet. This relationship is illustrated in Figure 10-A.

To set up the Circulation: Month-by-Month template, follow the cell-by-cell instructions which appear below, creating a generic template. Refer as needed to the general instructions and guidelines in Chapter 2, "Design and Modification of Spreadsheets." Most of the columns are set at the default of nine spaces. Column B is set at 10 spaces, while columns AA-AN are set at varying widths sufficient to display the texts of the menu macros.

Begin by keyboarding the organizational statement.

CIRCULATION SPREADSHEET—MONTH BY MONTH: CELL-BY-CELL INSTRUCTIONS

```
         A          B          C          D          E          F          G          H
    |----|-------------|---------|---------|---------|---------|---------|--------|
01       ||================================================================|
02       ||                                                                |
03       ||    C I R C U L A T I O N  -  1 9 9 3                            |
04       ||                                                                |
05       ||    This spreadsheet contains day-by-day, class-by-            |
06       ||    class data grouped in month-by-month blocks for           |
07       ||    the following service point or category of                |
08       ||    materials:                                                 |
09       ||                                                                |
10       ||              [name of service point]                          |
11       ||                                                                |
12       ||    The spreadsheet is arranged as follows:                    |
13       ||                                                                |
14       ||         January     February    March       April            |
15       ||                                                                |
16       ||         May         June        July        August           |
17       ||                                                                |
18       ||         September   October     November    December         |
19       ||                                                                |
20       ||         Total       (total)                                   |
21       ||                                                                |
22       ||    Within each month, the spreadsheet has a row for           |
23       ||    each day and a column for each class of materials.         |
24       ||    Row and column data are totaled for each day and           |
25       ||    for each class.  The beginning address for each            |
26       ||    month is as follows:                                       |
27       ||                                                                |
28       ||         A101        Q101        AG101       AW101             |
29       ||                                                                |
30       ||         A139        Q139        AG139       AW139             |
31       ||                                                                |
32       ||         A177        Q177        AG177       AW177             |
33       ||                                                                |
34       ||    The monthly totals are combined in a separate              |
35       ||    section beginning at A215.  The range name for             |
36       ||    this section is SOURCE.                                     |
37       ||                                                                |
38       ||    These same totals are displayed as values beginning        |
39       ||    at Q215.  The range name for this section is               |
40       ||    SUMMARY.                                                    |
41       ||                                                                |
42       ||    To speed data entry, turn off automatic recalcu-          |
43       ||    lation.  However, be sure to recalculate the              |
44       ||    spreadsheet before converting values, saving, or          |
45       ||    printing.                                                  |
46       ||                                                                |
47       ||    This spreadsheet is designed to be used in                 |
48       ||    conjunction with other spreadsheets for other             |
49       ||    service points and/or categories of materials             |
50       ||    (e.g., Young Adult, CD-ROMs, and/or branches).            |
51       ||    The totals for each of these are combined in              |
52       ||    another spreadsheet (CIRC1TOT.WK1) which draws            |
53       ||    its data from the SUMMARY range of each spread-           |
54       ||    sheet.                                                     |
55       ||                                                                |
56       ||    Use of this spreadsheet is assisted by a menu              |
57       ||    which can be invoked by simultaneously pressing           |
58       ||    [ALT] and the letter "a".  The macros which drive         |
59       ||    the menu begin at CA1.                                      |
60       ||                                                                |
61       ||================================================================|
62       [filename]
63       [date]
```

Keyboard the basic template into columns A–O, rows 101-135. Only the beginning and ending rows are shown below. Copy the zeros and formula in C103-C133 into rows D through N. Enter the appropriate class number at the head of each column. Use the data fill command (/df) to enter the dates. The beginning and end values for the months in 1993 are:

January 1 = 33970	January 31 = 34000
February 1 = 34001	February 28 = 34028
March 1 = 34029	March 31 = 34059
April 1 = 34060	April 30 = 34089
May 1 = 34090	May 31 = 34120
June 1 = 34121	June 30 = 34150
July 1 = 34151	July 31 = 34181
August 1 = 34182	August 31 = 34212
September 1 = 34213	September 30 = 34242
October 1 = 34243	October 31 = 34273
November 1 = 34274	November 30 = 34303
December 1 = 34304	December 31 = 34334

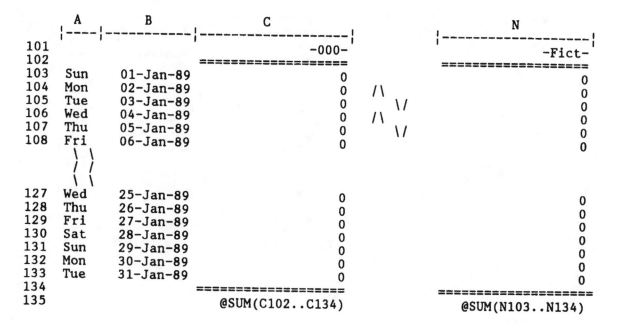

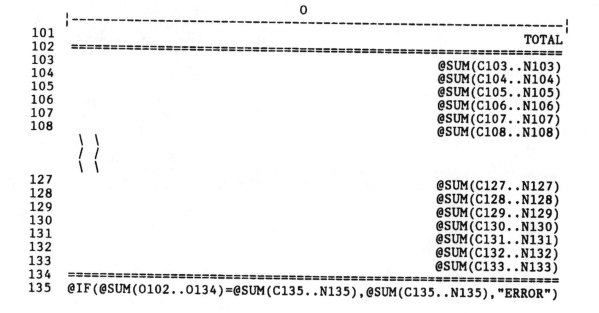

Copy the range A101-O135 into each of the following locations; fill in the correct dates and the days of the week.

	Q101	AG101	AW101
A139	Q139	AG139	AW139
A177	Q177	AG177	AW177

After keyboarding the Summary Table into columns A-O, rows 215-231, name the range C218-N229 "SOURCE." This will be used in the updating process to transfer values to the SUMMARY range.

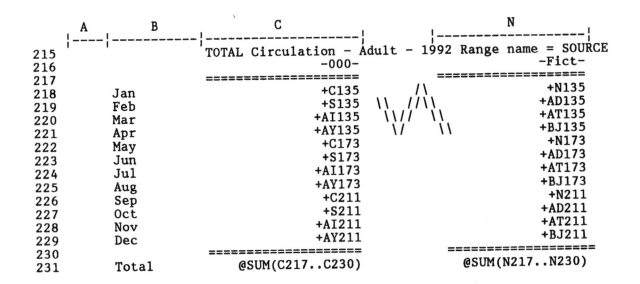

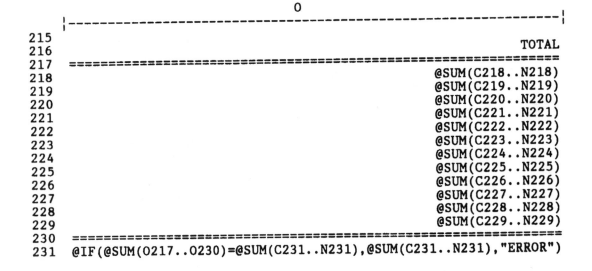

After keyboarding the Dummy File into columns R-AD, rows 216-229, name the range S218-AD229 "SUMMARY." This range is referenced by the spreadsheet CIRC1T.WK1 in which year-to-date cumulations are gathered.

```
            R            S                        AD
         !--------!--------!            !--------!
216               TOTAL - dummy file (range name = SUMMARY)
217               (values created from file at left using "/RV")
218     Jan       0                              0
219     Feb       0                              0
220     Mar       0        /\                     0
221     Apr       0          \/                   0
222     May       0        /\                     0
223     Jun       0          \/                   0
224     Jul       0                              0
225     Aug       0                              0
226     Sep       0                              0
227     Oct       0                              0
228     Nov       0                              0
229     Dec       0                              0
```

After keyboarding columns CA-CN, rows 1-66, name the range CB1 "\0" so that the organizational statement will be displayed whenever the spreadsheet is loaded. Name the range CE1 "\a" so that the menu will be displayed when [ALT] and "a" are pressed simultaneously.

```
         CA    |     CB      |   CC    |   CD    |       CE
    |---------|-------------|--------|--------|-------------------|
01  \0         /WTC                    \a        {MENUBRANCH CG1}~
02             {GOTO}A1~
03             {QUIT}
04
```

```
                           CG
    |----------------------------------------------------------|
01  Freeze
02  Holds date and class titles on screen
03  {MENUBRANCH CG15}~
04
05
            \ \
             / /
            \ \
15  January
16  Freezes row and column titles for month of January
17  /WTC
18  {GOTO}A101~
19  {RIGHT 2}~
20  {DOWN 2}
21  /WTB
22  {QUIT}
            \ \
             / /
            \ \
30  August
31  Freezes row and column titles for month of August
32  /WTC
33  {GOTO}AW139~
34  {RIGHT 2}~
35  {DOWN 2}
36  /WTB
37  {QUIT}
            \ \
             / /
            \ \
45  January
46  Prints data for month of January
47  /WTC
48  /PPR
49  A101..O135~
50  G
51  P
52  Q
53  {QUIT}
```

```
                              CG
    !----------------------------------------------------!
         \ \
          / /
         \ \
60   August
61   Prints data for month of August
62   /WTC
63   /PPR
64   AW139..BK173~
65   GPQ
66   {QUIT}



                              CH
    !----------------------------------------------------!
01   Recalculate
02   Recalculates the spreadsheet
03   {CALC}
04   {QUIT}
          \ \
           / /
          \ \
15   February
16   Freezes row and column titles for month of February
17   /WTC
18   {GOTO}Q101~
19   {RIGHT 2}~
20   {DOWN 2}~
21   /WTB
22   {QUIT}
          \ \
           / /
          \ \
30   September
31   Freezes row and column titles for month of September
32   /WTC
33   {GOTO}A177~
34   {RIGHT 2}~
35   {DOWN 2}~
36   /WTB
37   {QUIT}
          \ \
           / /
          \ \
45   February
46   Prints data for month of February
47   /WTC
48   /PPR
49   Q101..AE135~
50   G
51   P
52   Q
53   {QUIT}
          \ \
           / /
          \ \
```

```
                              CH
   !----------------------------------------------------!
60   September
61   Prints data for month for September
62   /WTC
63   /PPR
64   A177..O211~
65   GPQ
66   {QUIT}


                               CI
   !----------------------------------------------------!
01   Update
02   Recalculates spreadsheet and updates summary range values
03   {CALC}
04   /RV
05   Source~
06   Summary~
07   {QUIT}
            \  \
             /  /
             \  \
15   March
16   Freezes row and column titles for month of March
17   /WTC
18   {GOTO}AG101~
19   {RIGHT 2}~
20   {DOWN 2}
21   /WTB
22   {QUIT}
            \  \
             /  /
             \  \
30   October
31   Freezes row and column titles for month of October
32   /WTC
33   {GOTO}Q177~
34   {RIGHT 2}~
35   {DOWN 2}
36   /WTB
37   {QUIT}
            \  \
             /  /
             \  \
```

```
                               CI
  |----------------------------------------------------------|
  |----------------------------------------------------------|
45  March
46  Prints data for month of March
47  /WTC
48  /PPR
49  AG101..AU135~
50  GPQ
51  {QUIT}
            \  \
             /  /
            \  \
60  October
61  Prints data for month of October
62  /WTC
63  /PPR
64  Q177..AE211~
65  GPQ
66  {QUIT}


                               CJ
  |--------------------------------------------------------|
  |--------------------------------------------------------|
01  Save
02  Saves the spreadsheet to disk
03  /WTC
04  /FS{?}~
05  {QUIT}
            \  \
             /  /
            \  \
15  April
16  Freezes row and column titles for month of April
17  /WTC
18  {GOTO}AW101~
19  {RIGHT 2}~
20  {DOWN 2}
21  /WTB
22  {QUIT}
            \  \
             /  /
            \  \
30  November
31  Freezes row and column titles for month of November
32  /WTC
33  {GOTO}AG177~
34  {RIGHT 2}~
35  {DOWN 2}
36  /WTB
37  {QUIT}
            \  \
             /  /
            \  \
                               CJ
  |------------------------------------------------------|
45  April
46  Prints data for month of April
47  /WTC
48  /PPR
49  AW101..BK135~
50  GPQ
51  {QUIT}
```

```
                    \ \
                    / /
                    \ \
      60  November
      61  Prints data for month of November
      62  /WTC
      63  /PPR
      64  AG177..AU211~
      65  GPQ
      66  {QUIT}


                                      CK
      |----------------------------------------------------|
      01  Print
      02  Prints months and the year-to-date summary
      03  {MENUBRANCH CG45}~
                    \ \
                    / /
                    \ \
      15  -May
      16  Freezes row and column titles for month of May
      17  /WTC
      18  {GOTO}A139~
      19  {RIGHT 2}~
      20  {DOWN 2}
      21  /WTB
      22  {QUIT}
                    \ \
                    / /
                    \ \
      30  December
      31  Freezes row and column titles for month of December
      32  /WTC
      33  {GOTO}AW177~
      34  {RIGHT 2}~
      35  {DOWN 2}
      36  /WTB
      37  {QUIT}
                    \ \
                    / /
                    \ \
      45  -June
      46  Prints data for month of June
      47  /WTC
      48  /PPR
      49  Q139..AE173~
      50  GPQ
      51  {QUIT}
```

```
                              CK
   |------------------------------------------------------------|
45 -May
46 Prints data for month of May
47 /WTC
48 /PPR
49 A139..0173~
50 GPQ
51 {QUIT}
           \  \
            /  /
           \  \
60 December
61 Prints data for month of December
62 /WTC
63 /PPR
64 AW177..BK211~
65 GPQ
66 {QUIT}

                              CL
   |------------------------------------------------------------|
01 Quit
02 Exits Lotus 1-2-3. RECALCULATE, UPDATE, and SAVE FILES FIRST!
03 /WTC
04 /QY
05 {QUIT}
           \  \
            /  /
           \  \
15 -June
16 Freezes row and column titles for month of June
17 /WTC
18 {GOTO}Q139~
19 {RIGHT 2}~
20 {DOWN 2}
21 /WTB
22 {QUIT}
           \  \
            /  /
           \  \
30 December
31 Freezes row and column titles for month of December
32 /WTC
33 {GOTO}AW177~
34 {RIGHT 2}~
35 {DOWN 2}
36 /WTB
37 {QUIT}
           \  \
            /  /
           \  \
45 -June
46 Prints data for month of June
47 /WTC
48 /PPR
49 Q139..AE173~
50 GPQ
51 {QUIT}
```

```
         \ \
         / /
         \ \
60   Total
61   Prints year-to-date total
62   /WTC
63   /PPR
64   A215..O231~
65   GPQ
66   {QUIT}
```

```
                              CM
|------------------------------------------------------------|
01   Macro
02   Utility to move the cursor to the beginning of the menu program
03   /WTC
04   {GOTO}CA1~
05   {QUIT}
         \ \
         / /
         \ \
15   =July
16   Freezes row and column titles for month of July
17   /WTC
18   {GOTO}AG139~
19   {RIGHT 2}~
20   {DOWN 2}~
21   /WTB
22   {QUIT}
         \ \
         / /
         \ \
45   =July
46   Prints data for month of July
47   /WTC
48   /PPR
49   AG139..AU173~
50   GPQ
53   {QUIT}
```

```
                              CN
|------------------------------------------------------|
         \ \
         / /
         \ \
15   Other
16   Freezes row and column titles for July-December
17   {MENUBRANCH CG30}~
         \ \
         / /
         \ \
45   Other
46   Prints July-December and year-to-date totals
47   {MENUBRANCH CG60}~
```

Save this generic template. Make a copy for each service point for data entry and analysis, and label each with the appropriate title and date.

The next step is to create the summary template. Begin by keyboarding the organizational statement in columns B-D, rows 1-18.

SUMMARY SPREADSHEET: CELL-BY-CELL INSTRUCTIONS

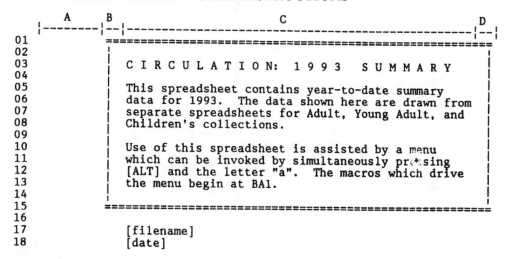

```
        A      B                        C                              D
    !---------!--!----------------------------------------------!--!
01  !         !  !============================================== !  !
02            |  |
03            |  |    C I R C U L A T I O N :   1 9 9 3   S U M M A R Y    |
04            |  |
05            |  |  This spreadsheet contains year-to-date summary  |
06            |  |  data for 1993.  The data shown here are drawn from  |
07            |  |  separate spreadsheets for Adult, Young Adult, and  |
08            |  |  Children's collections.  |
09            |  |
10            |  |  Use of this spreadsheet is assisted by a menu  |
11            |  |  which can be invoked by simultaneously pressing  |
12            |  |  [ALT] and the letter "a".  The macros which drive  |
13            |  |  the menu begin at BA1.  |
14            |  |
15            |  |  ==============================================  |
16
17            [filename]
18            [date]
```

Keyboard the labels, zeros, and formulas in columns A, B, and C, rows 101-163. Copy column C, rows 101-163, into columns D-N, correcting the class headings. Then keyboard column O. Note, as shown here, the template will accommodate data from spreadsheets for three service points. If additional service points are inserted, the formulas in rows 51-62 will need to be adjusted accordingly. Also, the Update macro (BE1..BE17) in the menu will need to recognize the filename used for each service point.

```
            A         B           C                                N
      !---------!------!---------------------!      !---------------------!
101   Adult
102             Month            -000-                        -Fict-
103             Jan                0                              0
104             Feb                0                              0
105             Mar                0                              0
106             Apr                0      /\                      0
107             May                0         \/                   0
108             Jun                0      /\                      0
109             Jul                0         \/                   0
110             Aug                0                              0
111             Sep                0                              0
112             Oct                0                              0
113             Nov                0                              0
114             Dec                0                              0
115             Total    @SUM(C103..C114)            @SUM(N103..N114)
116
117   Young Adult
118             Month            -000-                        -Fict-
119             Jan                0                              0
120             Feb                0                              0
121             Mar                0                              0
122             Apr                0                              0
123             May                0                              0
124             Jun                0                              0
125             Jul                0                              0
126             Aug                0                              0
127             Sep                0                              0
128             Oct                0                              0
129             Nov                0                              0
130             Dec                0                              0
131             Total    @SUM(C119..C130)            @SUM(N119..N130)
132
```

```
              A        B              C                              N
       |--------|------|---------------------|        |---------------------|
 133   Children's
 134            Month              -000-                              -Fict-
 135            Jan                  0                                   0
 136            Feb                  0                                   0
 137            Mar                  0    /\                             0
 138            Apr                  0       \/                          0
 139            May                  0    /\                             0
 140            Jun                  0       \/                          0
 141            Jul                  0                                   0
 142            Aug                  0                                   0
 143            Sep                  0                                   0
 144            Oct                  0                                   0
 145            Nov                  0                                   0
 146            Dec                  0                                   0
 147            Total       @SUM(C135..C146)              @SUM(N135..N146)
 148
 149   TOTAL Circulation - 1989
 150            Month              -000-                              -Fict-
 151            Jan         +C103+C119+C135              +N103+N119+N135
 152            Feb         +C104+C120+C136              +N104+N120+N136
 153            Mar         +C105+C121+C137              +N105+N121+N137
 154            Apr         +C106+C122+C138              +N106+N122+N138
 155            May         +C107+C123+C139              +N107+N123+N139
 156            Jun         +C108+C124+C140              +N108+N124+N140
 157            Jul         +C109+C125+C141              +N109+N125+N141
 158            Aug         +C110+C126+C142              +N110+N126+N142
 159            Sep         +C111+C127+C143              +N111+N127+N143
 160            Oct         +C112+C128+C144              +N112+N128+N144
 161            Nov         +C113+C129+C145              +N113+N129+N145
 162            Dec         +C114+C130+C146              +N114+N130+N146
 163            Total       @SUM(C151..C162)              @SUM(N151..N162)
```

```
                                       O
     |---------------------------------------------------------------|
101
102                                                            -Total-
103                                                 @SUM(C103..N103)
104                                                 @SUM(C104..N104)
105                                                 @SUM(C105..N105)
106                                                 @SUM(C106..N106)
107                                                 @SUM(C107..N107)
108                                                 @SUM(C108..N108)
109                                                 @SUM(C109..N109)
110                                                 @SUM(C110..N110)
111                                                 @SUM(C111..N111)
112                                                 @SUM(C112..N112)
113                                                 @SUM(C113..N113)
114                                                 @SUM(C114..N114)
115  @IF(@SUM(O103..O114)=@SUM(C115..N115),@SUM(C115..N115),"ERROR")
116
117
118                                                            -Total-
119                                                 @SUM(C119..N119)
120                                                 @SUM(C120..N120)
121                                                 @SUM(C121..N121)
122                                                 @SUM(C122..N122)
123                                                 @SUM(C123..N123)
124                                                 @SUM(C124..N124)
125                                                 @SUM(C125..N125)
126                                                 @SUM(C126..N126)
127                                                 @SUM(C127..N127)
128                                                 @SUM(C128..N128)
129                                                 @SUM(C129..N129)
130                                                 @SUM(C130..N130)
131  @IF(@SUM(O119..O130)=@SUM(C131..N131),@SUM(C131..N131),"ERROR")
132
133
134                                                            -Total-
135                                                 @SUM(C135..N135)
136                                                 @SUM(C136..N136)
137                                                 @SUM(C137..N137)
138                                                 @SUM(C138..N138)
139                                                 @SUM(C139..N139)
140                                                 @SUM(C140..N140)
141                                                 @SUM(C141..N141)
142                                                 @SUM(C142..N142)
143                                                 @SUM(C143..N143)
144                                                 @SUM(C144..N144)
145                                                 @SUM(C145..N145)
146                                                 @SUM(C146..N146)
147  @IF(@SUM(O135..O146)=@SUM(C147..N147),@SUM(C147..N147),"ERROR")
148
149
150                                                            -Total-
151                                                 @SUM(C151..N151)
152                                                 @SUM(C152..N152)
153                                                 @SUM(C153..N153)
154                                                 @SUM(C154..N154)
155                                                 @SUM(C155..N155)
156                                                 @SUM(C156..N156)
157                                                 @SUM(C157..N157)
158                                                 @SUM(C158..N158)
159                                                 @SUM(C159..N159)
160                                                 @SUM(C160..N160)
161                                                 @SUM(C161..N161)
162                                                 @SUM(C162..N162)
163  @IF(@SUM(O151..O162)=@SUM(C163..N163),@SUM(C163..N163),"ERROR")
```

After keyboarding columns BA-BJ, rows 1-51, name the range BB1 "\0" so that the instructional statement will be displayed whenever the spreadsheet is loaded. Name the range BD1 "\a" so that the menu will be displayed when [ALT] and "a" are pressed simultaneously. Supply the filenames referenced in BE (Update), matching those assigned to the source spreadsheets. Insert additional service points following row 15. Make room for additional service points using the Move command. DO NOT use the Insert Row command, as this may disrupt other parts of the spreadsheet.

```
          BA            BB          BC            BD
     |--------|--------------|--------|------------------|
  01  \0          /WTC          \a      {MENUBRANCH BE1}
  02              {GOTO}A1~
  03              {QUIT}
```

```
                  BE                                BF
     |----------------------------|------------------------------------|
  01  Update                        View
  02  Update spreadsheet            View selected portions of summary
  03  /WTC                          {MENUBRANCH BE30}~
  04  {GOTO}C103~
  05  /FCCN
  06  Summary~
  07  CIRC1A.WK1~
  08  {GOTO}C119~
  09  /FCCN
  10  Summary~
  11  CIRC1Y.WK1~
  12  {GOTO}C135~
  13  /FCCN
  14  Summary~
  15  CIRC1C.WK1~
  16  {GOTO}A101~
  17  {QUIT}
                \ \
                / /
                \ \
  30  Adult                         YA
  31  View adult summary            View Young Adult summary
  32  /WTC                          /WTC
  33  {RIGHT 7}~                    {GOTO}A117~
  34  {GOTO}A101~                   {DOWN 19}~
  35  {QUIT}                        {RIGHT 7}~
  36                                {GOTO}A117~
  37                                {QUIT}
                \ \
                / /
                \ \
  45  Adult                         YA
  46  Print Adult summary           Print Young Adult summary
  47  /WTC                          /WTC
  48  /PP                           /PP
  49  RAA1..0115~                   RA117..0131~
  50  GPQ                           GPQ
  51  {QUIT}                        {QUIT}
```

```
                        BG                      BH
      |---------------------------------|-----------------|
  01  Save                              Print
  02  Saves spreadsheet to disk         {MENUBRANCH BE45}~
  03  /WTC
  04  /FS{?}~
  05  {QUIT}
               \ \
               / /
               \ \
  30  Children's                        Total
  31  View Children's summary           View Total summary
  32  /WTC                              /WTC
  33  {GOTO}A133~                       {GOTO}A149~
  34  {DOWN 19}~                        {DOWN 19}~
  35  {RIGHT 7}~                        {RIGHT 7}~
  36  {GOTO}A133~                       {GOTO}A149~
  37  {QUIT}                            {QUIT}
               \ \
               / /
               \ \
  45  Children's                        Total
  46  Print Children's summary          Print Total summary
  47  /WTC                              /WTC
  48  /PP                               /PP
  49  RA133..0147~                      RA149..0163~
  50  GPQ                               GPQ
  51  {QUIT}                            {QUIT}


                             BI
      |----------------------------------------------------|
  01  Quit
  02  Exits Lotus 1-2-3.   SAVE FILES FIRST!
  03  /WTC
  04  /QY
  05  {QUIT}


                             BJ
      |-----------------------------------------------------------------|
  01  Macro
  02  Utility to move the cursor to the beginning of the menu program
  03  /WTC
  04  {GOTO}BA1~
  05  {QUIT}
```

Save this template. Make a copy, and label it with the appropriate title and date. The set of spreadsheets is now ready to use. The day-by-day activity for the month of January at one service point, using fictitious data, is displayed in Table 11-1; this was extracted from the spreadsheet for adult services. The total activity for the year at all service points, using fictitious data, is displayed in Table 11-2; this was printed from the Summary spreadsheet.

Table 11-1: Circulation—Main—Adult: January 1992

		000	100	200	300	400	500	600	700	800	900	Biog	Fict	TOTAL
Sun	01-Jan-92	0	0	0	0	0	0	0	0	0	0	0	0	0
Mon	02-Jan-92	367	249	257	340	397	134	316	172	315	167	370	314	3397
Tue	03-Jan-92	119	215	302	238	66	302	175	124	221	53	160	117	2091
Wed	04-Jan-92	312	57	365	276	260	235	95	232	61	341	337	218	2682
Thu	05-Jan-92	152	266	150	147	298	251	385	255	68	235	373	218	2798
Fri	06-Jan-92	238	366	53	52	295	50	93	332	64	151	110	345	2148
Sat	07-Jan-92	131	82	307	291	137	224	350	208	180	79	314	304	2607
Sun	08-Jan-92	135	144	129	143	201	265	372	224	182	393	67	101	2356
Mon	09-Jan-92	257	297	368	254	326	79	102	198	188	211	115	223	2617
Tue	10-Jan-92	240	114	202	115	187	87	59	61	344	299	264	170	2142
Wed	11-Jan-92	277	150	132	105	366	293	137	139	143	388	281	139	2549
Thu	12-Jan-92	337	306	83	367	271	388	148	391	200	328	85	258	3162
Fri	13-Jan-92	185	285	299	51	265	211	369	342	170	199	298	173	2846
Sat	14-Jan-92	104	54	137	388	279	210	343	66	173	70	340	381	2545
Sun	15-Jan-92	219	302	370	85	192	147	122	120	113	111	377	62	2220
Mon	16-Jan-92	0	0	0	0	0	0	0	0	0	0	0	0	0
Tue	17-Jan-92	205	70	128	310	199	55	55	391	97	137	114	385	2146
Wed	18-Jan-92	248	147	206	127	118	239	280	357	92	392	88	234	2527
Thu	19-Jan-92	323	316	169	51	294	248	361	285	213	225	383	322	3191
Fri	20-Jan-92	262	76	385	285	312	369	247	171	398	183	110	69	2867
Sat	21-Jan-92	215	210	122	222	67	322	198	366	264	316	261	237	2800
Sun	22-Jan-92	114	125	367	126	400	282	150	137	162	200	202	79	2343
Mon	23-Jan-92	261	271	305	388	372	60	245	302	121	250	183	94	2853
Tue	24-Jan-92	132	257	320	329	138	260	399	217	72	290	347	337	3098
Wed	25-Jan-92	356	274	372	206	342	73	119	164	294	179	307	267	2954
Thu	26-Jan-92	55	350	107	104	157	303	172	153	54	133	120	209	1917
Fri	27-Jan-92	192	374	214	342	199	357	312	365	397	246	84	157	3239
Sat	28-Jan-92	110	66	209	147	345	352	388	367	367	108	97	314	2871
Sun	29-Jan-92	201	137	82	114	137	252	86	176	178	203	396	142	2102
Mon	30-Jan-92	240	366	292	159	259	142	184	89	281	98	334	245	2691
Tue	31-Jan-92	301	108	152	262	219	57	254	216	116	269	142	111	2206
		6288	6032	6584	6023	7097	6248	6514	6621	5528	6255	6660	6116	75967

Table 11-2: Circulation: 1991 Y-T-D Totals

Adult

Month	-000-	-100-	-200-	-300-	-400-	-500-	-600-	-700-	-800-	-900-	-Biog-	-Fict-	-Total-
Jan	6630	6888	7358	6364	6248	7151	6958	6782	6937	8072	6941	6727	83055
Feb	6513	5999	5423	6678	5814	5537	8008	6383	5422	4400	6362	6188	72728
Mar	6178	7522	7006	7061	6771	6670	6263	7214	7013	6095	6874	6075	80741
Apr	6293	7407	7090	7085	6340	6714	6230	6433	7067	7364	6918	6894	81835
May	5960	8440	7494	7195	6651	6395	7100	7529	4988	6752	6265	7497	82266
Jun	6498	6407	6547	5625	6822	6756	6972	6417	7238	6603	6926	7102	79912
Jul	6280	6710	6393	6506	7046	7724	6432	6849	6117	7480	6620	7571	81729
Aug	7164	6724	6809	6527	6841	6577	6408	7377	7280	6761	6670	7677	82815
Sep	6483	6122	7067	6425	7571	6159	5723	6873	5772	5787	6447	6149	76579
Oct	7896	6714	6235	6592	7299	7171	6976	7230	7085	6322	6935	6766	83221
Nov	6421	5726	5754	6026	6163	6452	6001	6943	6194	5955	6398	5919	73952
Dec	6335	6537	6225	5955	6586	7041	6244	6098	7005	6207	6960	7081	78273
Total	78650	81197	79400	78039	80152	80346	79314	82128	78119	77798	80316	81646	957106

Young Adult

Month	-000-	-100-	-200-	-300-	-400-	-500-	-600-	-700-	-800-	-900-	-Biog-	-Fict-	-Total-
Jan	6414	5655	7903	6496	7205	5847	8304	7550	7909	6884	6264	6179	82610
Feb	5395	6567	6830	6763	6052	6257	6089	5916	5962	6540	7175	6169	75716
Mar	7122	6458	6692	7184	7270	7157	6765	7263	5723	6140	6940	6223	80937
Apr	5481	7165	6886	7043	6566	7925	7458	6980	6796	7590	5665	7170	82724
May	7008	7059	6957	6433	6994	6854	7719	7764	7502	7326	7240	7986	86842
Jun	6764	6237	6645	7551	7315	6515	7662	6081	5817	6608	5444	7188	79827
Jul	6350	7296	6409	7190	6405	6868	7104	5968	7212	7958	7092	7595	83446
Aug	7426	6551	6472	5913	6892	6004	5609	7147	7173	7768	7088	6915	80957
Sep	7577	7471	7511	7263	6004	7534	7143	7389	6915	6884	6763	6861	85314
Oct	7281	6148	7748	6931	7693	6587	7173	7032	7726	7186	5931	6672	84109
Nov	6202	7145	6489	5626	5829	7311	6635	6228	6679	6635	7855	6951	79585
Dec	6713	6938	6974	6755	7563	6810	7319	7183	7066	6888	7134	6343	83686
Total	79732	80691	83516	81148	81788	81668	84978	82502	82481	84407	80592	82252	985755

Children's

Month	-000-	-100-	-200-	-300-	-400-	-500-	-600-	-700-	-800-	-900-	-Biog-	-Fict-	-Total-
Jan	6414	5655	7903	6496	7205	5847	8304	7550	7909	6884	6264	6179	82610
Feb	5395	6567	6830	6763	6052	6257	6089	5916	5962	6540	7175	6169	75716
Mar	7122	6458	6692	7184	7270	7157	6765	7263	5723	6140	6940	6223	80937
Apr	5481	7165	6886	7043	6566	7925	7458	6980	6796	7590	5665	7170	82724
May	7008	7059	6957	6433	6994	6854	7719	7764	7502	7326	7240	7986	86842
Jun	6764	6237	6645	7551	7315	6515	7662	6081	5817	6608	5444	7188	79827
Jul	6350	7296	6409	7190	6405	6868	7104	5968	7212	7958	7092	7595	83446
Aug	7426	6551	6472	5913	6892	6004	5609	7147	7173	7768	7088	6915	80957
Sep	7577	7471	7511	7263	6004	7534	7143	7389	6915	6884	6763	6861	85314
Oct	7281	6148	7748	6931	7693	6587	7173	7032	7726	7186	5931	6672	84109
Nov	6202	7145	6489	5626	5829	7311	6635	6228	6679	6635	7855	6951	79585
Dec	6713	6938	6974	6755	7563	6810	7319	7183	7066	6888	7134	6343	83686
Total	79732	80691	83516	81148	81788	81668	84978	82502	82481	84407	80592	82252	985755

TOTAL Circulation - 1991

Month	-000-	-100-	-200-	-300-	-400-	-500-	-600-	-700-	-800-	-900-	-Biog-	-Fict-	-Total-
Jan	19457	18199	23163	19356	20658	18845	23565	21882	22756	21840	19469	19086	248275
Feb	17303	19134	19084	20204	17919	18052	20187	18215	17347	17479	20712	18526	224160
Mar	20421	20438	20390	21428	21312	20983	19792	21741	18458	18376	20755	18520	242615
Apr	17254	21737	20861	21171	19471	22563	21146	20394	20660	22544	18248	21233	247283
May	19975	22559	21408	20060	20638	20104	22537	23058	19991	21405	20745	23469	255949
Jun	20026	18882	19837	20727	21452	19785	22297	18580	18871	19818	17814	21478	239567
Jul	18980	21301	19210	20887	19856	21459	20639	18786	20542	23396	20805	22760	248621
Aug	22016	19825	19752	18353	20626	18584	17625	21671	21627	22297	20846	21507	244730
Sep	21637	21065	22089	20951	19578	21226	20009	21651	19601	19555	19973	19871	247207
Oct	22457	19009	21732	20454	22686	20345	21322	21294	22538	20694	18798	20110	251440
Nov	18826	20016	18733	17278	17821	21074	19271	19398	19552	19225	22107	19821	233123
Dec	19760	20414	20172	19466	21712	20660	20881	20464	21138	19983	21228	19767	245645
Total	238114	242580	246431	240335	243729	243682	249271	247132	243081	246612	241499	246149	2928615

Chapter 12
Circulation in 2-D: Monthly

In this third 2-D model, data for several service points are brought together in a separate spreadsheet for each month. (LC class letters can be substituted for the Decimal Classification numbers, although this will require that additional columns be inserted and that the menu macros be moved and appropriately altered.) A matching spreadsheet is assigned to each month of the year, and the year-to-date totals are brought together in a summary spreadsheet. This relationship is illustrated below in Figure 12-A.

To set up the Circulation: Monthly template follow the cell-by-cell instructions that appear below, creating a generic template. Refer as needed to the general instructions and guidelines in Chapter 2, "Design and Modification of Spreadsheets." Most of the columns are set at the default of nine spaces. Column B is set at 10 spaces, while columns AA-AN are set at varying widths sufficient to display the texts of the menu macros.

Begin by keyboarding the organizational statement.

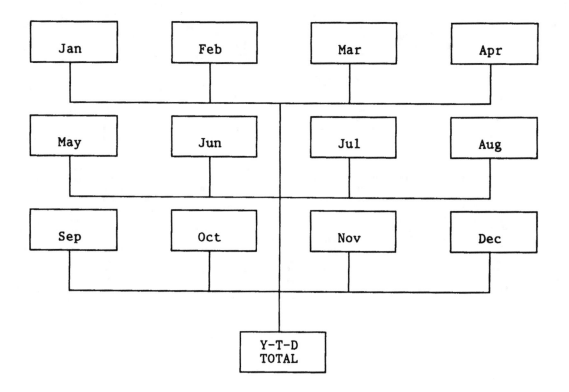

Figure 12-A: Relationship of Monthly Circulation Spreadsheets to Year-to-Date Total Spreadsheet

CIRCULATION SPREADSHEET—MONTHLY: CELL-BY-CELL INSTRUCTIONS

```
      A        B         C         D         E         F         G         H
    !----!--------!--------!--------!--------!--------!--------!--------!
01  !    !========================================================!
02  !    !                                                        !
03  !    !      C I R C U L A T I O N  -  January  1 9 9 3        !
04  !    !                                                        !
05  !    !   This spreadsheet contains day-by-day, class-by-      !
06  !    !   class data for January 1993 grouped in blocks for    !
07  !    !   the service points and categories of materials       !
08  !    !   shown below.  These are arranged as follows:         !
09  !    !                                                        !
10  !    !   Adult       Young Adult  Children's   Films          !
11  !    !                                                        !
12  !    !   East        West         North        South          !
13  !    !                                                        !
14  !    !      Total       (total)                               !
15  !    !                                                        !
16  !    !   Within each group, the spreadsheet has a row for     !
17  !    !   each day and a column for each class of materials.    !
18  !    !   Row and column data are totaled for each day and     !
19  !    !   for each class.  The beginning address for each      !
20  !    !   group is as follows:                                 !
21  !    !                                                        !
22  !    !      A101        Q101        AG101       AW101          !
23  !    !                                                        !
24  !    !      A139        Q139        AG139       AW139          !
25  !    !                                                        !
26  !    !   The group totals are combined in a separate          !
27  !    !   section beginning at A215.  The range name for      !
28  !    !   this section is SOURCE.                              !
29  !    !                                                        !
30  !    !   These same totals are displayed as values beginning  !
31  !    !   at Q215.  The range name for this section is        !
32  !    !   SUMMARY.                                             !
33  !    !                                                        !
34  !    !   To speed data entry, turn off automatic recalcu-     !
35  !    !   lation.  However, be sure to recalculate the        !
36  !    !   spreadsheet before converting values, saving, or     !
37  !    !   printing.                                            !
38  !    !                                                        !
39  !    !   This spreadsheet is designed to be used in           !
40  !    !   conjunction with other spreadsheets, one for each    !
41  !    !   month of the year.  The totals for each of these    !
42  !    !   are combined in a summary spreadsheet                !
43  !    !   (CIRCTOT.WK1) which draws its data from the          !
44  !    !   SUMMARY range of each spreadsheet.                   !
45  !    !                                                        !
46  !    !   Use of this spreadsheet is assisted by a menu        !
47  !    !   which can be invoked by simultaneously pressing      !
48  !    !   [ALT] and the letter "a".  The macros which drive   !
49  !    !   the menu begin at CA1.                               !
50  !    !                                                        !
51  !    !========================================================!
52  !    !
53       [filename]
54       [date]
```

Keyboard the basic template into columns A-O, rows 101-135. Only the beginning and ending rows are shown below. Copy the zeros and formula in C103-C135 into rows D through N. Enter the appropriate class number at the head of each column. Use the data fill command (/df) to enter the dates. The beginning and end values for the months in 1993 are:

January 1 = 33970   January 31 = 34000
February 1 = 34001   February 28 = 34028
March 1 = 34029   March 31 = 34059

April 1 = 34060   April 30 = 34089
May 1 = 34090   May 31 = 34120
June 1 = 34121   June 30 = 34150
July 1 = 34151   July 31 = 34181
August 1 = 34182   August 31 = 34212
September 1 = 34213   September 30 = 34242
October 1 = 34243   October 31 = 34273
November 1 = 34274   November 30 = 34303
December 1 = 34304   December 31 = 34334

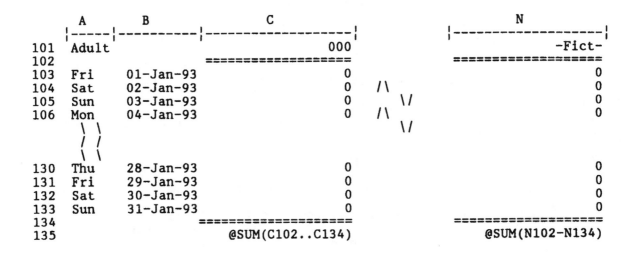

```
            A        B               C                                    N
         |-----|----------|-------------------|          |-------------------|
  101    Adult                            000                         -Fict-
  102              =================          =================
  103    Fri    01-Jan-93               0    /\                           0
  104    Sat    02-Jan-93               0   /\     \/                     0
  105    Sun    03-Jan-93               0          \/                     0
  106    Mon    04-Jan-93               0    /\                           0
                  \ \                                \/
                  / /
                  \ \
  130    Thu    28-Jan-93               0                                 0
  131    Fri    29-Jan-93               0                                 0
  132    Sat    30-Jan-93               0                                 0
  133    Sun    31-Jan-93               0                                 0
  134              =================          =================
  135             @SUM(C102..C134)              @SUM(N102-N134)
```

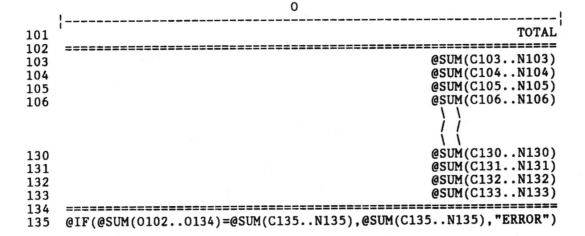

```
                                      O
         |-------------------------------------------------------|
  101                                                      TOTAL
  102     ===================================================
  103                                               @SUM(C103..N103)
  104                                               @SUM(C104..N104)
  105                                               @SUM(C105..N105)
  106                                               @SUM(C106..N106)
                                                        \ \
                                                        / /
                                                        \ \
  130                                               @SUM(C130..N130)
  131                                               @SUM(C131..N131)
  132                                               @SUM(C132..N132)
  133                                               @SUM(C133..N133)
  134     ===================================================
  135     @IF(@SUM(O102..O134)=@SUM(C135..N135),@SUM(C135..N135),"ERROR")
```

Copy columns A-O, rows 101-135 into Q101, AG101, AW101, A139, Q139, AG139, and AW139. Keyboard columns A-O, rows 177-189. Name the range

C180-N187 "SOURCE" which will be used in the updating process as values are transferred to the SUMMARY range.

```
            A         B               C                                       N
          |-----|----------|-------------------|    |-----------------------|
177                        TOTAL Circulation - January, 1993 - Range name = SOURCE
178                                000                                    -Fict-
179                        ===================    ======================
180         Adult                     +C135                                 +N135
181         Young Adult               +S135                                +AD135
182         Children's               +AI135      \\  /\                     +AT135
183         Films                    +AY135      \\//\\                     +BJ135
184         East                      +C173       \/  \\                     +N173
185         West                      +S173                                +AD173
186         North                    +AI173                                +AT173
187         South                    +AY173                                +BJ173
188                        ===================    ======================
189         Total          @SUM(C179..C188)            @SUM(N179..N188)
```

```
                                        O
          |-------------------------------------------------------------|
178                                                                 TOTAL
179       =============================================================
180                                                       @SUM(C180..N180)
181                                                       @SUM(C181..N181)
182                                                       @SUM(C182..N182)
183                                                       @SUM(C183..N183)
184                                                       @SUM(C184..N184)
185                                                       @SUM(C185..N185)
186                                                       @SUM(C186..N186)
187                                                       @SUM(C187..N187)
188       =============================================================
189       @IF(@SUM(O179..O188)=@SUM(C189..N189),@SUM(C189..N189),"ERROR")
```

After keyboarding the labels and zeros in columns R-AD, rows 178-187, name the range S180..AD187 "SUMMARY." This range is referenced by the spread-

sheet CIRCTOT.WK1 in which year-to-date cumulations are gathered.

```
            R              S                                  AD
          |--------------|-----------------|    |-----------------|
178                      TOTAL - dummy file (range name = SUMMARY)
179                      (values created from file at left using "/RV")
180       Adult          0                                      0
181       Young Adult    0                                      0
182       Children's     0              /\                      0
183       Films          0               \/                     0
184       East           0              /\                      0
185       West           0               \/                     0
186       North          0                                      0
187       South          0                                      0
```

After keyboarding columns CA-CN, rows 1-51, name the range CB1 "\0." This will cause the instructional statement to be displayed whenever the spreadsheet is loaded. Name the range CE1 "\a." This will allow the menu to be displayed when [ALT] and "a" are pressed simultaneously.

```
        CA          CB          CC        CD           CE
   !---------!------------!--------!--------!------------------!
01  \0          /WTC                 \a       {MENUBRANCH CG1}~
                {GOTO}A1~
                {QUIT}
```

```
                          CG
   !----------------------------------------------------!
01  Freeze
02  Holds date and class titles on screen
03  {MENUBRANCH CG15}~
         \ \
         / /
         \ \
15  Adult
16  Freezes row and column titles for Adult group
17  /WTC
18  {GOTO}A101~
19  {RIGHT 2}~
20  {DOWN 2}
21  /WTB
22  {QUIT}
         \ \
         / /
         \ \
45  Adult
46  Prints data for Adult group
47  /WTC
48  /PPR
49  A101..O135~
50  GPQ
51  {QUIT}
```

```
                 CH
   !----------------------------!
01  Recalculate
02  Recalculates the spreadsheet
03  {CALC}
04  {QUIT}
         \ \
         / /
         \ \
```

```
15  YA
16  Freezes row and column titles for Young Adult group
17  /WTC
18  {GOTO}Q101~
19  {RIGHT 2}~
20  {DOWN 2}
21  /WTB
22  {QUIT}
        \ \
         / /
         \ \
45  YA
46  Prints data for Young Adult group
47  /WTC
48  /PPR
49  Q101..AE135~
50  GPQ
51  {QUIT}
```

```
                          CI
    !---------------------------------------------------!
01  Update
02  Recalculates spreadsheet and updates summary range values
03  {CALC}
04  /RV
05  Source~
06  Summary~
07  {QUIT}
        \ \
         / /
         \ \
15  Children's
16  Freezes row and column titles for Children's group
17  /WTC
18  {GOTO}AG101~
19  {RIGHT 2}~
20  {DOWN 2}
21  /WTB
22  {QUIT}
        \ \
         / /
         \ \
45  Children's
46  Prints data for Children's group
47  /WTC
48  /PPR
49  AG101..AU135~
50  GPQ
51  {QUIT}
```

```
                          CJ
    !---------------------------------------------!
01  Save
02  Saves the spreadsheet to disk
03  /WTC
04  /FS{?}~
05  {QUIT}
        \ \
         / /
         \ \
```

```
15   Films
16   Freezes row and column titles for Films group
17   /WTC
18   {GOTO}AW101~
19   {RIGHT 2}~
20   {DOWN 2}
21   /WTB
22   {QUIT}
          \  \
           /  /
          \  \
45   Films
46   Prints data for Films group
47   /WTC
48   /PPR
49   AW101..BK135~
50   GPQ
51   {QUIT}
```

```
                        CK
     |----------------------------------------------|
     |                                              |
01   Print
02   Prints groups and the year-to-date summary
03   {MENUBRANCH CG45}~
          \  \
           /  /
          \  \
15   East
16   Freezes row and column titles for East group
17   /WTC
18   {GOTO}A139~
19   {RIGHT 2}~
20   {DOWN 2}
21   /WTB
22   {QUIT}
          \  \
           /  /
          \  \
45   East
46   Prints data for East group
47   /WTC
48   /PPR
49   A139..O173~
50   GPQ
51   {QUIT}
```

```
                CL
     |--------------------------|
01   Total
02   Prints year-to-date total
03   /WTC
04   /PPR
05   A215..O231~
06   GPQ
07   {QUIT}
          \  \
           /  /
          \  \
```

```
15   West
16   Freezes row and column titles for West group
17   /WTC
18   {GOTO}Q139~
19   {RIGHT 2}~
20   {DOWN 2}~
21   /WTB
22   {QUIT}
        \  \
         /  /
        \  \
45   West
46   Prints data for West group
47   /WTC
48   /PPR
49   Q139..AE173~
50   GPQ
51   {QUIT}
```

```
                          CM
|--------------------------------------------------------------|
01   Quit
02   Exits Lotus 1-2-3.   RECALCULATE, UPDATE, and SAVE FILES FIRST!
03   /WTC
04   /QY
05   {QUIT}
        \  \
         /  /
        \  \
15   North
16   Freezes row and column titles for North group
17   /WTC
18   {GOTO}AG139~
19   {RIGHT 2}~
20   {DOWN 2}~
21   /WTB
22   {QUIT}
        \  \
         /  /
        \  \
45   North
46   Prints data for North group
47   /WTC
48   /PPR
49   AG139..AU173~
50   GPQ
51   {QUIT}
```

```
                          CN
|--------------------------------------------------------------|
01   Macro
02   Utility to move the cursor to the beginning of the menu program
03   /WTC
04   {GOTO}CA1~
05   {QUIT}
        \  \
         /  /
        \  \
```

```
15   South
16   Freezes row and column titles for South group
17   /WTC
18   {GOTO}AW139~
19   {RIGHT 2}~
20   {DOWN 2}
21   /WTB
22   {QUIT}
        \  \
         /  /
        \  \
45   South
46   Prints data for South group
47   /WTC
48   /PPR
49   AW139..BK173~
50   GPQ
51   {QUIT}
```

Save this generic template. Make a copy for each month of the year, and assign each with an appropriate filename.

The next step is to create the summary template. Begin by keyboarding the organizational statement in columns A-H, rows 1-27.

SUMMARY SPREADSHEET: CELL-BY-CELL INSTRUCTIONS

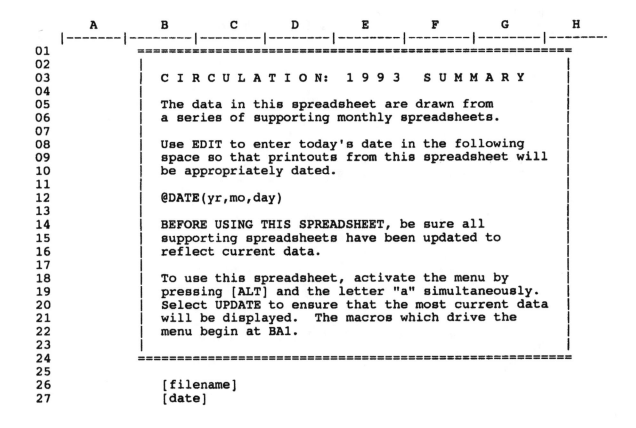

```
         A        B        C        D        E        F        G        H
   |-------|--------|--------|--------|--------|--------|--------|-------—-
01          ================================================================
02          |                                                              |
03          |    C I R C U L A T I O N:   1 9 9 3   S U M M A R Y          |
04          |                                                              |
05          |    The data in this spreadsheet are drawn from               |
06          |    a series of supporting monthly spreadsheets.              |
07          |                                                              |
08          |    Use EDIT to enter today's date in the following           |
09          |    space so that printouts from this spreadsheet will        |
10          |    be appropriately dated.                                   |
11          |                                                              |
12          |    @DATE(yr,mo,day)                                          |
13          |                                                              |
14          |    BEFORE USING THIS SPREADSHEET, be sure all                |
15          |    supporting spreadsheets have been updated to              |
16          |    reflect current data.                                     |
17          |                                                              |
18          |    To use this spreadsheet, activate the menu by             |
19          |    pressing [ALT] and the letter "a" simultaneously.         |
20          |    Select UPDATE to ensure that the most current data        |
21          |    will be displayed.  The macros which drive the            |
22          |    menu begin at BA1.                                        |
23          |                                                              |
24          ================================================================
25
26          [filename]
27          [date]
```

Keyboard the labels, zeros, and formulas in columns 101-255. Only the January, February, December, and total rows are shown below. Fill in the March through November sections following the same pattern. Copy column C, rows 102-255, into columns D-N. Enter the appropriate class numbers for each month and for the Total section in each column. Then keyboard column O.

```
         A            B              C                                    N
    !---------!-------------!------------------!              !-----------------!
101  January Circulation - 1993      +$C$12
102           Group              -000-            /\              -Fict-
103           Adult                  0           //\\               0
104           YA                     0        \\//  \\             0
105           Children's             0         \/                  0
106           Films                  0                             0
107           East                   0                             0
108           West                   0                             0
109           North                  0                             0
110           South                  0                             0
111           Total          @SUM(C103..C110)          @SUM(N103..N110)
112
113  February Circulation - 1993     +$C$12
114           Group              -000-                             -Fict-
115           Adult                  0                             0
116           YA                     0                             0
117           Children's             0                             0
118           Films                  0                             0
119           East                   0                             0
120           West                   0                             0
121           North                  0                             0
122           South                  0                             0
123           Total          @SUM(C115..C122)          @SUM(N115..N122)
           \  \
            /  /
            \  \
233  December Circulation - 1993   1 +$C$12
234           Group              -000-                             -Fict-
235           Adult                  0                             0
236           YA                     0                             0
237           Children's             0                             0
238           Films                  0                             0
239           East                   0                             0
240           West                   0                             0
241           North                  0                             0
242           South                  0                             0
243           Total          @SUM(C235..C242)          @SUM(N235..N242)


         A        B                                    C
    !--------!------------!-------------------------------------------------------!
245  Total Circulation - 1993                                              +$C$12
246           Group                                                        -000-
247           Adult      +C103+C115+C127+C139+C151+C163+C175+C187+C199+C211+C223+C235
248           YA         +C104+C116+C128+C140+C152+C164+C176+C188+C200+C212+C224+C236
249           Children's +C105+C117+C129+C141+C153+C165+C177+C189+C201+C213+C225+C237
250           Films      +C106+C118+C130+C142+C154+C166+C178+C190+C202+C214+C226+C238
251           East       +C107+C119+C131+C143+C155+C167+C179+C191+C203+C215+C227+C239
252           West       +C108+C120+C132+C144+C156+C168+C180+C192+C204+C216+C228+C240
253           North      +C109+C121+C133+C145+C157+C169+C181+C193+C205+C217+C229+C241
254           South      +C110+C122+C134+C146+C158+C170+C182+C194+C206+C218+C230+C242
255           Total                                              @SUM(C247..C254)
```

```
                                    N
      !-----------------------------------------------------------!
      !                                                  -Fict-
247    +N103+N115+N127+N139+N151+N163+N175+N187+N199+N211+N223+N235
248    +N104+N116+N128+N140+N152+N164+N176+N188+N200+N212+N224+N236
249    +N105+N117+N129+N141+N153+N165+N177+N189+N201+N213+N225+N237
250    +N106+N118+N130+N142+N154+N166+N178+N190+N202+N214+N226+N238
251    +N107+N119+N131+N143+N155+N167+N179+N191+N203+N215+N227+N239
252    +N108+N120+N132+N144+N156+N168+N180+N192+N204+N216+N228+N240
253    +N109+N121+N133+N145+N157+N169+N181+N193+N205+N217+N229+N241
254    +N110+N122+N134+N146+N158+N170+N182+N194+N206+N218+N230+N242
255                                                    @SUM(N247..N254)


                                    O
      !-----------------------------------------------------------!
101   !-----------------------------------------------------------!
102                                                        -Total-
103                                                    @SUM(C103..N103)
104                                                    @SUM(C104..N104)
105                                                    @SUM(C105..N105)
106                                                    @SUM(C106..N106)
107                                                    @SUM(C107..N107)
108                                                    @SUM(C108..N108)
109                                                    @SUM(C109..N109)
110                                                    @SUM(C110..N110)
111        @IF(@SUM(O103..O110)=@SUM(C111..N111),@SUM(C111..N111),"ERROR")
112
113                                                        -Total-
114
115                                                    @SUM(C115..N115)
116                                                    @SUM(C116..N116)
117                                                    @SUM(C117..N117)
118                                                    @SUM(C118..N118)
119                                                    @SUM(C119..N119)
120                                                    @SUM(C120..N120)
121                                                    @SUM(C121..N121)
122                                                    @SUM(C122..N122)
123        @IF(@SUM(O115..O122)=@SUM(C123..N123),@SUM(C123..N123),"ERROR")
          \ \
          / /
          \ \
134                                                        -Total-
135                                                    @SUM(C235..N235)
136                                                    @SUM(C236..N236)
137                                                    @SUM(C237..N237)
138                                                    @SUM(C238..N238)
139                                                    @SUM(C239..N239)
140                                                    @SUM(C240..N240)
141                                                    @SUM(C241..N241)
142                                                    @SUM(C242..N242)
143        @IF(@SUM(O235..O242)=@SUM(C243..N243),@SUM(C243..N243),"ERROR")
144
145                                                        -Total-
146
147                                                    @SUM(C247..N247)
148                                                    @SUM(C248..N248)
149                                                    @SUM(C249..N249)
150                                                    @SUM(C250..N250)
151                                                    @SUM(C251..N251)
152                                                    @SUM(C252..N252)
153                                                    @SUM(C253..N253)
154                                                    @SUM(C254..N254)
155        @IF(@SUM(O247..O254)=@SUM(C255..N255),@SUM(C255..N255),"ERROR")
```

After keyboarding columns BA-CA, rows 1-53, name the range BB1 "\0." This will cause the instructional statement to be displayed whenever the spreadsheet is loaded. Name the range BD1 "\a." This will allow the menu to be displayed when [ALT] and "a" are pressed simultaneously. Supply the filenames referenced in BE (Update), using the filenames assigned to the source spreadsheets.

```
       BA            BB            BC            BD
    |--------|------------|--------|------------------|
 01  \0          /WTC        \a        {MENUBRANCH BE1}~
```

```
                              BE
    |----------------------------------------------------------|
 01  Update
 02  Updates totals by importing data from supporting spreadsheets
 03  /WTC
 04  {GOTO}C103~
 05  /FCCN
 06  SUMMARY~
 07  CIRCJAN.WK1~
 08  {GOTO}C115~
 09  /FCCN
 10  SUMMARY~
 11  CIRCFEB.WK1~
 12  {GOTO}C127~
 13  /FCCN
 14  SUMMARY~
 15  CIRCMAR.WK1~
 16  {GOTO}C139~
 17  /FCCN
 18  SUMMARY~
 19  CIRCAPR.WK1~
 20  {GOTO}C151~
 21  /FCCN
 22  SUMMARY~
 23  CIRCMAY.WK1~
 24  {GOTO}C163~
 25  /FCCN
 26  SUMMARY~
 27  CIRCJUN.WK1~
 28  {GOTO}C175~
 29  /FCCN
 30  SUMMARY~
 31  CIRCJUL.WK1~
 32  {GOTO}C187~
 33  /FCCN
 34  SUMMARY~
 35  CIRCAUG.WK1~
 36  {GOTO}C199~
 37  /FCCN
 38  SUMMARY~
 39  CIRCSEP.WK1~
 40  {GOTO}C211~
 41  /FCCN
 42  SUMMARY~
 43  CIRCOCT.WK1~
 44  {GOTO}C223~
 45  /FCCN
 46  SUMMARY~
 47  CIRCNOV.WK1~
 48  {GOTO}C235~
 49  /FCCN
 50  SUMMARY~
 51  CIRCDEC.WK1~
 52  {GOTO}A101~
 53  {QUIT}
```

```
                 BF                                    BG
    |--------------------------|--------------------------------------------|
01  View                       Save
02  See summary data           Writes the year-to-date totals to disk
03  /WTC                       /WTC
04  {GOTO}AA1~                 /FS{?}~
05  {QUIT}                     {QUIT}
```

```
                 BH                                    BI
    |--------------------------|--------------------------------------------|
01  Print                      Quit
02  Prints year-to-date totals Exits Lotus 1-2-3.   SAVE FILES FIRST!
03  {MENUBRANCH BL1}~          /WTC
04  /FS{?}~                    /QY
05  {QUIT}                     {QUIT}
```

```
                                BJ
    |--------------------------------------------------------------------|
01  Macro
02  Utility to move the cursor to the beginning of the menu program
03  /WTC
04  {GOTO}BA1~
05  {QUIT}
```

```
                 BL                                    BM
    |------------------------------|------------------------------------|
01  January                        February
02  Prints January year-to-date totals  Prints February year-to-date totals
03  /WTC                           /WTC
04  /PP                            /PP
05  RA101..O111~                   RA113..O123~
06  GPQ                            GPQ
07  {QUIT}                         {QUIT}
```

```
                 BN                                    BO
    |------------------------------|------------------------------------|
01  March                          April
02  Prints March year-to-date totals    Prints April year-to-date totals
03  /WTC                           /WTC
04  /PP                            /PP
05  RA125..O137~                   RA139..O151~
06  GPQ                            GPQ
07  {QUIT}                         {QUIT}
```

```
                 BP                                    BQ
    |------------------------------|------------------------------------|
01  +May                           -June
02  Prints May year-to-date totals      Prints June year-to-date totals
03  /WTC                           /WTC
04  /PP                            /PP
05  RA153..O165~                   RA167..O179~
06  GPQ                            GPQ
07  {QUIT}                         {QUIT}
```

```
                       BR                                         BS
   |-----------------------------------|-------------------------------------|
01 |=July                              |Other                                |
02 Prints July year-to-date totals     August-December, Summary, and Totals
03 /WTC                                 {MENUBRANCH BU1}~
04 /PP
05 RA181..O193~
06 GPQ
07 {QUIT}


                       BU                                         BV
   |-----------------------------------|-------------------------------------|
01 August                              September
02 Prints August year-to-date totals   Prints September year-to-date totals
03 /WTC                                 /WTC
04 /PP                                  /PP
05 RA195..O207~                         RA209..O221~
06 GPQ                                  GPQ
07 {QUIT}                               {QUIT}


                       BW                                         BX
   |------------------------------------|------------------------------------|
01    October                              November
02 Prints October year-to-date totals   Prints November year-to-date totals
03 /WTC                                  /WTC
04 /PP                                   /PP
05 RA223..O235~                          RA237..O249~
06 GPQ                                   GPQ
07 {QUIT}                                {QUIT}


                       BY                                         BZ
   |------------------------------------|------------------------------|
01 December                             Summary
02 Prints December year-to-date totals  Prints year-to-date summary
03 /WTC                                 /WTC
04 /PP                                  /PP
05 RA251..O263~                         RA265..A277~
06 GPQ                                  GPQ
07 {QUIT}                               {QUIT}


                       CA
   |-------------------------------|
01 Totals
02 Prints all year-to-date totals
03 /WTC
04 /PP
05 RA101..O277~
06 GPQ
07 {QUIT}
```

Save this template. Make a copy, and label it with the appropriate title and date. The set of spreadsheets is now ready to use. The day-by-day activity for the month of January at one service point, using fictitious data, is displayed in Table 12-1; this was extracted from the spreadsheet for adult services. The total activity for the year at all service points, using fictitious data, is displayed in Table 12-2; this was printed from the Summary spreadsheet.

Table 12-1: Circulation—Monthly: January 1993

Adult		000	100	200	300	400	500	600	700	800	900	Biog	Fict	TOTAL
Fri	01-Jan-93	0	0	0	0	0	0	0	0	0	0	0	0	0
Sat	02-Jan-93	162	118	380	379	126	161	129	314	116	372	93	353	2701
Sun	03-Jan-93	307	124	155	195	223	323	370	374	341	313	301	230	3256
Mon	04-Jan-93	330	129	321	350	155	236	248	85	354	120	146	359	2834
Tue	05-Jan-93	389	369	173	368	303	263	222	104	163	233	296	332	3216
Wed	06-Jan-93	204	198	392	395	255	377	252	152	117	243	169	133	2887
Thr	07-Jan-93	219	382	181	173	315	362	81	83	313	135	319	163	2726
Fri	08-Jan-93	307	147	347	108	215	359	221	262	356	136	271	206	2936
Sat	09-Jan-93	233	175	90	243	272	365	138	182	170	214	200	157	2439
Sun	10-Jan-93	114	352	80	285	95	77	284	236	105	271	172	391	2462
Mon	11-Jan-93	175	312	298	320	103	138	285	343	346	343	76	384	3120
Tue	12-Jan-93	159	339	317	137	222	237	271	314	325	96	257	136	2809
Wed	13-Jan-93	140	158	289	302	356	355	114	230	230	72	50	193	2490
Thr	14-Jan-93	279	187	176	79	139	262	59	109	61	138	169	271	1929
Fri	15-Jan-93	233	331	386	249	98	61	313	280	94	379	185	322	2932
Sat	16-Jan-93	317	179	309	336	360	389	275	354	287	250	216	211	3484
Sun	17-Jan-93	211	251	347	378	63	162	222	298	390	169	156	88	2736
Mon	18-Jan-93	0	0	0	0	0	0	0	0	0	0	0	0	0
Tue	19-Jan-93	122	97	104	244	265	271	195	104	56	314	315	55	2144
Wed	20-Jan-93	190	241	66	364	203	281	280	162	350	124	299	194	2753
Thr	21-Jan-93	249	280	138	343	202	374	196	232	355	239	347	234	3189
Fri	22-Jan-93	288	127	276	391	387	153	274	169	86	253	212	276	2893
Sat	23-Jan-93	208	214	73	286	89	230	351	287	248	309	152	113	2560
Sun	24-Jan-93	281	285	94	103	54	331	392	340	243	244	156	303	2826
Mon	25-Jan-93	213	292	58	232	108	186	84	236	381	139	235	91	2255
Tue	26-Jan-93	298	245	176	351	310	81	168	65	242	161	352	230	2679
Wed	27-Jan-93	135	57	380	148	364	353	269	116	181	68	360	202	2633
Thr	28-Jan-93	127	90	263	395	78	185	238	205	390	96	283	342	2692
Fri	29-Jan-93	200	304	60	163	176	257	79	389	305	114	254	110	2411
Sat	30-Jan-93	218	180	94	157	380	261	88	60	364	348	268	152	2569
Sun	31-Jan-93	130	243	96	265	184	262	187	86	187	224	333	358	2556
		6438	6405	6120	7738	6102	7354	6286	6172	7154	6117	6642	6589	79116

Table 12-2: Circulation—Monthly: Total 1993

January Circulation - 1993 12/31/93

Group	-000-	-100-	-200-	-300-	-400-	-500-	-600-	-700-	-800-	-900-	-Biog-	-Fict-	-Total-
Adult	7008	5820	7716	7018	6678	6718	6692	6963	5727	6326	5775	5507	77947
YA	6305	6414	5946	5382	5919	6130	6133	5593	5959	6678	4736	5784	70978
Children'	6818	6195	6944	7133	6288	6586	6193	6000	6654	6601	6934	6624	78972
Films	6631	6126	7005	6722	5889	6102	5234	6294	5645	5757	6419	6028	73852
East	6247	5732	6521	6511	6928	6808	6246	6620	6230	6597	6383	6772	77596
West	6393	6668	6632	6256	6400	7446	5831	5856	6243	6227	5398	6492	75841
North	7126	6460	6243	5881	5937	7164	7338	6896	5949	6581	6379	7546	79501
South	6676	6467	5903	5460	6258	5720	7015	6353	5992	6760	7166	5383	75154
Total	53203	49884	52911	50363	50297	52674	50682	50576	48398	51527	49190	50135	609841

February Circulation - 1993 12/31/93

Group	-000-	-100-	-200-	-300-	-400-	-500-	-600-	-700-	-800-	-900-	-Biog-	-Fict-	-Total-
Adult	7008	5820	7716	7018	6678	6718	6692	6963	5727	6326	5775	5507	77947
YA	6305	6414	5946	5382	5919	6130	6133	5593	5959	6678	4736	5784	70978
Children'	6818	6195	6944	7133	6288	6586	6193	6000	6654	6601	6934	6624	78972
Films	6631	6126	7005	6722	5889	6102	5234	6294	5645	5757	6419	6028	73852
East	6247	5732	6521	6511	6928	6808	6246	6620	6230	6597	6383	6772	77596
West	6393	6668	6632	6256	6400	7446	5831	5856	6243	6227	5398	6492	75841
North	7126	6460	6243	5881	5937	7164	7338	6896	5949	6581	6379	7546	79501
South	6676	6467	5903	5460	6258	5720	7015	6353	5992	6760	7166	5383	75154
Total	53203	49884	52911	50363	50297	52674	50682	50576	48398	51527	49190	50135	609841

March Circulation - 1993 12/31/93

Group	-000-	-100-	-200-	-300-	-400-	-500-	-600-	-700-	-800-	-900-	-Biog-	-Fict-	-Total-
Adult	7735	7176	7556	6912	6686	7108	7884	6676	7755	7499	8068	6838	87893
YA	6753	8017	6112	7221	7531	8435	6302	6899	7163	7055	7621	7160	86269
Children'	6574	7456	7307	8461	6598	7026	6815	6037	6881	7150	7370	7346	85020
Films	7190	6722	6400	6362	6817	7590	7715	6177	8592	8092	7129	6386	85170
East	6911	6248	6850	7588	6903	6886	6237	6653	7633	6961	7232	6861	82964
West	6801	7296	7577	7244	6831	7958	7229	7784	6360	6861	6842	5763	84548
North	6008	6687	7035	6959	6850	6352	7451	6952	7121	6349	7128	7013	81905
South	6911	6964	8417	6548	6689	7037	6468	7539	7801	5896	7468	6945	84685
Total	54885	56566	57255	57296	54906	58393	56102	54715	59305	55863	58857	54311	678453

April Circulation - 1993 12/31/93

Group	-000-	-100-	-200-	-300-	-400-	-500-	-600-	-700-	-800-	-900-	-Biog-	-Fict-	-Total-
Adult	6791	5728	7158	6280	6562	5520	6816	7555	6079	7134	6962	6545	79130
YA	6548	7065	6871	7087	6978	6803	6016	6267	7980	6863	7285	7530	83294
Children'	6558	7197	6532	5616	6117	6637	6927	6945	6297	6787	6756	6133	78503
Films	6351	6490	8159	6320	6333	7376	6606	6597	6678	6297	6692	6696	80594
East	6864	6646	6000	7277	5303	6157	5987	7364	7493	7088	7394	7161	80735
West	5691	6562	6869	6452	7163	7534	6624	6065	6551	7714	7449	7460	82134
North	6697	6637	7769	7188	7334	6653	6823	6059	6233	6414	6308	5761	79876
South	6765	6186	6776	6442	7026	6739	6462	8279	6907	6300	7932	7697	83509
Total	52265	52511	56134	52662	52816	53419	52260	55131	54218	54597	56778	54983	647775

May Circulation - 1993 12/31/93

Group	-000-	-100-	-200-	-300-	-400-	-500-	-600-	-700-	-800-	-900-	-Biog-	-Fict-	-Total-
Adult	6194	6938	8001	7880	7427	7562	6882	5991	7665	6659	6812	7858	85869
YA	6653	6295	7039	5383	7249	6582	7199	7633	5976	6654	7466	6904	81034
Children'	6136	6703	7481	7572	6057	6562	7701	7484	7867	7221	6405	6959	84148
Films	7084	7492	6623	6407	6248	7307	6621	6642	7153	6932	7839	7214	83561
East	7286	6795	7268	7414	6981	7746	6723	7506	6928	6816	7102	6809	85375
West	7015	7891	7320	6729	6973	7531	7403	6641	6958	6820	7131	7223	85636
North	6229	7316	7041	7210	6471	7068	6336	6998	6357	6378	6592	7284	81281
South	5967	6719	6559	6757	7328	6767	6438	7374	6958	5959	7110	7307	81243
Total	52565	56152	57333	55353	54733	57125	55303	56269	55861	53439	56457	57557	668147

Table 12-2: Circulation—Monthly: Total 1993 (Continued)

June Circulation - 1993 (12/31/93 above -200-)

Group	-000-	-100-	-200-	-300-	-400-	-500-	-600-	-700-	-800-	-900-	-Biog-	-Fict-	-Total-
Adult	7076	7416	7062	7091	6320	6578	5617	6682	6779	6914	7031	6885	81450
YA	6842	6351	6999	6282	5955	8014	6068	7014	6624	6717	7094	7710	81671
Children'	6118	6719	6800	7362	7103	7382	6507	6172	5904	5681	6990	7477	80215
Films	7326	6273	6734	7065	6893	6640	6288	7147	6823	6214	6791	7361	81555
East	6863	6442	6380	6267	7767	7191	7251	7066	6821	5966	6626	6640	81280
West	6765	6290	6828	7499	6311	7835	7682	7523	6706	6290	7868	7078	84675
North	6316	7232	5842	6168	6404	6921	6725	7531	6785	6875	6541	7124	80465
South	6015	5887	5642	6008	6013	6454	6872	6985	5989	7960	6513	6899	77237
Total	53322	52610	52287	53741	52767	57014	53009	56120	52430	52618	55454	57175	648547

July Circulation - 1993 (12/31/93 above -200-)

Group	-000-	-100-	-200-	-300-	-400-	-500-	-600-	-700-	-800-	-900-	-Biog-	-Fict-	-Total-
Adult	6416	6458	6660	6816	6520	6842	6542	7137	6386	6645	5845	5774	78040
YA	7421	6327	5880	6583	6230	5080	7260	6938	6016	5723	6500	6972	76929
Children'	6362	6417	7165	7246	6897	6074	6584	6685	6158	5730	5520	6065	76902
Films	6517	6797	5599	7082	6579	6569	7802	5462	6898	5970	7407	6611	79295
East	6269	6695	7418	6683	5959	6649	6612	6929	5920	6976	6927	5879	78916
West	5838	7211	7643	5936	7042	7189	6182	6368	5534	6660	6071	6572	78246
North	7880	6112	7543	6346	6761	6634	6779	5570	6074	6312	7134	5741	78887
South	6763	6778	6123	6603	6218	6412	6301	6564	6123	6775	6903	8104	79667
Total	53466	52795	54031	53295	52206	51448	54062	51653	49109	50791	52308	51717	626881

August Circulation - 1993 (12/31/93 above -200-)

Group	-000-	-100-	-200-	-300-	-400-	-500-	-600-	-700-	-800-	-900-	-Biog-	-Fict-	-Total-
Adult	6363	7165	6030	6612	7755	7171	5585	6651	6267	5664	7373	7644	80280
YA	6630	6819	7191	6861	6420	6582	6143	6299	6984	6237	6635	6352	79152
Children'	6590	6392	6425	7658	6481	6285	5894	7491	7535	6709	6682	6652	80794
Films	6387	7099	6626	6119	6090	6337	5769	6808	6557	6480	6566	7431	78270
East	6267	5679	6106	5806	6913	6579	6277	6006	5707	7377	5687	5584	73988
West	6849	7694	6756	6326	7015	6676	6367	5488	6075	7222	6793	6003	79265
North	6746	6645	7055	6269	6536	6924	6074	6888	5990	6747	6812	7227	79913
South	7324	6267	6014	7081	7281	6660	6265	6091	6522	6785	6508	6968	79767
Total	53156	53761	52204	52732	54491	53214	48373	51723	51637	53221	53057	53861	631430

September Circulation - 1993 (12/31/93 above -200-)

Group	-000-	-100-	-200-	-300-	-400-	-500-	-600-	-700-	-800-	-900-	-Biog-	-Fict-	-Total-
Adult	6370	5459	6883	6158	6022	6395	5883	5682	6707	6199	5683	6751	74193
YA	5914	6444	6280	5663	6209	6256	6389	6366	6054	6742	6451	5598	74367
Children'	6078	6793	6737	6789	6275	7093	6382	5752	5692	6803	6910	6587	77893
Films	6202	6951	7123	6073	7043	7072	6100	5976	6660	7731	6342	7002	80277
East	4691	6117	5473	5376	5914	6895	6698	6510	6035	6475	5387	5971	71540
West	5527	6331	5832	5646	6310	6753	6897	6941	6217	5612	5250	6305	73619
North	6297	6333	6875	5641	6746	6047	7043	6167	6294	6235	6284	5905	75867
South	6961	5943	6184	5703	5914	6666	6114	6856	6893	7211	6954	6803	78202
Total	48041	50369	51387	47049	50434	53177	51506	50250	50552	53009	49262	50922	605959

October Circulation - 1993 (12/31/93 above -200-)

Group	-000-	-100-	-200-	-300-	-400-	-500-	-600-	-700-	-800-	-900-	Biog-	-Fict-	-Total-
Adult	6271	5708	7927	7186	6319	6946	6522	6429	6254	6382	6563	8013	80520
YA	6578	6618	6634	7145	6245	6334	5590	7037	7137	6879	6386	6054	78636
Children'	7244	7171	6601	6737	6148	6733	6055	6910	7007	6898	5791	6041	79335
Films	6845	6704	6868	6521	7426	6430	6989	6622	7135	6613	6940	6261	81354
East	6215	5780	5946	7010	5988	5684	6545	5760	6438	6805	6863	6465	75497
West	7154	6106	6467	6402	7169	6636	6045	6894	6518	6291	6238	6925	78845
North	7594	6113	7860	6605	6275	6878	6916	5597	5568	6390	5572	6388	77756
South	6131	6230	6765	7107	6830	6709	6774	6413	6219	6034	5751	6324	77288
Total	54031	50429	55069	54713	52399	52349	51435	51661	52277	52292	50105	52470	629231

Table 12-2: Circulation—Monthly: Total 1993 (Continued)

November Circulation - 1993   12/31/93

Group	-000-	-100-	-200-	-300-	-400-	-500-	-600-	-700-	-800-	-900-	-Biog-	-Fict-	-Total-
Adult	5901	6479	6176	5394	5805	6415	6708	6394	5731	5332	5878	6226	72441
YA	6817	6621	6351	5667	5623	5987	6402	6634	6785	6224	7023	5927	76061
Children'	6746	6486	6941	6625	6628	6419	6504	6979	6141	6413	5310	6810	78002
Films	5890	5610	5689	6731	5224	6579	6033	5646	6710	6486	5739	5388	71726
East	5524	5733	6519	5988	6637	6856	6039	4870	6086	5709	6042	5808	71812
West	5768	6382	6491	6130	7021	6279	5593	6343	6646	5994	6135	6323	75107
North	6777	6895	7043	5203	6595	6503	6882	5571	6427	6567	6591	5796	76850
South	5551	5610	5057	6473	6945	6457	6541	6331	5795	5832	6104	6358	73055
Total	48976	49816	50267	48211	50479	51497	50702	48768	50322	48557	48821	48638	595053

December Circulation - 1993   12/31/93

Group	-000-	-100-	-200-	-300-	-400-	-500-	-600-	-700-	-800-	-900-	-Biog-	-Fict-	-Total-
Adult	7210	6320	6904	5827	7129	6587	6651	6023	5551	7102	7409	5846	78560
YA	6638	5749	5996	7165	6753	6856	6934	6286	6303	6702	6823	6229	78433
Children'	6862	6397	5855	7310	7267	6774	7578	6266	6013	6463	6583	5488	78856
Films	6221	6321	6754	6058	7161	6566	6620	6762	6414	7542	6521	6409	79349
East	6710	6300	6115	6533	6094	6617	7054	5769	5709	6530	6185	6451	77066
West	6070	5973	5854	6272	7117	5925	6900	5193	5706	6280	5926	5518	72735
North	5817	6339	7761	6805	7204	7010	6317	6030	5549	5731	7151	6557	78271
South	6587	6608	6624	6622	6960	5803	5658	5494	7154	6608	7012	6404	77535
Total	52113	50006	51864	52592	55685	52139	53712	47823	48398	52959	53610	48902	619805

Total Circulation - 1993   12/31/93

Group	-000-	-100-	-200-	-300-	-400-	-500-	-600-	-700-	-800-	-900-	-Biog-	-Fict-	-Total-
Adult	80343	76487	85790	80192	79903	80560	78474	79147	76626	78183	79175	79391	954271
YA	79403	79135	77246	75820	77030	79188	76568	78559	78939	79152	78755	78006	937801
Children'	78905	80121	81732	85642	78148	80158	79334	78719	78805	79057	78185	78806	957612
Films	79275	78711	80584	78182	77592	80671	77010	76427	80910	79872	80803	78815	948853
East	76094	73899	77118	78964	78314	80877	77915	77673	77231	79897	78211	77171	933365
West	76265	81072	80902	77148	81753	85206	78584	76952	75756	78199	76500	78154	946491
North	80615	79229	84311	76156	79050	81319	82021	77156	74295	77161	78873	79889	950074
South	78327	76126	75969	76266	79720	77144	77923	80633	78343	78882	82587	80575	942495
Total	629228	624781	643653	628370	631509	645123	627829	625266	620906	630402	633089	630807	7570963

Chapter 13
Circulation in 3-D

In contrast to the templates developed in Chapters 10, 11, and 12, the templates in this chapter are three-dimensional, i.e., each is made up of several pages. In each monthly template, each week is presented on a separate page, and daily circulation data are arranged by date, day of the week, and Library of Congress Classification letter groups. (Decimal Classification numbers can be substituted for LC Class letters, although this would require that some columns be deleted.) If the template is rotated and viewed from the top, the data for the month can be viewed by day of the week, or, if rotated and viewed from the right, the data can be viewed by LC class. A matching spreadsheet is assigned to each month of the year, and the year-to-date totals are brought together in a summary spreadsheet. This relationship is illustrated in Figure 12-A at the beginning of Chapter 12.

To set up the Circulation in 3-D template, follow the cell-by-cell instructions that appear below, creating a generic template. Refer as needed to the general instructions and guidelines in Chapter 2, "Design and Modification of Spreadsheets." Most of the columns are set at the default of nine spaces. Note that cell addresses are identified by column letter, row number, and page number. Thus, C5;10 refers to the cell in column C, row 5, of page 10.

Begin by keyboarding the instructional statement.

3-D CIRCULATION SPREADSHEET: CELL-BY-CELL INSTRUCTIONS

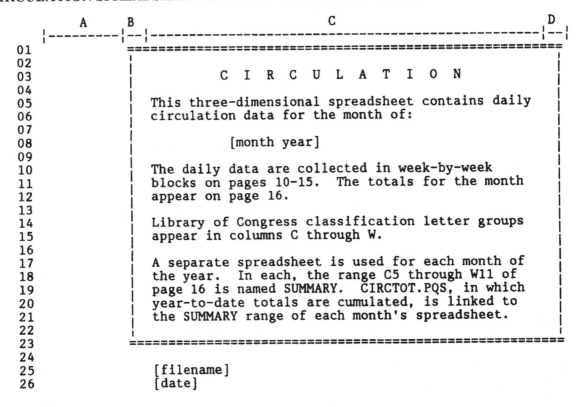

Keyboard the first page of the template into columns A-X, rows 1-13, page 10. Copy the lines, zeros, and formulas in C4-C13 into rows D through W. Enter the appropriate LC class letter at the head of each column. Then, keyboard the following in column X of page 10.

```
          A            B              C                            W
     |---------|---------|----------------------|     |--------------------|
01   |     CIRCULATION
02
03   DAY        DATE                 A                            Z
04                          --------------------         --------------------
05   Sun      [date]                 0                            0
06   Mon      [date]                 0   /\  /                    0
07   Tues     [date]                 0  /  \/                     0
08   Wed      [date]                 0   /\  /                    0
09   Thur     [date]                 0  /   \/                    0
10   Fri      [date]                 0                            0
11   Sat      [date]                 0                            0
12                          --------------------         --------------------
13                          @SUM(C4;10..C12;10)          @SUM(W4;10..W12;10)


                                          X
     |----------------------------------------------------------------------|
01   |
02
03                               -Total-
04   --------------------------------------------------------------------------
05                                                  @SUM(C5;10..W5;10)
06                                                  @SUM(C6;10..W6;10)
07                                                  @SUM(C7;10..W7;10)
08                                                  @SUM(C8;10..W8;10)
09                                                  @SUM(C9;10..W9;10)
10                                                @SUM(C10;10..W10;10)
11                                                @SUM(C11;10..W11;10)
12   --------------------------------------------------------------------------
13   @IF(@SUM(X4;10..X12;10)=@SUM(C13;10..W13;10),@SUM(C13;10..W13;10),"ERROR")
```

Copy the range A1;10..X13;10 into pages 11 through 15. Then, keyboard the labels and summary formulas in columns A-X, rows 1-13, in page 16. Copy the lines, zeros, and formulas in C4-C13 into columns D through W. Enter the appropriate LC class letter at the head of each column.

```
          A            B                    C                              W
    |-------|------------|-----------------------------|     |---------------------|
01               CIRCULATION
02               TOTAL
03     DAY       January              A                                   Z
04                             ----------------------         ---------------------
05     Sun                     @SUM(C5;10..C5;15)             @SUM(W5;10..W5;15)
06     Mon                     @SUM(C6;10..C6;15)  /\   /     @SUM(W6;10..W6;15)
07     Tues                    @SUM(C7;10..C7;15)     \/      @SUM(W7;10..W7;15)
08     Wed                     @SUM(C8;10..C8;15)  /\   /     @SUM(W8;10..W8;15)
09     Thur                    @SUM(C9;10..C9;15)     \/      @SUM(W9;10..W9;15)
10     Fri                    @SUM(C10;10..C10;15)            @SUM(W10;10..W10;15)
11     Sat                    @SUM(C11;10..C11;15)            @SUM(W11;10..W11;15)
12                             ----------------------         ---------------------
13                             @SUM(C4;16..C12;16)            @SUM(W4;16..W12;16)


                                           X
    |-----------------------------------------------------------------------------|
01
02
03                             -Total-
04  -----------------------------------------------------------------------------
05                                                      @SUM(C5;16..W5;16)
06                                                      @SUM(C6;16..W6;16)
07                                                      @SUM(C7;16..W7;16)
08                                                      @SUM(C8;16..W8;16)
09                                                      @SUM(C9;16..W9;16)
10                                                     @SUM(C10;16..W10;16)
11                                                     @SUM(C11;16..W11;16)
12  -----------------------------------------------------------------------------
13  @IF(@SUM(X4;16..X12;16)=@SUM(C13;16..W13;16),@SUM(C13;16..W13;16),"ERROR")
```

Save this generic template. Make a copy for each month of the year, label each with the appropriate month, and enter the dates for each day. In each, name the range C5;16..W11;16 "SUMMARY" which will be used in the updating process as year-to-date data are cumulated in the

Total template. Save each of these with appropriate file names, e.g., CIRCJAN, CIRCFEB, etc.

Create a generic Y-T-D Total template as directed below. Begin by keyboarding the instructional statement in page 1.

TOTAL Y-T-D CIRCULATION SPREADSHEET: CELL-BY-CELL INSTRUCTIONS

```
              A        B                         C                          D
      !-----------!--!----------------------------------------------!--!
01    !           !  !================================================!  !
02    !           !  !                                              '  !
03    !           !  !   T O T A L      C I R C U L A T I O N           !
04    !           !  !                                                  !
05    !           !  !   This three-dimensional spreadsheet contains year- !
06    !           !  !   to-date circulation data for the year 1993.   !
07    !           !  !   These data are drawn from the SUMMARY range of  !
08    !           !  !   each of 12 monthly spreadsheets, one for each   !
09    !           !  !   month.  This spreadsheet is linked to each of   !
10    !           !  !   these SUMMARY ranges.                           !
11    !           !  !                                                  !
12    !           !  !   In each of the monthly spreadsheets, daily data !
13    !           !  !   are collected in week-by-week blocks and cumulated !
14    !           !  !   for the month.                                 !
15    !           !  !                                                  !
16    !           !  !   Library of Congress classification letter groups !
17    !           !  !   appear in columns C through W in each monthly   !
18    !           !  !   spreadsheet as well as this year-to-date spread- !
19    !           !  !   sheet.                                          !
20    !           !  !                                                  !
21    !           !  !   Summary data begin on page 10 for the month of  !
22    !           !  !   January and continue through page 21 for the    !
23    !           !  !   month of December.  Totals for the year appear on !
24    !           !  !   page 22.                                        !
25    !           !  !                                                  !
26    !           !  !================================================!  !
27    !           !                                                      !
28    !           !  [filename]                                          !
29    !           !  [date]                                              !
```

Keyboard the first page of the template into columns A-X, rows 1-13, in page 10. Copy the lines, zeros, and formulas in C4-C13 into rows D through W. Enter the appropriate LC class letter at the head of each column. Then, keyboard the following in column X of page 10.

```
          A            B              C                          W
    |---------|--------------|---------------------|     |-------------------|
01                  CIRCULATION
02                  1993
03    DAY         January             A                            Z
04                               -------------------     -------------------
05    Sun                                          0                        0
06    Mon                                          0  /\    \ /             0
07    Tues                                         0     \/                 0
08    Wed                                          0  /\    \ /             0
09    Thur                                         0     \/                 0
10    Fri                                          0                        0
11    Sat                                          0                        0
12                               -------------------     -------------------
13                        @SUM(C4;10..C12;10)          @SUM(W4;10..W12;10)


                                          X
    |-----------------------------------------------------------------------|
01
02
03                                                                   -Total-
04  -----------------------------------------------------------------------
05                                                          @SUM(C5;10..W5;10)
06                                                          @SUM(C6;10..W6;10)
07                                                          @SUM(C7;10..W7;10)
08                                                          @SUM(C8;10..W8;10)
09                                                          @SUM(C9;10..W9;10)
10                                                         @SUM(C10;10..W10;10)
11                                                         @SUM(C11;10..W11;10)
12  -----------------------------------------------------------------------
13  IF(@SUM(X4;10..X12;10)=@SUM(C13;10..W13;10),@SUM(C13;10..W13;10),"ERROR")
```

Copy the range A1;10..X13;10 into pages 11 through 21. Change the month on each page. Then, keyboard the summary labels and formulas in columns A-X, rows 1-13, in page 22. Copy the lines, zeros, and formulas in C4-C13 into columns D through W. Enter the appropriate LC class letter at the head of each column. Keyboard the following in column X.

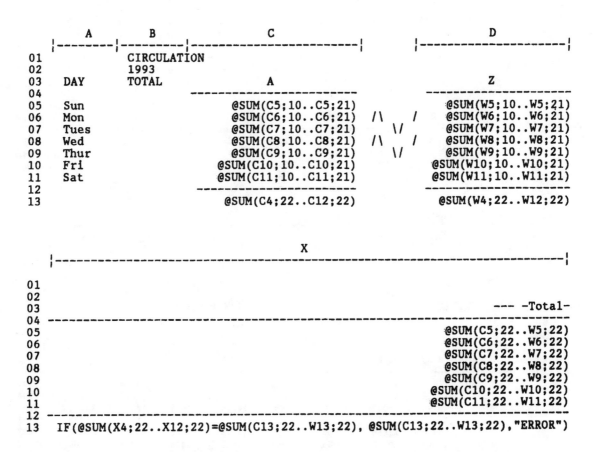

```
            A          B              C                                    D
01                 CIRCULATION
02                 1993
03       DAY       TOTAL              A                                    Z
04                           ----------------------      ----------------------
05       Sun                 @SUM(C5;10..C5;21)    /\    /  @SUM(W5;10..W5;21)
06       Mon                 @SUM(C6;10..C6;21)    /\   \/   @SUM(W6;10..W6;21)
07       Tues                @SUM(C7;10..C7;21)         \/   @SUM(W7;10..W7;21)
08       Wed                 @SUM(C8;10..C8;21)    /\   /   @SUM(W8;10..W8;21)
09       Thur                @SUM(C9;10..C9;21)    /\   \/   @SUM(W9;10..W9;21)
10       Fri                @SUM(C10;10..C10;21)        @SUM(W10;10..W10;21)
11       Sat                @SUM(C11;10..C11;21)        @SUM(W11;10..W11;21)
12                           ----------------------      ----------------------
13                           @SUM(C4;22..C12;22)        @SUM(W4;22..W12;22)


                                            X
        |--------------------------------------------------------------------|
01
02
03                                                               --- -Total-
04      ----------------------------------------------------------------------
05                                                          @SUM(C5;22..W5;22)
06                                                          @SUM(C6;22..W6;22)
07                                                          @SUM(C7;22..W7;22)
08                                                          @SUM(C8;22..W8;22)
09                                                          @SUM(C9;22..W9;22)
10                                                         @SUM(C10;22..W10;22)
11                                                         @SUM(C11;22..W11;22)
12      ----------------------------------------------------------------------
13      IF(@SUM(X4;22..X12;22)=@SUM(C13;22..W13;22), @SUM(C13;22..W13;22),"ERROR")
```

Save this generic template, make a working copy, and save it with an appropriate filename, e.g., CIRCTOT. In the working copy, place the cursor in cell C5 on page 10 (C5;10) and link this cell with the "SUMMARY" range in the spreadsheet CIRCJAN. Next, place the cursor in cell C5 on page 11 (C5;11) and link this cell with the "SUMMARY" range in the spreadsheet CIRCFEB. Do the same with pages 12 through 21 with the spreadsheets for March through December. Save the spreadsheet.

Enter the monthly data in the appropriate monthly spreadsheets. Then, whenever the CIRCTOT spreadsheet is loaded, it will reflect the year-to-date totals, because the links between the 12 monthly spreadsheets and the monthly pages of CIRCTOT automatically update the summary data.

Selected sample pages from these spreadsheets are shown below. The appearance of one page from the December spreadsheet, using fictitious data, is shown in Table 13-1, while another page of the same spreadsheet with totals for the entire month is shown in Table 13-2. The totals for the month of January, using fictitious data, are extracted from the Total spreadsheet in Table 13-3, while the grand totals for the year are shown in Table 13-4. An example of how the spreadsheet will appear when rotated and viewed from the right side is shown in Table 13-5.

Three examples of graphic presentations of these fictitious data are also shown. The annual circulation for each day of the week is displayed as a circle graph in Figure 13-A, while the same data are displayed as a bar graph in Figure 13-B. The percentage of annual circulation by LC letter group is displayed as a circle graph in Figure 13-C.

Table 13-1: Circulation by LC Class for Week of December 5, 1993—Front View, Page 11

DAY	DATE	A	B-BJ	BL-BX	C	D	E-F	G	H	J	K
Sun	05-Dec-93	6	17	4	6	11	18	4	4	6	4
Mon	06-Dec-93	15	16	8	12	9	14	10	7	16	16
Tues	07-Dec-93	7	7	13	13	17	7	10	6	15	14
Wed	08-Dec-93	2	11	13	2	18	16	13	18	6	14
Thur	09-Dec-93	3	17	11	14	3	13	1	7	17	11
Fri	10-Dec-93	10	3	17	8	5	16	12	3	12	18
Sat	11-Dec-93	14	4	5	17	14	9	19	4	2	4
		57	75	71	72	77	93	69	49	74	81

L	M	N	P	Q	R	S	T	U	V	Z	-Total-
11	10	6	4	12	14	14	2	2	2	3	160
4	3	2	2	4	13	5	11	6	8	16	197
11	14	8	11	12	17	13	3	9	8	3	218
14	10	13	4	5	18	8	3	19	7	2	216
7	9	17	7	7	10	2	16	15	4	18	209
11	7	9	5	4	13	19	112	13	11	3	311
1	8	8	8	2	9	10	9	13	16	11	187
59	61	63	41	46	94	71	156	77	56	56	1498

Table 13-2: December 1993 Circulation by LC Class—Front View, Page 16

DAY	TOTAL December	A	B-BJ	BL-BX	C	D	E-F	G	H	J	K
Sun		6466	12635	12366	12010	11706	11392	11068	10788	10528	10200
Mon		5638	11019	10791	10480	10222	9944	9655	9412	9186	8904
Tues		11266	16394	15953	15329	14806	14265	13698	13208	12741	12180
Wed		10496	14887	14478	13909	13418	12921	12388	11927	11480	10953
Thur		9518	12953	12566	12060	11608	11173	10684	10275	9889	9403
Fri		8444	10864	10523	10065	9642	9235	8804	8433	8102	7672
Sat		7360	8754	8443	8044	7674	7321	6946	6631	6337	5973
		59188	87506	85120	81897	79076	76251	73243	70673	68263	65284

L	M	N	P	Q	R	S	T	U	V	Z	-Total-
9878	9566	9239	8969	8652	8346	8006	7688	7387	7070	6773	200734
8618	8343	8058	7820	7532	7259	6969	6691	6435	6166	5903	175046
11624	11077	10510	10031	9465	8918	8329	7753	7247	6681	6163	237637
10437	9918	9389	8953	8420	7914	7375	6847	6366	5849	5362	213686
8938	8467	7986	7597	7110	6637	6164	5688	5250	4795	4349	183107
7264	6848	6429	6081	5654	5239	4823	4392	4020	3628	3231	149391
5605	5254	4882	4574	4207	3862	3489	3117	2781	2432	2096	115779
62363	59473	56492	54025	51040	48174	45155	42175	39486	36620	33877	1275381

Table 13-3: January 1993 Total Circulation by LC Class and Day of Week—Front View, Page 10

DAY	CIRCULATION 1993 January	A	B-BJ	BL-BX	C	D	E-F	G	H	J	K
Sun		53	37	37	52	62	42	53	44	53	35
Mon		40	44	45	50	43	41	59	45	56	43
Tues		31	23	30	34	49	31	36	46	51	26
Wed		37	35	47	35	39	44	70	40	42	50
Thur		49	42	46	45	44	22	52	43	45	26
Fri		27	48	51	34	45	42	27	46	30	45
Sat		65	59	68	51	57	33	42	41	55	54
		301	290	324	302	339	256	339	305	332	279

L	M	N	P	Q	R	S	T	U	V	Z	-Total-
49	60	32	67	41	73	38	62	41	25	46	1004
50	36	39	43	40	37	46	31	44	40	30	904
28	27	47	39	30	46	29	23	58	39	46	770
57	38	62	57	52	52	49	32	27	51	37	952
32	32	47	67	36	51	45	47	45	48	38	903
26	25	35	50	50	44	29	56	23	50	36	817
55	73	46	56	41	29	31	48	49	66	71	1089
296	291	309	377	291	331	267	298	288	320	305	6439

Table 13-4: 1993 Year-to-Date Total Circulation by LC Class and Day of Week—Front View, Page 22

DAY	CIRCULATION 1993 TOTAL	A	B-BJ	BL-BX	C	D	E-F	G	H	J	K
Sun		537	425	470	555	592	439	501	444	498	398
Mon		499	587	563	604	583	562	691	542	689	567
Tues		445	334	436	413	604	450	473	552	628	418
Wed		458	454	602	464	535	554	770	510	536	613
Thur		609	506	571	540	542	402	630	526	540	415
Fri		424	545	604	449	537	532	394	465	483	582
Sat		617	559	638	490	610	406	505	418	536	555
		3588	3410	3883	3514	4002	3345	3964	3456	3909	3548

L	M	N	P	Q	R	S	T	U	V	Z	-Total-
526	571	379	626	479	727	408	592	507	332	521	10527
645	475	494	562	497	517	587	454	550	490	429	11585
431	395	593	536	443	576	406	383	705	497	572	10290
671	512	693	675	628	625	632	462	387	592	491	11864
422	495	553	782	485	637	589	590	565	580	491	11470
414	390	436	592	564	527	442	629	363	620	491	10482
530	695	498	585	442	357	328	541	499	668	653	11130
3639	3533	3646	4357	3537	3968	3392	3651	3577	3779	3649	77348

Table 13-5: 1993 Year-to-Date Total Circulation for LC Class T by Day of Week and Month—Right-Side View, Page 20

	T	T	T	T	T	T	T	T	T	T	T	T	T
Sun	62	26	48	50	62	50	50	63	50	62	26	45	592
Mon	31	39	45	31	45	31	31	43	31	31	47	51	454
Tues	23	48	37	23	23	29	23	31	23	23	72	26	383
Wed	32	37	46	32	32	42	32	39	38	32	54	44	462
Thur	47	30	47	65	47	37	65	44	55	47	44	63	590
Fri	56	48	56	50	56	52	64	49	54	60	49	36	629
Sat	48	51	38	53	48	50	56	41	45	45	31	35	541
	298	278	316	305	312	290	323	309	297	299	323	301	3651
	(Jan)	(Feb)	(Mar)	(Apr)	(May)	(Jun)	(Jul)	(Aug)	(Sep)	(Oct)	(Nov)	(Dec)	(Total)

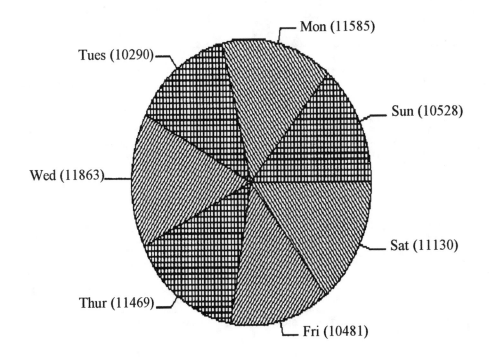

Figure 13-A: 1993 Circulation by Day of Week; Circle Graph

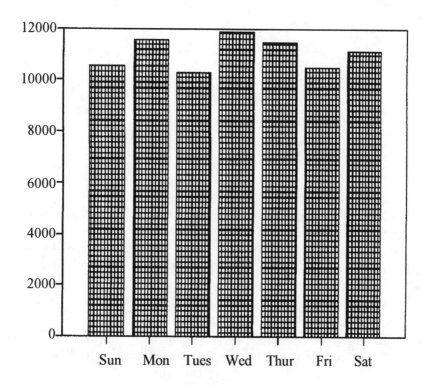

Figure 13-B: 1993 Circulation by Day of Week; Bar Graph

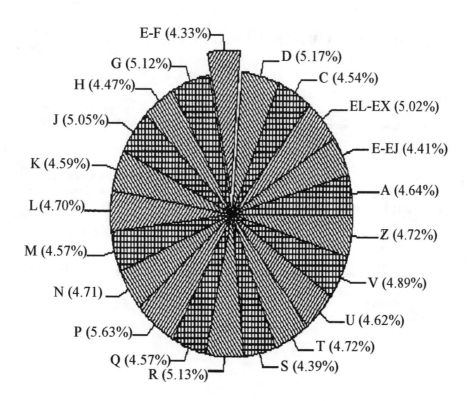

Figure 13-C: 1993 Circulation by LC Classes (Percentage); Circle Graph

Chapter 14
CD-ROM Use

The three-dimensional template shown in this chapter can be used for recording month-by-month use of six CD-ROM databases by five categories of users. The data for each month are recorded on a separate page, and the year-to-date totals are recorded on a final page. If additional databases or categories of users are needed, step-by-step instructions for expanding this spreadsheet to accommodate 20 databases and seven categories of users are provided in Chapter 2, "Design and Modification of Spreadsheets." Further expansion is possible by using these instructions as a guide.

If the template is rotated and viewed from the top, the data for the month can be viewed by database, or, if rotated and viewed from the right, the data can be viewed by user category.

To set up the CD-ROM Use template, follow the cell-by-cell instructions that appear below, creating a generic template. Refer as needed to the general instructions and guidelines in Chapter 2, "Design and Modification of Spreadsheets." Most of the columns are set at the default of nine spaces. Note that cell addresses are identified by column letter, row number, and page number. Thus, C5;10 refers to the cell in column C, row 5, of page 10.

Begin by keyboarding the organizational statement shown below into page one.

CD-ROM USE SPREADSHEET: CELL-BY-CELL INSTRUCTIONS

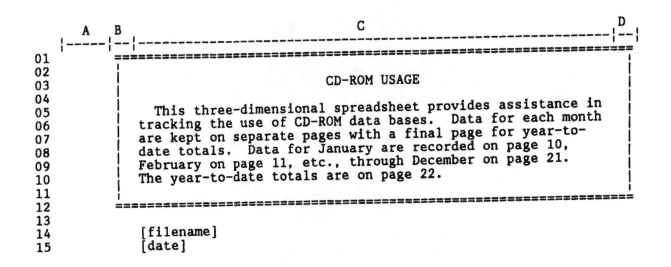

Keyboard the first page of the template into columns A-G, rows 1-18, in page 10. Enter the appropriate user category at the head of each column. Copy the labels in rows A8;10..A17;10 into columns B-G of page 9. These and "(Jan)," which appears in several columns of row 18, are useful when viewing the spreadsheet from the right.

	A	B	C	D
01	CD-ROM USAGE			
02		January	1993	
03				
04			U s e r s	
05				
06		Students		
07				
08	Data Base	Undergrad	Graduate	Faculty
09				
10	xxxxxx	0	0	0
11	xxxxxx	0	0	0
12	xxxxxx	0	0	0
13	xxxxxx	0	0	0
14	xxxxxx	0	0	0
15	xxxxxx	0	0	0
16				
17	Total	@SUM(B9;10..B16;10)	@SUM(C9;10..C16;10)	@SUM(D9;10..D16;10)
18		(Jan)	(Jan)	(Jan)

	E	F	G
01			
02			
03			
04			
05			
06			
07			
08	Librarians	Other	TOTAL
09			
10	0	0	@SUM(B10;10..F10;10)
11	0	0	@SUM(B11;10..F11;10)
12	0	0	@SUM(B12;10..F12;10)
13	0	0	@SUM(B13;10..F13;10)
14	0	0	@SUM(B14;10..F14;10)
15	0	0	@SUM(B15;10..F15;10)
16			
17	@SUM(E9;10..E16;10)	@SUM(F9;10..F16;10)	
18	(Jan)	(Jan)	

	G
17	@IF(@SUM(B17;10..F17;10)=@SUM(G9;10..G16;10),@SUM(G9;10..G16;10),"ERROR")
18	(Jan)

Copy the range A1;10..G18;10 onto pages 11 through 21. Change the names of the months. Keyboard the summary labels and formulas in columns AL-G, rows 1-18, on page 22.

```
                A                    B                       C
    |------------------|--------------------|----------------------|
01    CD-ROM USAGE
02                     TOTAL             1993
03
04                              U   s   e   r   s
05                     --------------------------------------------
06                                  Students
07                     --------------------------------------------
08    Data Base                  Undergrad                Graduate
09    ----------------------------------------------------------------
10    DIALOG         @SUM(B10;10..B10;21)    @SUM(C10;10..C10;21)
11    ERIC           @SUM(B11;10..B11;21)    @SUM(C11;10..C11;21)
12    WilsonLine     @SUM(B12;10..B12;21)    @SUM(C12;10..C12;21)
13    Infotrac       @SUM(B13;10..B13;21)    @SUM(C13;10..C13;21)
14    AgriSci        @SUM(B14;10..B14;21)    @SUM(C14;10..C14;21)
15    PsychLit       @SUM(B15;10..B15;21)    @SUM(C15;10..C15;21)
16                   --------------------------------------------
17       Total       @SUM(B9;22..B16;22)     @SUM(C9;22..C16;22)
18                        (Total)                 (Total)
```

```
                D                    E                       F
    |--------------------|--------------------|----------------------|
01
02
03
04
05    -------------------
06
07
08             Faculty              Librarians                Other
09    ----------------------------------------------------------------
10    @SUM(D10;10..D10;21)  @SUM(E10;10..E10;21)  @SUM(F10;10..F10;21)
11    @SUM(D11;10..D11;21)  @SUM(E11;10..E11;21)  @SUM(F11;10..F11;21)
12    @SUM(D12;10..D12;21)  @SUM(E12;10..E12;21)  @SUM(F12;10..F12;21)
13    @SUM(D13;10..D13;21)  @SUM(E13;10..E13;21)  @SUM(F13;10..F13;21)
14    @SUM(D14;10..D14;21)  @SUM(E14;10..E14;21)  @SUM(F14;10..F14;21)
15    @SUM(D15;10..D15;21)  @SUM(E14;10..E14;21)  @SUM(F15;10..F15;21)
16    ----------------------------------------------------------------
17    @SUM(D9;22..D16;22)   @SUM(E9;22..E16;22)   @SUM(F9;22..F16;22)
18        (Total)               (Total)               (Total)
```

```
                                 G
    |---------------------------------------------------------------|
08                                                            TOTAL
09    ----------------------------------------------------------------
10                                          @SUM(B10;22..F10;22)
11                                          @SUM(B11;22..F11;22)
12                                          @SUM(B12;22..F12;22)
13                                          @SUM(B13;22..F13;22)
14                                          @SUM(B14;22..F14;22)
15                                          @SUM(B15;22..F15;22)
16    ----------------------------------------------------------------
17    @IF(@SUM(B17;22..F17;22)=@SUM(G9;22..G16;22),@SUM(G9;22..G16;22),"ERROR")
18                                              (Total)
```

Save this generic template and make a working copy.

Examples of two pages from this spreadsheet are shown below. Data (entirely fictitious) for the month of January 1993 are displayed in Table 14-1, while the year-to-date totals for the year are shown in Table 14-2.

Two examples of graphic presentations of these fictitious data are also shown. The percentage of use by CD-ROM titles is displayed as a circle graph in Figure 14-A. The number of users of CD-ROM databases in each user group are displayed as a circle graph in Figure 14-B.

Table 14-1: CD-ROM Usage for January 1993—Front View, Page 6

CD-ROM USAGE

January   1993

U s e r s

Data Base	Students		Faculty	Librarians	Other	TOTAL
	Undergrad	Graduate				
DIALOG	22	11	9	5	2	49
ERIC	31	15	14	8	3	71
WilsonLine	20	10	5	2	3	40
Infotrac	65	22	3	3	4	97
AgriSci	17	14	11	7	6	55
PsychLit	28	31	23	9	2	93
Total	183	103	65	34	20	405
	(Jan)	(Jan)	(Jan)	(Jan)	(Jan)	(Jan)

Table 14-2: Total CD-ROM Usage for 1993—Front View, Page 18

CD-ROM USAGE

TOTAL   1993

U s e r s

Data Base	Students		Faculty	Librarians	Other	TOTAL
	Undergrad	Graduate				
DIALOG	457	252	186	105	41	1041
ERIC	656	323	302	168	64	1513
WilsonLine	420	221	107	46	66	860
Infotrac	731	244	36	35	42	1088
AgriSci	198	158	111	85	73	625
PsychLit	207	334	248	98	27	914
Total	2669	1532	990	537	313	6041
	(Total)	(Total)	(Total)	(Total)	(Total)	(Total)

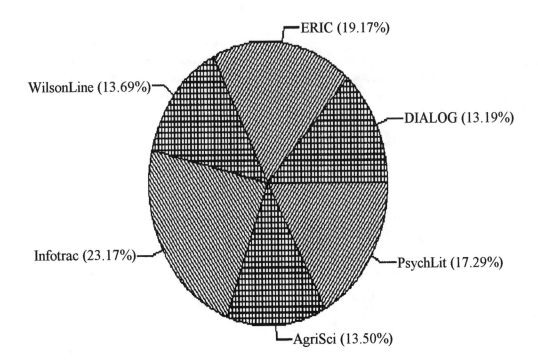

Figure 14-A: CD-ROM Usage (Percentage) by Title; Circle Graph

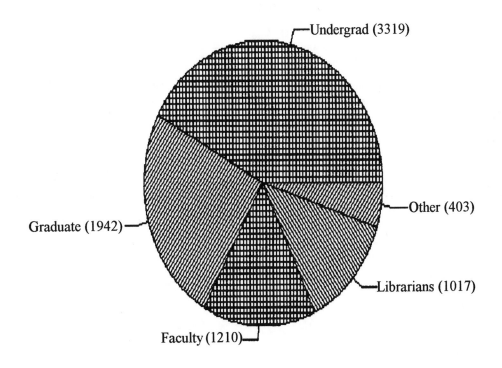

Figure 14-B: CD-ROM Usage by User Group; Circle Graph

Chapter 15
Estimating Shelving Capacity

Three spreadsheets for estimating shelving capacity were included in *Electronic Spreadsheets for Libraries*. Another approach to dealing with the problem of keeping track of full and empty shelves is presented in this chapter. CASMS (Computer Assisted Shelf Management System) is adapted from a spreadsheet originally designed by Norman Holmes as a part of his final project for the Certificate of Advanced Study degree.

To set up the Shelf Management template, follow the general instructions and guidelines in Chapter 2, "Design and Modification of Spreadsheets." The template, as presented, provides spaces for the 10 Dewey Decimal Classification classes plus Biography and Fiction. The classes can be subdivided by inserting additional lines and copying the formulas into these new lines. Or, Library of Congress Classification letter groups could be substituted.

Most of the columns are set at the default of nine spaces. Columns set at other widths are: B and D = 3; C = 50; AC, AF, and AI = 3; and BA-BJ = 20-65, depending on need.

Begin by keyboarding the instructional statement.

ESTIMATING SHELVING CAPACITY SPREADSHEET: CELL-BY-CELL INSTRUCTIONS

```
          A        B                          C                          D
    !--------!---!---------------------------------------------------!---!
01  !        !=======================================================!===!
02  !        !                                                           !
03  !        !      CASMS - Computer Assisted Shelf Management System    !
04  !        !                                                           !
05  !        !     CASMS, a management tool, is designed to help make    !
06  !        ! optimum use of available shelving by providing            !
07  !        ! assistance in determining the total amount of shelf       !
08  !        ! space available, the amount currently being used, and     !
09  !        ! the amount remaining.                                     !
10  !        !                                                           !
11  !        !     The four spreadsheet areas and beginning addresses    !
12  !        ! are:                                                      !
13  !        !                                                           !
14  !        ! CLASSES &       ORIGINAL      CURRENT         FUTURE      !
15  !        ! LOCATIONS       SPACES        TRANSACTIONS                !
16  !        ! A101            F101          K101            R101        !
17  !        !                                                           !
18  !        !     The Classes & Locations area contains classification  !
19  !        ! groups, floors, and ranges.                               !
20  !        !                                                           !
21  !        !     The Original Spaces area contains the total linear     !
22  !        ! feet available, the linear feet used, the percent          !
23  !        ! used, and the linear feet remaining.                       !
24  !        !                                                           !
25  !        !     The Current Transactions area contains the average     !
26  !        ! width of the volumes in each classification group, the     !
27  !        ! number of volumes being added, the number of volumes       !
28  !        ! being withdrawn, the linear feet now used, the percent     !
29  !        ! used, and the linear feet remaining.                       !
30  !        !                                                           !
31  !        !     The Future area contains the projected growth in       !
32  !        ! volumes, the linear feet this represents, the total        !
33  !        ! projection of linear feet used, and the linear feet        !
34  !        ! remaining.                                                 !
35  !        !                                                           !
36  !        !     To speed data entry, turn off automatic recalcula-     !
37  !        ! tion.  However, be sure to recalculate before saving       !
38  !        ! or printing the spreadsheet.                               !
39  !        !                                                           !
40  !        !     Use of this spreadsheet is assisted by a menu which    !
41  !        ! can be invoked by simultaneously pressing [ALT] and        !
42  !        ! the letter "a".  The macros which drive the menu           !
43  !        ! begin at BA1.                                              !
44  !        !                                                           !
45  !        !=======================================================!===!
46  !
47           [filename]
48           [date]
```

Keyboard the basic template into columns A-U, rows 101-137.

	A	B	C	D	E	F	G
101	C L A S S E S & L O C A T I O N S					O R I G I N A L S P A C E	
102							
103						Total	Amount
104			Begin	End		Avail	Used
105	Class #	Floor	Range	Range		(feet)	(feet)
106							
107	000-099	0	0	0		0	0
108							
109	100-199	0	0	0		0	0
110							
111	200-299	0	0	0		0	0
112							
113	300-399	0	0	0		0	0
114							
115	400-499	0	0	0		0	0
116							
117	500-599	0	0	0		0	0
118							
119	600-699	0	0	0		0	0
120							
121	700-799	0	0	0		0	0
122							
123	800-899	0	0	0		0	0
124							
125	900-999	0	0	0		0	0
126							
127	Biography	0	0	0		0	0
128							
129	Fiction	0	0	0		0	0
130							
131						@SUM(F106..F130)	@SUM(G106..G130)

	H	I	J	K	L
101					
102					
103		Amount		Average	
104	Used	Remaining		Width	Added
105	(percent)	(feet)		(inches)	(volumes)
106					
107	+G107/F107	+F107-G107		0	0
108					
109	+G109/F109	+F109-G109		0	0
110					
111	+G111/F111	+F111-G111		0	0
112					
113	+G113/F113	+F113-G113		0	0
114					
115	+A115/F115	+F115-G115		0	0
116					
117	+G117/F117	+F117-G117		0	0
118					
119	+G119/F119	+F119-G119		0	0
120					
121	+G121/F121	+F121-G121		0	0
122					
123	+G123/F123	+F123-G123		0	0
124					
125	+G125/F125	+F125-G125		0	0
126					
127	+G127/F127	+F127-G127		0	0
128					
129	+G129/F129	+F129-G129		0	0
130					
131	+G131/F131	@SUM(I116..I130)		@AVG(K107..K129)	@SUM(L106..L130)

```
              M                    N                        O
     !----------------!--------------------------------!-----------------!
101  C U R R E N T   T R A N S A C T I O N S
102  -----------------------------------------------------------------------
103                                              Amount              Add'1
104            Withdrawn                           Used               Used
105            (volumes)                         (feet)  (percent)
106  ================================================================
107                    0    +((K107*L107)-(K107*M107))/12    +(N107/F107)
108
109                    0    +((K109*L109)-(K109*M109))/12    +(N109/F109)
110
111                    0    +((K111*L111)-(K111*M111))/12    +(N111/F111)
112
113                    0    +((K113*L113)-(K113*M113))/12    +(N113/F113)
114
115                    0    +((K115*A115)-(K115*M115))/12    +(N115/F115)
116
117                    0    +((K117*L117)-(K117*M117))/12    +(N117/F117)
118
119                    0    +((K119*L119)-(K119*M119))/12    +(N119/F119)
120
121                    0    +((K121*L121)-(K121*M121))/12    +(N121/F121)
122
123                    0    +((K123*L123)-(K123*M123))/12    +(N123/F123)
124
125                    0    +((K125*L125)-(K125*M125))/12    +(N125/F125)
126
127                    0    +((K127*L127)-(K127*M127))/12    +(N127/F127)
128
129                    0    +((K129*L129)-(K129*M129))/12    +(N129/F129)
130
     ----------------------------------------------------------------------
131  @SUM(AM6..AM30)             @SUM(N106..N130)        +(N131/F131)


              P          Q      R                 S
     !------------------!---!-----------------!----------------------!
101                             F U T U R E
102  -------------------     -------------------------------------------
103             Amount             Projected             Amount
104          Remaining                Growth               Used
105             (feet)             (volumes)             (feet)
106  ==================     ===========================================
107  +F107-(G107+N107)               0         +(K107*R107)/12
108
109  +F109-(G109+N109)               0         +(K109*R109)/12
110
111  +F111-(G111+N111)               0         +(K111*R111)/12
112
113  +F113-(G113+N113)               0         +(K113*R113)/12
114
115  +F115-(G115+N115)               0         +(K115*R115)/12
116
117  +F117-(G117+N117)               0         +(K117*R117)/12
118
119  +F119-(G119+N119)               0         +(K119*R119)/12
120
121  +F121-(G121+N121)               0         +(K121*R121)/12
122
123  +F123-(G123+N123)               0         +(K123*R123)/12
124
125  +F125-(G125+N125)               0         +(K125*R125)/12
126
127  +F127-(G127+N127)               0         +(K127*R127)/12
128
129  +F129-(G129+N129)               0         +(K129*R129)/12
130  -------------------     -------------------------------------------
131  @SUM(P106..P130)    @SUM(R106..R130)    @SUM(S106..S130)
132
133
134  -----------------------------------------------------------------------
135  Average free shelving
136  Standard Deviation
137  -----------------------------------------------------------------------
```

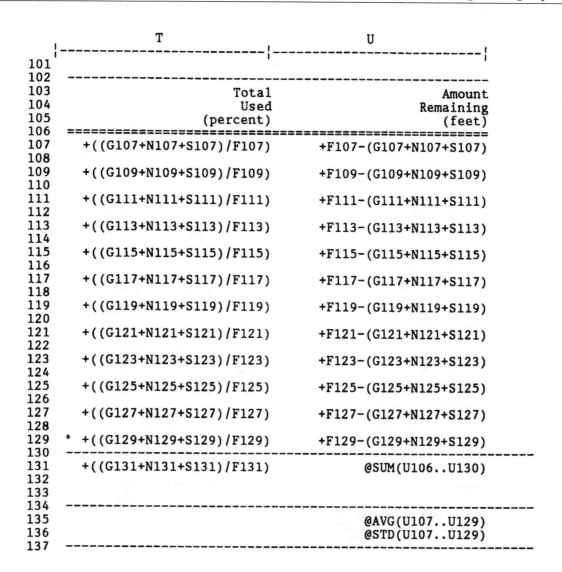

```
                  T                                U
    |------------------------------|------------------------------|
101 |                              |                              |
102 |------------------------------------------------------------- 
103                   Total                            Amount
104                   Used                           Remaining
105                 (percent)                          (feet)
106 ===============================================================
107    +((G107+N107+S107)/F107)      +F107-(G107+N107+S107)
108
109    +((G109+N109+S109)/F109)      +F109-(G109+N109+S109)
110
111    +((G111+N111+S111)/F111)      +F111-(G111+N111+S111)
112
113    +((G113+N113+S113)/F113)      +F113-(G113+N113+S113)
114
115    +((G115+N115+S115)/F115)      +F115-(G115+N115+S115)
116
117    +((G117+N117+S117)/F117)      +F117-(G117+N117+S117)
118
119    +((G119+N119+S119)/F119)      +F119-(G119+N119+S119)
120
121    +((G121+N121+S121)/F121)      +F121-(G121+N121+S121)
122
123    +((G123+N123+S123)/F123)      +F123-(G123+N123+S123)
124
125    +((G125+N125+S125)/F125)      +F125-(G125+N125+S125)
126
127    +((G127+N127+S127)/F127)      +F127-(G127+N127+S127)
128
129  * +((G129+N129+S129)/F129)      +F129-(G129+N129+S129)
130 -------------------------------------------------------------
131    +((G131+N131+S131)/F131)         @SUM(U106..U130)
132
133
134 -------------------------------------------------------------
135                                     @AVG(U107..U129)
136                                     @STD(U107..U129)
137 -------------------------------------------------------------
```

After keyboarding columns BA-BN, rows 1-12, name the range BB1 "\0." This will cause the organizational statement to be displayed whenever the spreadsheet is loaded. Name the range BD1 "\a." This will display the menu when [ALT] and "a" are pressed simultaneously.

```
        BA           BB            BC            BD
    |--------|-------------------|--------|-------------------|
01  \0        {WINDOWSOFF}~       \a        {MENUBRANCH BE1}~
02            /WTC
03            {GOTO}A1~
04            {RIGHT 2}~
05            {DOWN 4}~
06            {WINDOWSON}~
07            {QUIT}
```

```
                         BE
 |----------------------------------------------|
 |                                              |
01  Organize
02  Go to classification and range areas
03  /WTC
04  {WINDOWSOFF}~
05  {GOTO}A101
06  {RIGHT}~
07  {DOWN 6}~
08  /WTB
09  {WINDOWSON}~
10  {QUIT}
```

```
                         BF
 |---------------------------------------------|
 |                                             |
01  Data
02  Go to Original, Current, and Future data areas
03  {MENUBRANCH BL1}~
```

```
              BG                        BH
 |----------------------------|  |----------------------------------|
 |                            |  |                                  |
01  Recalculate                 Save
02  Recalculated the spreadsheet Saves the spreadsheet to disk
03  /WTC                        /WTC~
04  {CALC}                      /FS{?}~
05  {QUIT}                      {QUIT}
```

```
              BI                        BJ
 |----------------------------|  |--------------------------------|
 |                            |  |                                |
01  Print                       Quit
02  Print the spreadsheet       Exits Lotus 1-2-3.  SAVE FILES FIRST!
03  /WTC                        /WTC
04  /PP                         /QY
05  RA101..I131~                {QUIT}
06  GP
07  RK101..V137~
08  GPQ
09  {QUIT}
```

```
                         BK
 |------------------------------------------------------------|
 |                                                            |
01  Macro
02  Utility to move the cursor to the beginning of the menu program
03  /WTC
04  {GOTO}BA1~
05  {QUIT}
```

```
                    BL                               BM
   |-------------------------------|  |----------------------------------|
01 Original                           Current
02 Original or starting space         Current transactions or changes
03 /WTC                               /WTC
04 {WINDOWSOFF}~                       {WINDOWSOFF}~
05 {GOTO}A101~                         {GOTO}A101~
06 {RIGHT}~                            {RIGHT}~
07 {DOWN 6}~                           {DOWN 6}~
08 /WTB                               /WTB
09 {GOTO}L107~                         {GOTO}R107~
10 {LEFT 6}~                           {LEFT 7}~
11 {WINDOWSON}~                        {WINDOWSON}~
12 {QUIT}                              {QUIT}
```

```
                    BN
   |----------------------------|
01 Future
02 Future anticipated changes
03 /WTC
04 {WINDOWSOFF}~
05 {GOTO}A101~
06 {RIGHT}~
07 {DOWN 6}~
08 /WTB
09 {GOTO}Y107~
10 {LEFT 7}~
11 {WINDOWSON}~
12 {QUIT}
```

Save the completed template and make a working copy. An example of a completed CASMS spreadsheet, using fictitious data, is shown in Table 15-1. An example of a graphic presentation of these fictitious data is shown in Figure 15-A.

Table 15-1: CASMS (Computer Assisted Shelf Management System)

| | | | | ORIGINAL SPACE | | | | CURRENT TRANSACTIONS | | | | | | FUTURE | | | |
| CLASSES & LOCATIONS | | | | Total Avail (feet) | Amount Used (feet) | Used (percent) | Amount Remaining (feet) | Average Width (inches) | Added (volumes) | Subtract (volumes) | Amount Used (feet) | Add'l Used (percent) | Amount Remaining (feet) | Projected Growth (volumes) | Amount Used (feet) | Total Used (percent) | Amount Remaining (feet) |
Class #	Floor	Begin Range	End Range														
000's	1	1	75	72	47	65%	25	1.50	14	3	1.38	2%	23.63	12	1.50	69%	22.13
100's	1	76	125	85	56	66%	29	1.25	75	4	7.40	9%	21.60	16	1.67	77%	19.94
200's	2	1	89	136	117	86%	19	1.00	35	2	2.75	2%	16.25	15	1.25	89%	15.00
300's	2	90	154	115	86	75%	29	1.25	134	14	12.50	11%	16.50	56	5.83	91%	10.67
400's	2	155	201	74	60	81%	14	1.50	37	5	4.00	5%	10.00	20	2.50	90%	7.50
500's	3	1	80	92	70	76%	22	1.00	89	8	6.75	7%	15.25	32	2.67	86%	12.58
600's	3	81	160	128	95	74%	33	1.00	129	43	7.17	6%	25.83	172	14.33	91%	11.50
700's	3	161	225	140	115	82%	25	1.50	74	9	8.13	6%	16.88	36	4.50	91%	12.38
800's	4	1	95	188	135	72%	53	1.00	145	89	4.67	2%	48.33	220	18.33	84%	30.00
900's	4	96	178	130	97	75%	33	1.25	121	14	11.15	9%	21.85	56	5.83	88%	16.02
Biog	5	1	80	93	77	83%	16	1.00	40	35	0.42	0%	15.58	65	5.42	89%	10.17
Fict	5	81	200	166	115	69%	51	1.00	200	120	6.67	4%	44.33	221	18.42	84%	25.92
				1419	1070	75%	349	1.19	1093	346	72.96	5%	276.04	921	82.25	86%	193.79

Average free shelving	16.15
Standard deviation	6.63

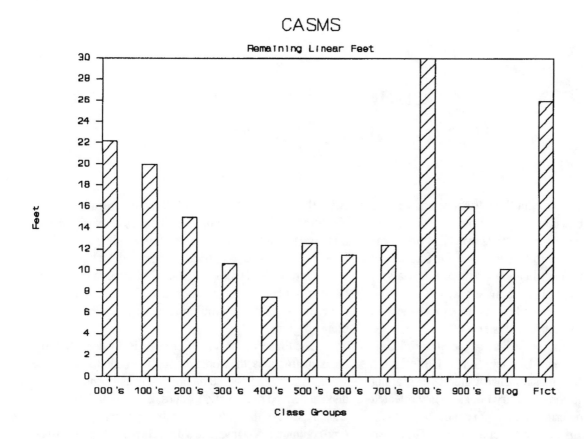

Figure 15-A: CASMS: Remaining Feet of Linear Shelving by Class; Bar Graph

Chapter 16
Preservation Values

Anyone who has seen the film *Slow Fires* or has walked through the stacks of a large library knows that there is no shortage of books and other materials in need of preservation attention if they are to be conserved for future use. One problem is the identification of these materials; a second problem is selecting the most needy items from among them. The Preservation Value spreadsheet is designed to be of assistance in this effort.

In their "Deterioration Survey of the Stanford University Libraries Green Library Stack Collection," Buchanan and Coleman established criteria for grading the level of deterioration of library books. They selected three categories of deterioration: paper condition, binding condition, and board and cover condition. (They also identified two other categories, insects and/or vermin and mildew/mold, which they did not include in their evaluation of deterioration, nor are these factors included in the spreadsheet here.) Each category was graded on the following scale:

0—good condition; needs no attention

1—moderate condition; evidence of deterioration, needs some attention

2—poor condition; rapid deterioration, needs immediate attention, should not be used

Users of this spreadsheet should refer to the explicit guidelines provided by Buchanan and Coleman for assigning the grades of conditions. In determining the preservation grade for an item, paper condition was given twice the weight of binding condition or board and cover condition. The formula used in this spreadsheet to determine preservation values retains this emphasis.

I am indebted to Patricia Palmer and Andrew Bullen who, as students, developed a PASCAL program based on the work of Buchanan and Coleman. They kindly agreed to permit me to develop this spreadsheet loosely based on their program.

The Preservation Value template is divided into three areas: instructions, the work area, and the menu/macros. The work area, containing the bibliographic and condition data and the derived preservation values, is set up and defined as a database. For this reason, the entries beginning in AA104 (and continuing downward to a theoretical AA8192) must be continuous, i.e., there should be no blank lines. If there is a blank line, the sort programs will stop at the preceding row. Also, AA104 must always have an entry even if it is only a dummy entry. Without an entry in AA104, the sort programs will not recognize the presence of any succeeding data.

To set up the Preservation Values template, follow the general instructions and guidelines in Chapter 2, "Design and Modification of Spreadsheets." The specifications, labels, and formulas for setting up the Preservation Values template are shown below.

Many of the columns are set at the default of nine spaces. Columns set at other widths are:

B	=	3	AH	=	1	AR	=	1
C	=	55	AI	=	5	AS	=	5
D	=	3	AJ	=	1	AT	=	1
AA	=	20	AK	=	15	AU	=	5
AB	=	1	AL	=	1	BB	=	12
AC	=	20	AM	=	5	BD	=	30
AD	=	1	AN	=	1	BE	=	40
AE	=	12	AO	=	7	BF	=	30
AF	=	12	AP	=	1	BG	=	60
AG	=	7	AQ	=	5	BH	=	50

BI	=	45
BJ	=	40
BK	=	70
BM	=	30
BN	=	30
BO	=	40
BP	=	40
BQ	=	40
BR	=	40

Turn off automatic recalculation. Set the display of numbers to Fixed with no digits after the decimal. For printing, set the left margin at 4 and the right margin at 136, and select compressed type, i.e., 17 characters per inch. Begin by keyboarding the organizational statement (B1-D56).

PRESERVATION VALUES SPREADSHEET: CELL-BY-CELL INSTRUCTIONS

```
       B                                  C                                    D
     |---|--------------------------------------------------------------|---|
01   |                    Priority Books for Preservation                   |
02
03   |==================================================================|
04   |                                                                    |
05   |      This spreadsheet provides assistance in identifying           |
06   |   books which are in need of preservation work and in             |
07   |   assigning priorities among these books.  Brief biblio-          |
08   |   graphic data is keyboarded for each item followed by            |
09   |   numeric values for 3 categories of deterioration:               |
10   |        paper condition,                                            |
11   |        binding condition, and                                      |
12   |        board and cover condition.                                  |
13   |   For each book, a numeric value is assigned in each of           |
14   |   these 3 categories:                                              |
15   |        0 = good condition; needs no attention                      |
16   |        1 = moderate condition; evidence of                         |
17   |            deterioration, needs some attention                     |
18   |        2 = poor condition; rapid deterioration,                    |
19   |            needs immediate attention, should                       |
20   |            not be used                                             |
21   |                                                                    |
22   |      To use the Priority Books for Preservation spread-           |
23   |   sheet, press [Alt] and "a" simultaneously, and the menu         |
24   |   will appear.                                                     |
25   |                                                                    |
26   |      The appropriate label prefixes are noted above certain       |
27   |   columns and should be used whenever entering numbers in         |
28   |   these columns.  This assures proper right and left              |
29   |   justification of these columns.                                  |
30   |                                                                    |
31   |      Because the working section of the spreadsheet               |
32   |   (columns AA-AQ) is a data base, there must be NO BLANK          |
33   |   ROWS or the sort program will not work properly.  DO           |
34   |   NOT leave blank rows when adding titles.  Close up             |
35   |   blank rows after deleting titles.  Also, always KEEP AT        |
36   |   LEAST ONE RECORD in the data base, even if it is a             |
37   |   dummy record.                                                    |
38   |                                                                    |
39   |      Set the numeric display to FIXED with no zeros to the        |
40   |   right of the decimal.                                            |
41   |                                                                    |
42   |      For printing, set the left margin at 2 and the right         |
43   |   margin at 136.  The setup string should be for                 |
44   |   condensed type, i.e., 17 characters per inch.                   |
45   |                                                                    |
46   |      The data base can be sorted by author, title, date of       |
47   |   publication, call number, value, or record number.             |
48   |                                                                    |
49   |      The menu and associated macro instructions are stored       |
50   |   in columns BA-BR, rows 1-15.  They may be viewed by           |
51   |   selecting "Macro" from the menu.                                 |
52   |                                                                    |
53   |==================================================================|
54
55   [filename]
56   [date]
```

Keyboard the data and analysis portions of the template beginning with columns AA-AU, rows 101-103.

```
            AA                AB              AC            AD         AE              AF
  |--------------------||------------------||--------------|------------|------------|
101|                    ||                  ||              ||          |            |
102
103 AUTHOR              TITLE                            PLACE OF PUB   PUBLISHER
```

```
      AG  AH AI AJ      AK        AL AM AN   AO   AP AQ AR AS AT AU
  |------||----||--------------||----||------||----||----||----|
101|     ||    ||              ||    ||   QUALITY
102                                    --------------------
103 DATE   PAGES CALL NUMBER      PAPER BINDING COVER VALUE REC#
```

Then, keyboard the following formula in cell AS104:

@IF(AM104=2,2,@IF(AM104=1#AND#@SUM(AM104..AQ4)=5,2,@IF(AN104=1,1,@IF(AO104+AQ104=4,2,@IF(AM104+AO104+AQ104<=1,0,1)))))

In the spreadsheet, this long formula is a continuous string of characters with no blank spaces or other breaks. This formula should be copied into additional rows of column AS as titles are added. Note that the cell addresses are relative so that the row numbers will change depending on which row of the spreadsheet is being used. However, the column designations should not change.

After keyboarding columns BA-BR, rows 1-14, name the range BB1 "\0" so that the organizational statement will be displayed automatically whenever this spreadsheet is loaded. Name the range BD1 "\a" so that the menu will be displayed when [ALT] and "a" are pressed simultaneously.

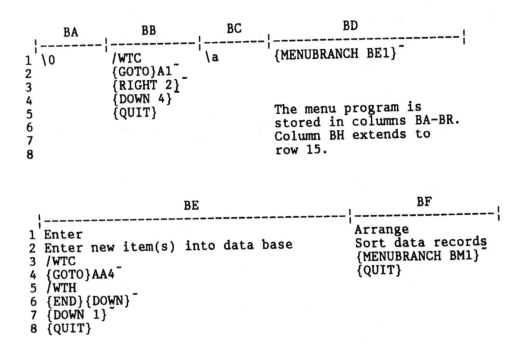

```
       BA              BB            BC              BD
  |-----------|-----------------|------------|-----------------------------|
1  \0          /WTC              \a           {MENUBRANCH BE1}~
2              {GOTO}A1~
3              {RIGHT 2}~
4              {DOWN 4}~
5              {QUIT}                          The menu program is
6                                              stored in columns BA-BR.
7                                              Column BH extends to
8                                              row 15.
```

```
                          BE                                    BF
  |----------------------------------------------------|--------------------|
1  Enter                                                 Arrange
2  Enter new item(s) into data base                     Sort data records
3  /WTC                                                  {MENUBRANCH BM1}~
4  {GOTO}AA4~                                            {QUIT}
5  /WTH
6  {END}{DOWN}~
7  {DOWN 1}~
8  {QUIT}
```

```
                              BG
|-----------------------------------------------------------|
1 Save
2 Saves the spreadsheet to disk.  Supply a filename as needed
3 /WTC
4 /FS{?}~
5 {QUIT}
```

```
                         BH
|----------------------------------------------|
 1 Print
 2 Sends the list of records to the printer
 3 {WINDOWSOFF}~
 4 /WTC
 5 /PP
 6 RAA1~
 7 R.
 8 {DOWN 2}
 9 {END}{DOWN}
10 {RIGHT 20}~
11 GPQ
12 {WINDOWSON}~
13 {QUIT}
```

```
                         BI
|----------------------------------------------|
 1 File
 2 Writes the list of records on a disk file
 3 {WINDOWSOFF}~
 4 /WTC
 5 /PF{?}~{?}~
 6 RAA1~
 7 R.
 8 {DOWN 2}
 9 {END}{DOWN}
10 {RIGHT 20}~
11 G
12 Q
13 {WINDOWSON}~
14 {QUIT}
```

```
                       BJ
|--------------------------------------|
1 Quit
2 Exits Lotus 1-2-3.  SAVE FILES FIRST!
3 /WTC
4 /QY
5 {QUIT}
```

```
                          BK
|----------------------------------------------------|
1 Macro
2 Utility to move the cursor to the beginning of the menu program
3 /WTC
4 {GOTO}BA1~
5 {QUIT}
```

```
                      BM                                BN
   |------------------------------|   |------------------------------|
 1 Author                             Title
 2 Sort data base by authors          Sort data base by titles
 3 /WTC                                /WTC
 4 /DS                                 /DS
 5 DAA4~                               DAA4~
 6 D.{END}{DOWN}                       D.{END}{DOWN}
 7 {RIGHT 20}~                         {RIGHT 20}~
 8 PAA4~                               PAC4~
 9 A~                                  A~
10 G                                   G
11 {GOTO}AA1~                          {GOTO}AA1~
12 {QUIT}                              {QUIT}
```

```
                           BO
      |------------------------------------------|
 1 Date
 2 Sort data base by dates of publication
 3 /WTC
 4 /DS
 5 DAA4~
 6 D.{END}{DOWN}
 7 {RIGHT 20}~
 8 PAG4~
 9 A~
10 G
11 {GOTO}AA1~
12 {QUIT}
```

```
                       BP
      |------------------------------------|
 1 Call#
 2 Sort data base by call numbers
 3 /WTC
 4 /DS
 5 DAA4~
 6 D.{END}{DOWN}
 7 {RIGHT 20}~
 8 PAJ4~
 9 A~
10 G
11 {GOTO}AA1~
12 {QUIT}
```

```
                       BQ
      |---------------------------------------|
 1 Value
 2 Sort data base by preservation values
 3 /WTC
 4 /DS
 5 DAA4~
 6 D.{END}{DOWN}
 7 {RIGHT 20}~
 8 PAS4~
 9 A~
10 G
11 {GOTO}AA1~
12 {QUIT}
```

```
                                    BR
     |------------------------------------------|
   1 Record#
   2 Sort data base by record numbers
   3 /WTC
   4 /DS
   5 DAA4~
   6 D.{END}{DOWN}
   7 {RIGHT 20}~
   8 PAU4~
   9 A~
  10 G
  11 {GOTO}AA1~
  12 {QUIT}
```

Save this template. Make a working copy and begin entering data.

An example of how the completed spreadsheet would appear, using fictitious data, is shown in Table 16-1.

Table 16-1: Preservation Values

AUTHOR	TITLE	PLACE	PUBLISHER	DATE	PAGES	CALL NUMBER	PAPER	BINDING	COVER	VALUE	REC#
Chagall	Lithographs	Monte Carlo	A. Sauret	1960	220	q769.944 C3461	0	1	2	1	1
Zahn	Silk screen methods	Chicago	Drake	1939	233	745.7 Z13s	2	1	1	2	2
Thompson	English monasteries	Cambridge	Univ Press	1923	158	726.7 T37e	0	1	2	1	3
Knight	Willian Shakespeare	New York	Collier	nd	553	PR2894.K5 1800z	2	1	0	2	4
Florida	Florida poets 1930	Newport, Ky	Intl Writers	1930	116	PS558.F6F6	0	1	0	0	5
Hergesheimer	Sheridan	Boston	Houghton Mif	1931	381	E467.1.S54H5	2	0	2	2	6
Stevenson	Song-book	New York	Scribner's	1897	119	784.624 CST48S	0	0	1	0	7
Goldsmith	Grecian history	Hartford	S. Andrus	1824	316	DF215.G615 1824	0	2	1	1	8
Irving	Alhambra	New York	Putnam's	1865	511	PS2056.A1 1865	2	2	0	2	9
Goldsmith	Misc. works	Philadelphia	Crissy and T	1841	527	PR3481.I7 1841	1	1	0	1	10
Irving	Alhambra	New York	Crowell	1851	376	PS2056.A1 1851	2	2	2	2	11
Stevenson	Suicide Club	New York	Scribner's	1896	174	PR5488.S9 a896	1	1	2	1	12
Marlowe	Hero and Leander	New York	Covici, Frie	1934	161	PR2670.H6 1934	0	1	1	1	13
Graves	Long week end	New York	Macmillan	1941	455	DA566.4.G7 1941	2	1	0	2	14
Marlowe	Plays	London	J.M. Dent	1941	488	PR2662.T4 1909	1	0	0	1	15
Graves	Fairies and fusiliers	New York	Folcroft	1918	97	PR6103.R35F3	2	1	2	2	16
Jefferson	Best letters	Boston	Houghton Mif	1926	300	E302.J443 c.1	1	0	2	1	17
Raleigh	Selections ... histor	Oxford	Clarendon	1917	212	D57.R183	0	1	2	1	18
Benson, E. F.	As we were	London	Longmans	1930	306	DA560.B4 1930a	0	2	1	1	19
Benson, E.F.	Life of Alcibiades	New York	Appleton	1929	324	DF230.A4B4x	1	2	0	1	20
Benson, A.C.	Hugh	New York	Longmans	1915	265	BX4705.B3B3 1915	1	0	2	1	21
Benson, A.C.	Alfred Tennyson	London	Methuen	1904	243	PR5581.B45	0	1	1	1	22
Benson, R.H.	Papers of a pariah	London	Murray	1907	211	BX1752.B38	2	0	0	2	23

Chapter 17
Reference Work Values

Aside from simple tallies of questions asked, reference work has proven to be relatively more difficult to measure and evaluate than many other library activities. Murfin and Wynar in their bibliography on reference service include only a few items on this topic. Altman observed in her careful essay on "Assessment of References Services" that "there is still no consensus on how to measure, let along evaluate, reference" (p. 170). Kesselman and Watstein present a complex method for collecting and analyzing reference services statistics and data, while Westbrook offers guidance for qualitative evaluations of reference services. Koren provides the most current bibliography.

The three-dimensional spreadsheet presented in this chapter is an attempt to quantify reference work and to provide a means of comparing and contrasting different levels of work and providing an indicator of the relative performance of different reference staff members. The key to valid use of this spreadsheet is to remember at all times that it provides only a measure of quantity, not a measure of quality. For example, any evaluation of the correctness or appropriateness of a worker's responses to reference questions must be determined through other measures not included in this spreadsheet.

This spreadsheet is based on the self-evident assumption that some reference questions are more difficult than others, that reference questions can be categorized according to their difficulty. Each of the five levels of reference question difficulty used in this spreadsheet is assigned a weight based on the relative difficulty and the amount of time required to respond to an inquiry. As presented in this chapter, each level is assigned a factor three times greater than the previous level. Thus, Level 1, directional inquiries and the like, is assigned a weighting factor of 1; Level 2, simple facts and basic instruction, is assigned a factor of 3; Level 3, moderate questions and instruction, is assigned a factor of 9; Level 4, complex questions and instruction, is assigned a factor of 27; and Level 5, extended searches and teaching classes, is assigned a factor of 81. Each of these weighting factors can be adjusted to match the pattern of locally posed questions and the expectations of the clientele.

To set up the Reference Work Values template, follow the general instructions and guidelines in Chapter 2, "Design and Modification of Spreadsheets." The specifications, labels, and formulas for setting up the Reference Work Values template are shown below. Most of the columns are set at the default of nine spaces. Note that cell addresses are identified by column letter, row number, and page number. Thus, C5;10 refers to the cell in column C, row 5, of page 10.

Begin by keyboarding the organizational statement. Note that the assigned weight values are constants and are in column D.

REFERENCE WORK VALUES SPREADSHEET: CELL-BY-CELL INSTRUCTIONS

```
        A    B                        C                        D    E
    !--------!--!---------------------------------------------!----!--!
01  !        !  !=============================================!    !  !
02  !        !  !                                             !    !  !
03  !        !  !        R e f e r e n c e   S e r v i c e s  !    !  !
04  !        !  !                                             !    !  !
05  !        !  !   This spreadsheet provides assistance in evaluating the !
06  !        !  ! quantity and quality of reference services.  Data gathered !
07  !        !  ! on tally sheets are transferred to this spreadsheet where !
08  !        !  ! they are accumulated, month by month, with a separate page !
09  !        !  ! for each reference worker.                   !
10  !        !  !                                             !
11  !        !  !   Five weighted levels of reference service are used in this !
12  !        !  ! spreadsheet.  The levels and the assigned weights are: !
13  !        !  !                                             !
14  !        !  !      level 1 - Directional inquiries              1 !
15  !        !  !      level 2 - Simple facts and basic instruction 3 !
16  !        !  !      level 3 - Moderate questions and instruction 9 !
17  !        !  !      level 4 - Complex questions and instruction 27 !
18  !        !  !      level 5 - Extended searches and teaching classes 81 !
19  !        !  !                                             !
20  !        !  ! The weighting is based on the relative difficulty and the !
21  !        !  ! amount of time required to respond to a typical inquiry on !
22  !        !  ! each level.  For each month, an adjusted value for each !
23  !        !  ! reference worker is calculated using the weighting factors !
24  !        !  ! as constants.  In addition, the cumulative year-to-date data !
25  !        !  ! and adjusted values are combined in a final summary sheet. !
26  !        !  ! The weighting factors can be adjusted by changing the !
27  !        !  ! figures shown above in cells D14-D18.  (An associated work !
28  !        !  ! area in cells F14-G19 supports this function.) !
29  !        !  !                                             !
30  !        !  !   This is a THREE-DIMENSIONAL spreadsheet.  In addition to !
31  !        !  ! ROWS and COLUMNS, this spreadsheet also has PAGES.  These !
32  !        !  ! instructions appear on page 1, a worksheet which may be !
33  !        !  ! printed and on which daily tallies may be recorded appears !
34  !        !  ! on page 3, while the data display and analysis area begins !
35  !        !  ! on page 10 and continues for several pages thereafter.  A !
36  !        !  ! summary of totals appears on the final page. !
37  !        !  !                                             !
38  !        !  !=============================================!
39
40           [filename]
41           [date]
```

Keyboard the following into F14;1..G19;1.

```
                F                        G
    !---------------------!---------------------!
14  !                     ! (100/F19;1)*D14;1   !
15  !                     ! (100/F19;1)*D15;1   !
16  !                     ! (100/F19;1)*D16;1   !
17  !                     ! (100/F19;1)*D17;1   !
18  !                     ! (100/F19;1)*D18;1   !
19  ! @SUM(D14;1..D18;1)  !                     !
```

Keyboard the following worksheet into page 3. Later, print a copy, photocopy it, and use it for gathering data.

```
          A      B            C        D        E        F    G      H       I        J     K         L
     |---------|-|--------------------|-|---------------|-|---------|-|-------|-|---------|-|
 01  Reference Question Tally                            Name:
 02  Daily Worksheet                                     Date:
 03  Hour               level 1            level 2       level 3   level 4   level 5
 04  ================================================================================
 05    8:00      |                |        |        |        |        |
 06                                                                              |
 07  --------------------------------------------------------------------------------
 08    9:00      |                |        |        |        |        |
 09                                                                              |
 10  --------------------------------------------------------------------------------
 11  10:00       |                |        |        |        |        |
 12                                                                              |
 13  --------------------------------------------------------------------------------
 14  11:00       |                |        |        |        |        |
 15                                                                              |
 16  --------------------------------------------------------------------------------
 17  12:00       |                |        |        |        |        |
 18                                                                              |
 19  --------------------------------------------------------------------------------
 20    1:00      |                |        |        |        |        |
 21                                                                              |
 22  --------------------------------------------------------------------------------
 23    2:00      |                |        |        |        |        |
 24                                                                              |
 25  --------------------------------------------------------------------------------
 26    3:00      |                |        |        |        |        |
 27                                                                              |
 28  --------------------------------------------------------------------------------
 29    4:00      |                |        |        |        |        |
 30                                                                              |
 31  --------------------------------------------------------------------------------
 32    5:00      |                |        |        |        |        |
 33                                                                              |
 34  --------------------------------------------------------------------------------
 35    6:00      |                |        |        |        |        |
 36                                                                              |
 37  --------------------------------------------------------------------------------
 38    7:00      |                |        |        |        |        |
 39                                                                              |
 40  --------------------------------------------------------------------------------
 41    8:00      |                |        |        |        |        |
 42                                                                              |
 43  --------------------------------------------------------------------------------
 44    9:00      |                |        |        |        |        |
 45                                                                              |
 46  --------------------------------------------------------------------------------
 47  10:00       |                |        |        |        |        |
 48                                                                              |
 49  --------------------------------------------------------------------------------
 50  11:00       |                |        |        |        |        |
 51                                                                              |
 52  ================================================================================
 53     TOTAL    |                |        |        |        |        |
```

Keyboard the basic template into columns A-H, rows 1-20, on page 10. Copy the labels in rows 1 through 20 (B1;10..B20;10) into columns B through G on page 8 (B1;8..G20;8). This will allow row titles to be displayed when the spreadsheet is rotated and viewed from the right side.

```
        A                B                          C
    |----------|----------------------|----------------------|
01  Reference Questions
02
03           N u m b e r   o f   Q u e s t i o n s
04  ------------------------------------------------------------
05  Month                 level 1                    level 2
06  ============================================================
07  January               0                          0
08  February              0                          0
09  March                 0                          0
10  April                 0                          0
11  May                   0                          0
12  June                  0                          0
13  July                  0                          0
14  August                0                          0
15  September             0                          0
16  October               0                          0
17  November              0                          0
18  December              0                          0
19  ============================================================
20  Total No.  @SUM(B6;10..B19;10)     @SUM(C6;10..C19;10)
```

```
           D                E                          F
    |----------------------|----------------------|----------------------|
01  Name:
02  Year:
03
04  ------------------------------------------------------------
05           level 3              level 4              level 5
06  ============================================================
07           0                    0                    0
08           0                    0                    0
09           0                    0                    0
10           0                    0                    0
11           0                    0                    0
12           0                    0                    0
13           0                    0                    0
14           0                    0                    0
15           0                    0                    0
16           0                    0                    0
17           0                    0                    0
18           0                    0                    0
19  ============================================================
20  @SUM(D6;10..D19;10)  @SUM(E6;10..E19;10)  @SUM(F6;10..F19;10)
```

```
                                                                    G
                                                           |————————————|
01 |————————————————————————————————————————————————————————————————————  FTE:
02
03                                                                      Adj.
04                                                                      Value
05
06 ════════════════════════════════════════════════════════════════════════════
07   (((B7;10*$G$14;$1)+(C7;10*$G$15;$1)+(D7;10*$G$16;$1)+(E7;10*$G$17;$1)+(F7;10*$G$18;$1))/100)/$H$1;10
08   (((B8;10*$G$14;$1)+(C8;10*$G$15;$1)+(D8;10*$G$16;$1)+(E8;10*$G$17;$1)+(F8;10*$G$18;$1))/100)/$H$1;10
09   (((B9;10*$G$14;$1)+(C9;10*$G$15;$1)+(D9;10*$G$16;$1)+(E9;10*$G$17;$1)+(F9;10*$G$18;$1))/100)/$H$1;10
10 (((B10;10*$G$14;$1)+(C10;10*$G$15;$1)+(D10;10*$G$16;$1)+(E10;10*$G$17;$1)+(F10;10*$G$18;$1))/100)/$H$1;10
11 (((B11;10*$G$14;$1)+(C11;10*$G$15;$1)+(D11;10*$G$16;$1)+(E11;10*$G$17;$1)+(F11;10*$G$18;$1))/100)/$H$1;10
12 (((B12;10*$G$14;$1)+(C12;10*$G$15;$1)+(D12;10*$G$16;$1)+(E12;10*$G$17;$1)+(F12;10*$G$18;$1))/100)/$H$1;10
13 (((B13;10*$G$14;$1)+(C13;10*$G$15;$1)+(D13;10*$G$16;$1)+(E13;10*$G$17;$1)+(F13;10*$G$18;$1))/100)/$H$1;10
14 (((B14;10*$G$14;$1)+(C14;10*$G$15;$1)+(D14;10*$G$16;$1)+(E14;10*$G$17;$1)+(F14;10*$G$18;$1))/100)/$H$1;10
15 (((B15;10*$G$14;$1)+(C15;10*$G$15;$1)+(D15;10*$G$16;$1)+(E15;10*$G$17;$1)+(F15;10*$G$18;$1))/100)/$H$1;10
16 (((B16;10*$G$14;$1)+(C16;10*$G$15;$1)+(D16;10*$G$16;$1)+(E16;10*$G$17;$1)+(F16;10*$G$18;$1))/100)/$H$1;10
17 (((B17;10*$G$14;$1)+(C17;10*$G$15;$1)+(D17;10*$G$16;$1)+(E17;10*$G$17;$1)+(F17;10*$G$18;$1))/100)/$H$1;10
18 (((B18;10*$G$14;$1)+(C18;10*$G$15;$1)+(D18;10*$G$16;$1)+(E18;10*$G$17;$1)+(F18;10*$G$18;$1))/100)/$H$1;10
19 ════════════════════════════════════════════════════════════════════════════
20                                                        (@SUM(G6;10..G19;10))/12


          H
      |————————|
01    |        0  |
```

Keyboard vertical lines in columns B-G, rows 7-20, on pages 9 and 15. Keyboard the labels and formulas for the Totals on page 16, columns A-H, rows 1-20.

	A	B	C
01	Reference Questions: Summary		
02			
03	T o t a l Q u e s t i o n s		
04			
05	Month	level 1	level 2
06	===		
07	January	@SUM(B7;9..B7;15)	@SUM(C7;9..C7;15)
08	February	@SUM(B8;9..B8;15)	@SUM(C8;9..C8;15)
09	March	@SUM(B9;9..B9;15)	@SUM(C9;9..C9;15)
10	April	@SUM(B10;9..B10;15)	@SUM(C10;9..C10;15)
11	May	@SUM(B11;9..B11;15)	@SUM(C11;9..C11;15)
12	June	@SUM(B12;9..B12;15)	@SUM(C12;9..C12;15)
13	July	@SUM(B13;9..B13;15)	@SUM(C13;9..C13;15)
14	August	@SUM(B14;9..B14;15)	@SUM(C14;9..C14;15)
15	September	@SUM(B15;9..B15;15)	@SUM(C15;9..C15;15)
16	October	@SUM(B16;9..B16;15)	@SUM(C16;9..C16;15)
17	November	@SUM(B17;9..B17;15)	@SUM(C17;9..C17;15)
18	December	@SUM(B18;9..B18;15)	@SUM(C18;9..C18;15)
19	===		
20	Total No.	@SUM(B6;16..B19;16)	@SUM(C6;16..C19;16)

	D	E	F
01			
02		Year:	
03			
04			
05	level 3	level 4	level 5
06	===		
07	@SUM(D7;9..D7;15)	@SUM(E7;9..E7;15)	@SUM(F7;9..F7;15)
08	@SUM(D8;9..D8;15)	@SUM(E8;9..E8;15)	@SUM(F8;9..F8;15)
09	@SUM(D9;9..D9;15)	@SUM(E9;9..E9;15)	@SUM(F9;9..F9;15)
10	@SUM(D10;9..D10;15)	@SUM(E10;9..E10;15)	@SUM(F10;9..F10;15)
11	@SUM(D11;9..D11;15)	@SUM(E11;9..E11;15)	@SUM(F11;9..F11;15)
12	@SUM(D12;9..D12;15)	@SUM(E12;9..E12;15)	@SUM(F12;9..F12;15)
13	@SUM(D13;9..D13;15)	@SUM(E13;9..E13;15)	@SUM(F13;9..F13;15)
14	@SUM(D14;9..D14;15)	@SUM(E14;9..E14;15)	@SUM(F14;9..F14;15)
15	@SUM(D15;9..D15;15)	@SUM(E15;9..E15;15)	@SUM(F15;9..F15;15)
16	@SUM(D16;9..D16;15)	@SUM(E16;9..E16;15)	@SUM(F16;9..F16;15)
17	@SUM(D17;9..D17;15)	@SUM(E17;9..E17;15)	@SUM(F17;9..F17;15)
18	@SUM(D18;9..D18;15)	@SUM(E18;9..E18;15)	@SUM(F18;9..F18;15)
19	===		
20	@SUM(D6;16..D19;16)	@SUM(E6;16..E19;16)	@SUM(F6;16..F19;16)

```
                                          G
|----------------------------------------------------------------------------------|
01                                                                      FTE Workers:
02
03                                                                              Adj.
04                                                                             Value
05 ================================================================================
06 ================================================================================
07      (((B7;16*$G$14;$1)+(C7;16*$G$15;$1)+(D7;16*$G$16;$1)+(E7;16*$G$17;$1)+(F7;16*$G$18;$1))/100)/$H$1;16
08      (((B8;16*$G$14;$1)+(C8;16*$G$15;$1)+(D8;16*$G$16;$1)+(E8;16*$G$17;$1)+(F8;16*$G$18;$1))/100)/$H$1;16
09      (((B9;16*$G$14;$1)+(C9;16*$G$15;$1)+(D9;16*$G$16;$1)+(E9;16*$G$17;$1)+(F9;16*$G$18;$1))/100)/$H$1;16
10  (((B10;16*$G$14;$1)+(C10;16*$G$15;$1)+(D10;16*$G$16;$1)+(E10;16*$G$17;$1)+(F10;16*$G$18;$1))/100)/$H$1;16
11  (((B11;16*$G$14;$1)+(C11;16*$G$15;$1)+(D11;16*$G$16;$1)+(E11;16*$G$17;$1)+(F11;16*$G$18;$1))/100)/$H$1;16
12  (((B12;16*$G$14;$1)+(C12;16*$G$15;$1)+(D12;16*$G$16;$1)+(E12;16*$G$17;$1)+(F12;16*$G$18;$1))/100)/$H$1;16
13  (((B13;16*$G$14;$1)+(C13;16*$G$15;$1)+(D13;16*$G$16;$1)+(E13;16*$G$17;$1)+(F13;16*$G$18;$1))/100)/$H$1;16
14  (((B14;16*$G$14;$1)+(C14;16*$G$15;$1)+(D14;16*$G$16;$1)+(E14;16*$G$17;$1)+(F14;16*$G$18;$1))/100)/$H$1;16
15  (((B15;16*$G$14;$1)+(C15;16*$G$15;$1)+(D15;16*$G$16;$1)+(E15;16*$G$17;$1)+(F15;16*$G$18;$1))/100)/$H$1;16
16  (((B16;16*$G$14;$1)+(C16;16*$G$15;$1)+(D16;16*$G$16;$1)+(E16;16*$G$17;$1)+(F16;16*$G$18;$1))/100)/$H$1;16
17  (((B17;16*$G$14;$1)+(C17;16*$G$15;$1)+(D17;16*$G$16;$1)+(E17;16*$G$17;$1)+(F17;16*$G$18;$1))/100)/$H$1;16
18  (((B18;16*$G$14;$1)+(C18;16*$G$15;$1)+(D18;16*$G$16;$1)+(E18;16*$G$17;$1)+(F18;16*$G$18;$1))/100)/$H$1;16
19 ================================================================================
                                                                  =(@SUM(G616..G19;16))/12
20
```

Keyboard the following in column H of page 16.

```
                  H
|----------------------|
01      @SUM(H1;9..H1;15)
```

Save this generic template. Make a working copy, and save it with an appropriate filename, e.g., REFWORK. In the working copy, insert pages as necessary for additional reference workers after page 9 and before page 15. Be sure the formulas on the final or total page include these additional pages. Then, enter the data in the appropriate workers' pages.

Two sample pages from this spreadsheet are shown below. A reference worker's page, using fictitious data, is shown in Table 17-1. The final page with totals for the entire year is shown in Table 17-2. An example of how the spreadsheet will appear when rotated and viewed from the right side is shown in Table 17-3, while the view from the top is shown in Table 17-4.

In Figure 17A, an example of graphic presentation of these fictitious data is shown with the percentage of total reference questions by level of difficulty displayed as a circle graph.

Table 17-1: Reference Work Values for Wayne Smith for 1993—Front View, Page 16

```
Reference Questions          Name:    Wayne Smith        FTE:        1
                             Year:      1993
          N u m b e r   o f   Q u e s t i o n s
          ------------------------------------------------   Adj.
Month     level 1   level 2   level 3   level 4   level 5    Value
==================================================================
January     251        84        27        10        4       11.1
February    297        98        35        14        5       14.0
March       263        88        30        11        4       11.7
April       229        73        25         9        3        9.6
May         317       113        38        12        4       13.6
June        331       117        39        13        4       14.1
July        152       103        19         7        2        8.1
August      153       101        17         5        2        7.5
September   348       119        41        14        5       15.3
October     327       114        38        13        4       13.9
November    338       117        39        14        5       15.1
December    261        86        28        10        3       10.6
==================================================================
Total No.  3267      1213       376       132       45       12.1
```

Table 17-2: Reference Work Values for All Workers for 1993—Front View, Page 16

```
Reference Questions: Summary              FTE Workers:     4.5
                                     Year:      1993
          T o t a l   Q u e s t i o n s
          ------------------------------------------------   Adj.
Month     level 1   level 2   level 3   level 4   level 5    Value
==================================================================
January    1132       379       122        45       18       11.1
February   1337       443       158        63       22       13.9
March      1284       398       135        50       18       11.9
April      1030       328       113        41       13        9.5
May        1422       509       171        54       18       13.6
June       1158       405       137        46       14       11.0
July        915       364       112        37       12        9.2
August      789       322        93        30       10        7.7
September  1568       535       185        63       23       15.4
October    1474       513       171        59       18       14.0
November   1531       526       176        63       23       15.2
December   1178       387       126        45       14       10.7
==================================================================
Total No. 14818      5109      1699       596      203       11.9
```

Table 17-3: Level 1 Reference Questions Month by Month and Worker by Worker—Right-Side View, Page 2

Month	level 1	level 1	level 1	level 1	level 1	level 1
January	251	251	251	128	251	1132
February	297	297	297	149	297	1337
March	263	263	263	232	263	1284
April	229	229	229	114	229	1030
May	317	317	317	154	317	1422
June	331	331	0	165	331	1158
July	152	305	305	153	0	915
August	153	0	331	0	305	789
September	348	348	348	176	348	1568
October	327	327	327	166	327	1474
November	338	338	338	179	338	1531
December	261	261	261	134	261	1178
Total No.	3267	3267	3267	1750	3267	14818
	(WKR 1)	(WKR 2)	(WKR 3)	(WKR 4)	(WKR 5)	(TOTAL)

Table 17-4: Reference Questions for January by Worker and Level of Difficulty—Top View, Page 7

	January	January	January	January	January	January	
January	251	251	251	128	251	1132	(Level 1)
January	84	84	84	43	84	379	(Level 2)
January	27	27	27	14	27	122	(Level 3)
January	10	10	10	5	10	45	(Level 4)
January	4	4	4	2	4	18	(Level 5)
January	11.1	11.1	11.1	5.6	11.1	11.1	(Total)
	(Wkr 1)	(Wkr 2)	(Wkr 3)	(Wkr 4)	(Wkr 5)	(Total)	

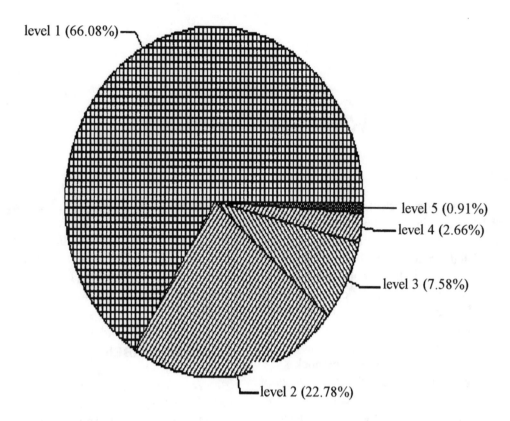

Figure 17-A: Percentage of Total Reference Questions by Level of Difficulty; Circle Graph

Chapter 18
Random Numbers

What distinguishes a randomly selected number from any other number? If, when selecting a number from a group (i.e., population) of numbers, each number in that group has an equal and independent probability of being selected, the selection is said to be random. One or more such numbers drawn from a population constitute a random sample. By extension, it is possible to draw a random sample of observations, events, or other data points. (For further discussion of random numbers and their selection, refer to a basic statistical textbook.)

Random numbers can be obtained from a number of sources. One is a table of random numbers. While most statistics texts include such tables, they are inconvenient to use in many applications. Special computer programs that generate lists of random numbers are handy but not always available. Another approach is to use the @RAND function available in most spreadsheet software packages. In its simplest form, the @RAND function generates a random number between 0 and 1. This number can be modified to be displayed as a whole number, and the maximum and minimum values can be set. This is customarily done by supplementing the @RAND function with a minimum value and a range.

USING RANDOM NUMBERS TO TEST A TEMPLATE

It is sometimes useful to insert fictitious data into a template in order to observe how it functions. When data are needed only to test the arithmetic of a formula, any convenient set of numbers can be inserted without regard for the reasonableness of the results. Or, if the data are to represent a particular situation, they will be selected to reflect certain desired characteristics. Composing fictitious numbers can be a laborious task, although little thought and imagination may be needed. An alternative way of testing a model is to use randomly selected numbers. This is done by placing the @RAND function in each cell requiring an entry.

Although @RAND looks much the same in various spreadsheet packages, it behaves differently. For example, with 1-2-3, each time the spreadsheet is recalculated, each @RAND function generates a new random number. This is in contrast to Quattro, which does not recalculate @RAND unless the function is moved to another cell.

RANDOM NUMBER LISTS

To produce a list of random numbers, simply copy the @RAND function into as many cells as numbers are needed. Set the range and minimum value as appropriate. (For example, with 1-2-3, the format for the range and minimum value is @RAND*[range]+[minimum value].) This list, which will be in random sequence, can be printed and used as is, although the list would be easier to use if it were arranged in ascending or descending order. To arrange a list of random numbers, it is necessary to sort them. One way would be to subject the file to a sort command (e.g., SORT in MS-DOS). Or, the file could be imported into a word processor and sorted there. Either way, the file must be moved around before it can be sorted, and, if the original file of @RANDs is recalculated, repeated moving of the list can be quite tiring.

A simpler approach is to sort the file within the spreadsheet program, using software (e.g., 1-2-3) in which automatic recalculation can be turned off for the @RAND function. (Quattro does not permit automatic recalculation to be turned off for the @RAND function.) If automatic recalculation is not turned off, the numbers will first be sorted and then recalculated. Thus, the newly calculated numbers will not be in a sorted sequence.

Also, because the Primary Sort-Key command operates logically on only one column, all of the @RAND values must appear in a single column. (A way around this limitation is demonstrated in Chapter 19.) If the @RAND is placed in more than one column, the entire block can be rearranged, but only by the sort done on the designated sort column; the remainder of the block will still be in a (different) random order.

The Random Number List shown below in Table18-1 illustrates the product of a spreadsheet designed to produce a customized and sorted list of random numbers. The numbers are created and sorted in a single column.

The Random Number List template is unusual because it creates and then sorts its own data. The template is a menu containing a series of macro commands which are explained in the instructions in columns B-D. To set up the Random Number List template, follow the general instructions and guidelines in Chapter 2, "Design and Modification of Spreadsheets." The specifications, la-

bels, and formulas for setting up the Random Number List template are shown below. Set the columns below at widths other than the default of nine spaces:

B	= 3	BG	= 60
C	= 55	BH	= 60
D	= 3	BI	= 45
BB	= 20	BJ	= 65
BD	= 20	BK	= 40
BE	= 45	BL	= 65
BF	= 55		

Set the display of numbers to Fixed with no digits after the decimal. Begin by keyboarding the organizational statement in columns B-D, rows 1-48.

After keyboarding columns BA-BL, rows 1-17,

RANDOM NUMBERS SPREADSHEET: CELL-BY-CELL INSTRUCTIONS

```
         B                             C                            D
     !---!-------------------------------------------------------!---!
   1 !===========================================================!
   2 !                                                           !
   3 !   Random Number Generator                                 !
   4 !                                                           !
   5 !     This spreadsheet generates a sorted list of random    !
   6 !   numbers.  It is interactive, asking the user for such   !
   7 !   items as the minimum and maximum values and the length  !
   8 !   of the list of numbers.  A menu of the different        !
   9 !   options available in this spreadsheet is provided.      !
  10 !                                                           !
  11 !     Before using the menu, be sure that automatic         !
  12 !   recalculation has been turned off, and set the number   !
  13 !   of digits to be displayed to the right of the decimal.  !
  14 !                                                           !
  15 !     To see the menu of options, press [Alt] and "a"       !
  16 !   simultaneously.                                         !
  17 !                                                           !
  18 !     To produce a list of random numbers, select "List"    !
  19 !   from the menu and follow the prompts entering the       !
  20 !   range and minimum value followed by pressing the ENTER  !
  21 !   key, thereby completing the @RAND function.  Then, move !
  22 !   the cursor down a sufficient number of rows to provide  !
  23 !   the desired length list.                                !
  24 !                                                           !
  25 !     In 1-2-3, the format for the range and minimum value  !
  26 !   is:    @RAND*[range]+[minimum value].                   !
  27 !                                                           !
  28 !     "Print" is based on the assumption that the entire    !
  29 !   list of random numbers will be printed.  "Page" is      !
  30 !   based on the same assumption, and a filename must be    !
  31 !   entered from the keyboard.                              !
  32 !                                                           !
  33 !     "Erase" erases the list of random numbers.  It is     !
  34 !   not necessary to use "Erase", but it is included for    !
  35 !   convenience.                                            !
  36 !                                                           !
  37 !     "Macro" places the cursor at the beginning of the     !
  38 !   menu program which is stored in columns BA-BL, rows     !
  39 !   1-17.                                                   !
  40 !                                                           !
  41 !     The list of random numbers begins at cell AA1.        !
  42 !                                                           !
  43 !===========================================================!
  44
  45    [filename]
  46    [date]
```

name the range BB1 "\0" so that the organizational statement will be displayed automatically whenever the spreadsheet is loaded. Name the range BD1 "\a" so that the menu will be displayed when [ALT] and "a" are pressed simultaneously.

```
     BA          BB          BC              BD
  |----|-----------|----|----------------------------------|
01 \0    {goto}A1~         \a    {MENUBRANCH BE1}
02       {RIGHT 2}~
03       {DOWN 2}
04       {QUIT}
05                               The menu program is
06                               stored in columns
07                               BA-BJ.  Column BC
08                               extends to row 17.
```

```
                               BE
  |--------------------------------------------------|
01 List
02 Generates a sorted list of random numbers
03 {GOTO}AA1~
04 /re.
05 {END}{DOWN}~
06 {GOTO}AA1~
07 @RAND{?}~
08 /C~{DOWN}
09 .{?}~
10 /DSR
11 D
12 AA1~
13 D.{END}{DOWN}~
14 PAA11~
15 A~
16 G
17 {QUIT}
```

```
                             BF
  |--------------------------------------------------|
01 Recalculate
02 Recalculates and resorts the list of random numbers
03 {GOTO}AA1~
04 {CALC}~
05 /DSR
06 D
07 AA1~
08 D.{END}{DOWN}~
09 PAA1~
10 A~
11 G
12 {QUIT}
```

```
                             BG
  |----------------------------------------------------|
01 Save
02 Saves the spreadsheet to disk.  Supply a filename as needed
03 /FS
04 {QUIT}
```

```
                             BH
  |----------------------------------------------------|
01 Print
02 Sends the list of sorted random numbers to the printer
03 /PPRAA1~
04 R.
05 {END}{DOWN}~
06 GPG
07 {QUIT}
```

```
                            BI
  !------------------------------------------------------!
01 File
02 Saves a page image of the list of sorted random numbers
03 /PF{?}~
04 RAA1~
05 R.
06 {END}{DOWN}~
07 G
08 P
09 Q
10 {QUIT}
                              BJ
  !---------------------------------------------------------!
01 Erase
02 Erases the list of sorted random numbers from the spreadsheet
03 {GOTO}AA1~
04 /re.
05 {END}{DOWN}~
06 {QUIT}

                       BK
  !-------------------------------------------!
01 Quit
02 Exits Lotus 1-2-3.   SAVE FILES FIRST!
03 /QY
04 {QUIT}


                             BL
  !----------------------------------------------------------------!
01 Macro
02 A utility to display the beginning of the menu program & macros
03 {GOTO}BA1~
04 {QUIT}
```

Save this generic template and then make a working copy. A very simple example of what can be produced with the completed spreadsheet is shown in Table 18-1. In this case, a random sample of 10 numbers between 12 and 20 has been drawn. In a typical application, the list would be longer, having been drawn from a greater range.

Table 18-1: Sorted List of Random Numbers

12
12
13
13
14
14
15
17
18
20

Chapter 19
Nested Random Numbers

Sometimes nested random numbers are called for. Imagine a 15-volume set of reference books in which each volume has a maximum of 600 pages, each page has four columns, and each column has a maximum of 12 entries. From this population we want a random sample of 20 entries. The chart shown in Table 19-1 provides such a sample. By varying the parameters for each column, this spreadsheet can be adapted to a wide range of possibilities. For example, the year of an annual publication could be substituted for the volume number. If fewer columns are needed, the unnecessary columns can be ignored.

The range and minimum value are set for each column. In 1-2-3, the format for the range and minimum value is @RAND*[range]+[minimum value].

The Nested Random Numbers template uses a special formula so that more than the primary sort key column can be sorted. For this formula to work it is necessary that the numbers be converted to labels before they are sorted. Also, leading zeros may need to be supplied so that all of the numbers in a column will be the same length. It is also desirable to eliminate the digits to the right of the decimal.

The conversion to labels and the elimination of digits to the right of the decimal are done automatically, but leading zeros must be entered from the keyboard. The [enter] key is pressed to accept each converted number.

To set up the Nested Random Number Chart template, follow the general instructions and guidelines in Chapter 2, "Design and Modification of Spreadsheets." The specifications, labels, and formulas for setting up the Nested Random Number Chart template are shown below. The following columns are set at widths other than the default of nine spaces:

B	=	3	CG = 65	
C	=	50	CH = 65	
D	=	3	CI = 70	
CB	=	20	CJ = 40	
CD	=	20	CK = 60	
CE	=	70		
CF	=	65		

Set the display of numbers to Fixed with no digits after the decimal. Begin by keyboarding the organizational statement in columns B-D, rows 1-68.

NESTED RANDOM NUMBERS SPREADSHEET: CELL-BY-CELL INSTRUCTIONS

```
      B                        C                           D
  !---!------------------------------------------------!---!
01 |     Nested Random Numbers                             |
02 |                                                       |
03 =========================================================
04 |     This spreadsheet generates four columns of        |
05 | nested, sorted random numbers.  It is interactive,    |
06 | pausing for the user to enter such items as the       |
07 | minimum and maximum values, the length of the list    |
08 | of numbers, and leading zeros.  A menu of the         |
09 | different options availabale in this spreadsheet      |
10 | is provided.                                          |
11 |                                                       |
12 |     As an example of the use of this spreadsheet,     |
13 | the first column could represent the volumes of a     |
14 | reference set, the second column could represent      |
15 | the pages in each volume of the set, the third        |
16 | column could represent the columns on each page,      |
17 | and the fourth column could represent the items in    |
18 | each column.  The numbers are sorted so the items     |
19 | are in sequence.  Each row of 4 numbers represents    |
20 | one item.  Thus, a sample of 50 items would           |
21 | require 50 rows of numbers.                           |
22 |                                                       |
23 |     Before using the menu, be sure that automatic     |
24 | recalculation has been turned off, and set the        |
25 | number of digits to be displayed to the right of      |
26 | the decimal to "0".                                   |
27 |                                                       |
28 |     To see the menu of options, press [ALT] and "a"   |
29 | simultaneously.                                       |
30 |                                                       |
31 |     To produce a list of nested random numbers,       |
32 | select "List" from the menu and follow the prompts    |
33 | entering the range and minimum values for each        |
34 | column.  (In 1-2-3, the format for the range and      |
35 | minimum value is @RAND*[range]+[minimum value].)      |
36 | Then, move the cursor down a sufficient number of     |
37 | rows to provide the desired length list.  Enter       |
38 | leading zeros as needed so that all of the numbers    |
39 | within a column have the same number of digits.       |
40 |                                                       |
41 |     The internal processes of creating and sorting    |
42 | the list require many steps, so PLEASE BE PATIENT.    |
43 | Depending on the length of the list, processing       |
44 | may require several minutes.                          |
45 |                                                       |
46 |     "Print" is based on the assumption that the       |
47 | entire list of random numbers will be printed.        |
48 | "Page" is based on the same assumption, and a         |
49 | filename must be entered from the keyboard.           |
50 |                                                       |
51 |     "Erase" erases the list of random numbers.  It    |
52 | is not necessary to use "Erase", but it is            |
53 | included for convenience.                             |
54 |                                                       |
55 |     "Macro" places the cursor at the beginning of     |
56 | the menu program which is stored beginning with       |
57 | CA1.                                                  |
58 |                                                       |
59 |     The list of sorted, nested random numbers         |
60 | begins at AA1.  The work area begins at BA1.          |
61 |                                                       |
62 |     The menu and associated macros which drive the    |
63 | menu begin at CA1.                                    |
64 |                                                       |
65 =========================================================
66
67    [filename]
68    [date]
```

After keyboarding columns CA-CK, rows 1-104, name the range CB1 "\0" so that the organizational statement will be displayed automatically whenever the template is loaded. Name the range CD1 "\a" so that the menu will be displayed when [ALT] and "a" are pressed simultaneously.

```
        CA              CB               CC            CD
   |--------|--------------------|--------|------------------|
01 |\0        {GOTO}A1~                   \a     {MENUBRANCH CE1}~
02          {RIGHT 2}~
03          {DOWN 3}~
04          {QUIT}
05
06
07
08
```

```
                                    CE
   |------------------------------------------------------------------|
01 |List
02 |Generates a sorted, nested list of random numbers
03 |{WINDOWSOFF}~
04 |{GOTO}AA1~
05 |/re.
06 |{END}{DOWN}
07 |{RIGHT 51}
08 |/wcdAE1~
09 |{WINDOWSON}~
10 |{GOTO}BA1~
11 |@RAND{?}~
12 |/c~{DOWN}
13 |.{?}~
14 |{GOTO}BB1~
15 |@RAND{?}~
16 |/c~{DOWN}
17 |.{LEFT}{END}{DOWN}{RIGHT}~
18 |{GOTO}BC1~
19 |@RAND{?}~
20 |/c~{DOWN}
21 |.{LEFT}{END}{DOWN}{RIGHT}~
22 |{GOTO}BD1~
23 |@RAND{?}~
24 |/c~{DOWN}
25 |.{LEFT}{END}{DOWN}{RIGHT}~
26 |{WINDOWSOFF}
27 |{GOTO}BA1~
28 |/rv
29 |{END}{DOWN}
30 |{END}{RIGHT}~
31 |AA1~
32 |{GOTO}AA1~
33 |{IF (@CELLPOINTER("CONTENTS")<>0){BRANCH CE70}
34 |{GOTO}AB1~
35 |{IF (@CELLPOINTER("CONTENTS")<>0){BRANCH CE80}
36 |{GOTO}AC1~
37 |{IF (@CELLPOINTER("CONTENTS")<>0){BRANCH CE90}
38 |{GOTO}AD1~
39 |{IF (@CELLPOINTER("CONTENTS")<>0){BRANCH CE100}
40 |{GOTO}AE1~
41 |+AA1&" "&AB1&" "&AC1&" "&AD1~
42 |/c~
43 |{DOWN}.
```

```
                                  CE
    |---------------------------------------------------------------|
 44 {LEFT}{END}{DOWN}{RIGHT}~
 45 {GOTO}AE1~
 46 /rv{END}{DOWN}~AE1~
 47 {WINDOWSON}~
 48 /DSRDAA1~
 49 D.{END}{DOWN}{RIGHT 4}~
 50 PAE1~
 51 A~G
 52 /wchAE1~
 53 {GOTO}AA1~
 54 {QUIT}


 70 {EDIT}{BACKSPACE}~
 71 {IF (@CELLPOINTER("CONTENTS"))/
    (@INT(@CELLPOINTER("CONTENTS")))>1}{BRANCH CE70}
 72 {EDIT}{HOME}'{?}
 73 {DOWN}
 74 {BRANCH CB33}


 80 {EDIT}{BACKSPACE}~
 81 {IF (@CELLPOINTER("CONTENTS"))/
    (@INT(@CELLPOINTER("CONTENTS")))>1}{BRANCH CE80}
 82 {EDIT}{HOME}'{?}
 83 {DOWN}
 84 {BRANCH CB35}


 90 {EDIT}{BACKSPACE}~
 91 {IF (@CELLPOINTER("CONTENTS"))/
    (@INT(@CELLPOINTER("CONTENTS")))>1}{BRANCH CE90}
 92 {EDIT}{HOME}'{?}
 93 {DOWN}
 94 {BRANCH CB37}


100 {EDIT}{BACKSPACE}~
101 {IF (@CELLPOINTER("CONTENTS"))/
    (@INT(@CELLPOINTER("CONTENTS")))>1}{BRANCH CE100}
102 {EDIT}{HOME}'{?}
103 {DOWN}
104 {BRANCH CB39}


                                  CF
    |---------------------------------------------------------------|
 01 Save
 02 Saves the spreadsheet to disk.  Supply a filename as needed
 03 /FS{?}~
 04 {QUIT}
```

```
                                 CG
|------------------------------------------------------------------|
01 Print
02 Sends the list of sorted, nested random numbers to the printer
03 /PPRAA1~
04 R.
05 {END}{DOWN}
06 {END}{RIGHT 3}~
07 GPQ
08 {QUIT}
```

```
                                 CH
|------------------------------------------------------------------|
01 File
02 Writes a page image of the list of numbers in a disk file
03 /PF{?}
04 {GOTO}AA1~
05 RAA1.
06 R.
07 {END}{DOWN}
08 {END}{RIGHT 3}~
09 G
10 Q
11 {QUIT}
```

```
                                 CI
|--------------------------------------------------------------------|
01 Erase
02 Erases the list of sorted, nested random numbers from the spreadsheet
03 {WINDOWSOFF}~
04 {GOTO}AA1~
05 /re.
06 {END}{DOWN}
07 {RIGHT 51}
08 {QUIT}
```

```
                      CJ
|------------------------------------------------|
01 Quit
02 Exits Lotus 1-2-3.  SAVE FILES FIRST!
03 /QY
04 {QUIT}
```

```
                               CK
|------------------------------------------------------------------|
01 Macro
02 Utility to move the cursor to beginning of the menu program
03 {GOTO}CA1~
04 {QUIT}
```

Save this generic template and then make a working copy.

An example of what can be produced with the completed spreadsheet is shown in Table 19-1.

Table 19-1: Sorted List of Nested Random Numbers

02	178	3	05
03	247	4	04
04	246	1	03
04	495	4	01
05	415	1	12
06	279	4	10
07	399	4	04
07	563	2	08
07	586	1	02
09	008	4	08
09	152	3	10
10	149	2	05
10	564	1	08
12	416	2	01
13	288	3	07
14	18	2	11
14	229	1	05
14	587	4	07
15	084	4	07
15	439	4	08

Note: This table represents a sample of 20 items from a 15-volume reference work (column 1), each volume containing a maximum of 600 pages (column 2), each page containing four columns (column 3), and each column containing a maximum of 12 entries (column 4).

Glossary

A number of terms are used with particular meanings in connection with spreadsheets. Definitions for some of the most important of these are listed below.

Address—The combination of column and row letters and numbers that identify a particular cell.

Backup Copy—An extra, spare copy of a file. Useful when a working copy of the file is spoiled. *See also* Working Copy.

Block—A designated cell or group of cells, also known as a range. Often, a block is assigned a name.

Cell—The space at the intersection of a column and a row. Designated by the column and row coordinates, e.g., C4 is the cell at the intersection of column C and row 4.

Column—A vertical sequence of cells. Columns follow the y axis of a spreadsheet.

Data—Numeric or alphabetic contents of a cell; not a label or a formula.

Documentation—Paper file containing the layout, specifications, block names, formulas, etc., about a spreadsheet, together with examples.

Fixed Address—In a formula, an address that does not change when the formula is copied to another cell(s). *See also* Relative Address.

Formula—A statement in a cell that performs a mathematical or logical operation on one or more cells. Uses arithmetic operators (+, -, *, /) and pre-programmed functions.

Label—A word(s), often at the head of a column or the beginning of a row, naming the contents of the column or row.

Link—A connection between two spreadsheets; changes in the first spreadsheet are reflected in the second spreadsheet.

Macro—A sequence of recorded keystrokes or commands that can be repeated on demand by pressing only two or three keys. Useful for executing repetitive tasks.

Menu—A specialized set of macros that displays a selection of choices.

Page Image—An alternate to the print command that creates a file instead of printing a page. The file can be printed or imported into text being prepared with a word processing program.

Range—*See* Block.

Relative Address—In a formula, an address that changes when the formula is copied to another cell(s), reflecting the new location(s). *See also* Fixed Address.

Rotation—Turning the matrix or cube of a 3-D spreadsheet so that it can be viewed from another of its six sides.

Row—A horizontal sequence of cells. Rows follow the x axis of a spreadsheet.

Spreadsheet—An array of labels and formulas with no data is a template. When data are added to a template, it becomes a spreadsheet.

Template—*See* Spreadsheet.

Value—*See* Data.

Working Copy—The copy of a file used for entering data. *See also* Backup Copy.

Bibliography

Abbott, Edwin Abbott. *Flatland; A Romance of Many Dimensions.* (London: Seeley, 1884), 100. This little book still holds its readers. Several reprint editions are available.

Altman, Ellen. "Assessment of Reference Services." In *The Service Imperative for Libraries: Essays in Honor of Margaret E. Monroe.* Gail A. Schlachter, Editor. (Littleton, CO: Libraries Unlimited, 1982), 169-85.

Auld, Lawrence W. S. *Electronic Spreadsheets for Libraries.* (Phoenix, AZ: Oryx Press, 1986), 168.

Buchanan, Sarah, and Sandra Coleman. "Deterioration Survey of the Stanford University Libraries Green Library Stack Collection." In *Preservation Planning Program Resource Notebook*, compiled by Pamela W. Darling; rev. ed. by Wesley L. Boomgaarden. (Washington, DC: Association of Research Libraries, Office of Management Studies, 1987), 189-221.

Ellis, Judith Compton. "Planning and Executing a Major Bookshift/ Move Using an Electronic Spreadsheet." *College & Research Libraries News* xx (May 1988): 282-87.

Kesselman, Martin A., and Sarah B. Watstein. "The Measurement of Reference and Information Services." *Journal of Academic Librarianship* 13 (March 1987): 24-30.

Koren, Johan. "Evaluation of Reference Services: A Chronological Bibliography, 1971-1991." *Christian Librarian* 34 (August 1991): 117-23.

Levy, Steven. "A Spreadsheet Way of Knowledge." *Harper's* 269 (November 1984): 58-64.

Murfin, Marjorie E., and Lubomyr Wynar. *Reference Service: An Annotated Bibliographic Guide.* (Littleton, CO: Libraries Unlimited, 1977), 294.

————. *Reference Service: An Annotated Bibliographic Guide Supplement, 1976-1982.* (Littleton, CO: Libraries Unlimited, 1984), 353.

Slow Fires: On the Preservation of the Human Record. A production of the American Film Foundation. Produced and directed by Terry Sanders. Written by Ben Maddow and Terry Sanders. (Santa Monica, CA: American Film Foundation, 1987), videorecording, 59 minutes.

Tufte, Edward R. *Envisioning Information.* (Cheshire, CT: Graphics Press, 1990), 126.

————. *The Visual Display of Quantitative Information.* (Cheshire, CT: Graphics Press, 1983), 197.

Turabian, Kate L. *A Manual for Writers of Term Papers, Theses, and Dissertations.* 5th ed. rev. and expanded by Bonnie Birtwistle Honigsblum. (Chicago: University of Chicago Press, 1987), 300.

Westbrook, Lynn. *Qualitative Evaluation Methods for Reference Services: An Introductory Manual.* (Washington, DC: Office of Management Services, Association of Research Libraries, 1989), 25.

Index